MOUNTAIN BIKE!
Vermont

MOUNTAIN BIKE!
Vermont

A GUIDE TO THE CLASSIC TRAILS

KATE CARTER

Menasha
Ridge
Press

© 1998 by Kate Carter
All rights reserved
Printed in the United States of America
Published by Menasha Ridge Press
First edition, first printing

Library of Congress Cataloging-in-Publication Data:
Carter, Kate, 1955-
Mountain bike! Vermont: a guide to the classic trails/
Kate Carter.—1st ed.
p.   cm.—(America by mountain bike)
Includes index.
ISBN 0-89732-267-3
1. All terrain cycling—Vermont—Guidebooks.
2. Bicycle trails—Vermont—Guidebooks.
3. Vermont—Guidebooks.
I. Title. II. Series: America by mountain bike series.
GV1045.5.V5C37 1998
917.4304'43—dc21 98-6082
CIP

Photos by the author unless otherwise credited
Maps by Stephen Jones and Jeff Goodwin
Cover and text design by Suzanne Holt
Cover Photo by Dennis Coello

Menasha Ridge Press
700 South 28th Street
Suite 206
Birmingham, Alabama 35233

All the trails described in this book are legal for mountain bikes. But rules can change—especially for off-road bicycles, the new kid on the outdoor recreation block. Land access issues and conflicts between bicyclists, hikers, equestrians, and other users can cause the rewriting of recreation regulations on public lands, sometimes resulting in a ban of mountain bike use on specific trails. That's why it's the responsibility of each rider to check and make sure that he or she rides only on trails where mountain biking is permitted.

CAUTION

Outdoor recreational activities are by their very nature potentially hazardous. All participants in such activities must assume the responsibility for their own actions and safety. The information contained in this guidebook cannot replace sound judgment and good decision-making skills, which help reduce risk exposure, nor does the scope of this book allow for disclosure of all the potential hazards and risks involved in such activities.

Learn as much as possible about the outdoor recreational activities in which you participate, prepare for the unexpected, and be cautious. The reward will be a safer and more enjoyable experience.

For all parents who teach their children to ride a bike.
Thanks, Dad.

CONTENTS

CENTRAL VERMONT

GREEN MOUNTAIN NATIONAL FOREST

NORTHERN VERMONT

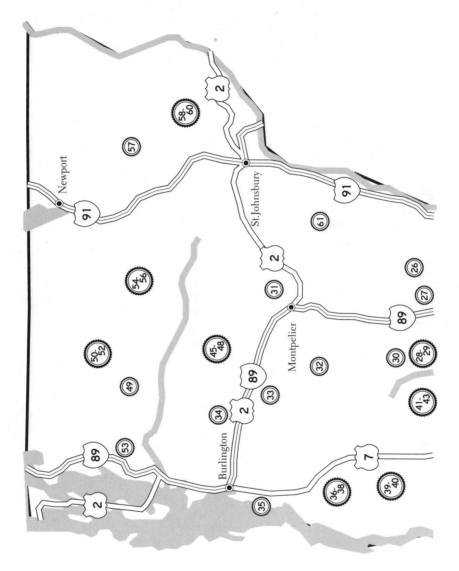

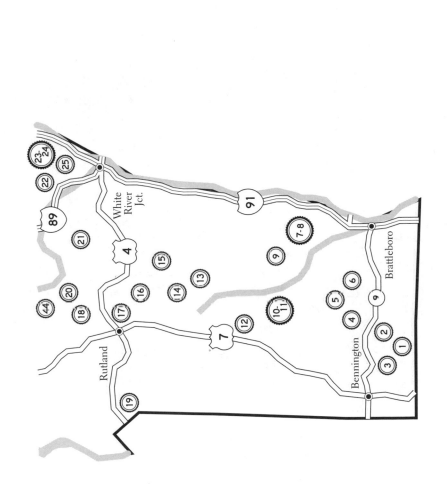

AMERICA BY MOUNTAIN BIKE   MAP LEGEND

Ride trailhead

Primary bike trail

Direction of travel

Optional bike trail and trailhead

Other trail

Hiking only trail

Interstate highways (with exit no.)

US routes

State routes

Other paved roads — Taylor Rd.

4WD — Unpaved, gravel or dirt roads (may be 4WD only)

US Forest Service roads — FR 726

Double-track

Burlington — Cities

Rutland — Towns or settlements

Dam — Lake

Intermittent stream

Perennial stream

0 ½ 1 MILES — Approximate scale in miles

True north

WILDERNESS AREA — Public lands*

State or county border

✈ Airport

♥ Archeological or historical site

Boat ramp

▲ Campground (CG)

≡ Cattle guard

† Cemetery or gravesite

♦ Church

Cliff, escarpment, or outcropping

Drinking water

Fire tower or lookout

Falls or rapids

Food

Gate

House or cabin

Lodging

Mountain or butte

Mountain pass

△ Mountain summit
3312 (elevation in feet)

✕ Mine or quarry

Observatory

Park office or ranger station

Picnic area

Power line or pipeline

Rest rooms

Spring

Stable, corral, or ranch

Swimming area

Transmission towers

Tunnel or bridge

*Remember, private property exists in and around our national forests.

LIST OF MAPS

ACKNOWLEDGMENTS

I had a lot of fun working on this book, but the best part was researching the rides. Occasionally I would go alone to check out a route, but solo excursions were never as much fun as riding with others. I want to thank all my friends who rode with me, posed for photos, and waited while I scrutinized maps and took notes. Special thanks go to Eric Ryea, who I believe had as much fun on "work rides" as I did, was always enthusiastic, and proved to be the perfect riding companion. Bette and Ernie Reuter became my good friends over the course of the summers, and lived up to their nickname, the "Ever-Ready" Reuters. Thanks to all my other friends who kept me company along the way—you know who you are.

Trek bicycles provided me with a Gary Fisher Hoo-Koo-E-Koo model to use during the first part of my research. Thanks for the loaner!

I would especially like to thank David Porter of the Winooski Bicycle Shop, who kept all of my bicycles—road and mountain—in working order, and provided me with replacement parts when I needed them. He is the very best bicycle mechanic a gal could have, and I am thankful for his skills, friendship, and company, on and off the bike. David also supplied me with a Seven Cycles mountain bike to use while I completed this book during a second summer. Seven Cycles is a new frame-building company in Topsfield, Massachusetts. They make exquisite steel and titanium frames, and it has been a pleasure for me to discover how sweet it is to ride state-of-the-art machinery. My beautiful purple Seven has certainly enhanced my mountain biking experience and led me to appreciate the value of good equipment. Thank you, Lisa Rodier, at Seven Cycles.

Finally, I thank the following people who helped me identify rides worthy of this book (all towns listed here are in Vermont unless otherwise noted): Sharon and John Ahern formerly of West Dover, now of Stowe; Dirk Anderson of Chelsea; Rob Barnard of Flick's (video store), Montgomery Center; Gina Campoli of the Craftsbury Outdoor Center, Craftsbury; Tom Cook of Wheels & Weights, Proctor; Jeff Hale, formerly of East Burke Sports, East Burke; Bob Harnish and Chuck Wagonheim of Cortina Inn/The Great Outdoors Adventure Bike Tours, Killington and Rutland; Robert Immler, author of *Mountain Biking the Ski Resorts of the Northeast* (Woodstock: Countryman Press); Dave King, author of *The Mountain Bike Experience* (New York: Henry Holt & Company); Colin Lawson of the Grafton Ponds Cross-Country Ski & Mountain Bike Center; Richard Montague of Brick Store Bicycles, Strafford; Neil Quinn of the West Hill Shop, Putney; Paul Rea of the White River Trails Association, Randolph; Andrea Riha of Shelburne; Chuck Schultz of Chuck's Bikes, Morrisville; and Dave Tier of the Bike & Ski Touring Center, Middlebury.

FOREWORD

Welcome to *America by Mountain Bike*, a series designed to provide all-terrain bikers with the information they need to find and ride the very best trails around. Whether you're new to the sport and don't know where to pedal, or an experienced mountain biker who wants to learn the classic trails in another region, this series is for you. Drop a few bucks for the book, spend an hour with the detailed maps and route descriptions, and you're prepared for the finest in off-road cycling.

My role as editor of this series was simple: First, find a mountain biker who knows the area and loves to ride. Second, ask that person to spend a year researching the most popular and very best rides around. And third, have that rider describe each trail in terms of difficulty, scenery, condition, elevation change, and all other categories of information that are important to trail riders. "Pretend you've just completed a ride and met up with fellow mountain bikers at the trailhead," I told each author. "Imagine their questions, be clear in your answers."

As I said, the *editorial* process — that of sending out riders and reading the submitted chapters — is a snap. But the work involved in finding, riding, and writing about each trail is enormous. In some instances our authors' tasks are made easier by the information contributed by local bike shops or cycling clubs, or even by the writers of local "where-to" guides. Credit for these contributions is provided, when appropriate, in each chapter, and our sincere thanks goes to all who have helped.

But the overwhelming majority of trails are discovered and pedaled by our authors themselves, then compared with dozens of other routes to determine if they qualify as "classic" — that area's best in scenery and cycling fun. If you've ever had the experience of pioneering a route from outdated topographic maps, or entering a bike shop to request information from local riders who would much prefer to keep their favorite trails secret, or know how it is to double- and triple-check data to be positive your trail info is correct, then you have an idea of how each of our authors has labored to bring about these books. You and I, and all the mountain bikers of America, are the richer for their efforts.

You'll get more out of this book if you take a moment to read the Introduction explaining how to read the trail listings. The "Topographic Maps" section will help you understand how useful topos will be on a ride, and will also tell you where to get them. And though this is a "where-to," not a "how-to" guide, those of you who have not traveled the backcountry might find "Hitting the Trail" of particular value.

In addition to the material above, newcomers to mountain biking might want to spend a minute with the Glossary, page 234, so that terms like *hardpack, single-track,* and *waterbars* won't throw you when you come across them in the text.

Finally, the tips in the Afterword on mountain biking etiquette and the land-use controversy might help us all enjoy the trails a little more.

All the best.

Dennis Coello
St. Louis

PREFACE

B ecause of its northern climate and mountainous terrain, Vermont is perfectly suited to a variety of winter sports. Most tourists come to Vermont during
the winter to ski, snowboard, and snowshoe. But most residents live here for the
lush, warm, romantic summers. Skiing is what brought *me* to Vermont, but summers are why I stay.

One of the reasons why Vermont summers are special to me is the diverse and
entertaining cycling I have done here, both on- and off-road. I am a road biker
at heart, but Vermont's dirt roads, logging roads, abandoned town roads, and
numerous other trails and right-of-ways have introduced me to a whole new
dimension in cycling. Inevitably, I have come to love mountain biking as much
as I love road biking.

A BRIEF HISTORY OF VERMONT'S ROADS AND TRAILS

For such a small state (9,609 square miles including inland water), Vermont
packs a walloping amount of off-road riding. As of 1996, the population of
Vermont was approximately 580,000, which means you don't have to go far to
find good mountain biking on trails where it is unlikely you will see another person, let alone another biker.

Vermont's agricultural and economic history accounts for the excellent off-
road riding now found throughout the state. The evolution of modern transportation meant the gradual abandonment of an extensive network of logging,
carriage, and stage roads. The remnants of these routes, some nearly 200 years
old, are ideal for mountain biking.

Consider the logging roads, for example. From as early as 1766, lumber has
been one of Vermont's greatest resources. The original pioneers' first cash crop was
potash, made from the ashes of burned logs. However, an influx of settlers in the
1790s brought about the reckless destruction of Vermont's forests. Lumber was used
for everything imaginable and was exported from the state at an amazing rate. By
1840, there were more than 1,000 sawmills in Vermont, and by 1874, Vermont's

Old farmhouses and apple orchards await mountain bikers who venture off-road in central Vermont.

railroad steam engines burned more than 500,000 cords of wood annually. During the 1880s, Burlington was the third-largest lumber port in the world.

Unrestrained cutting and burning of timber for farmland left Vermont stripped of virgin forests, ending the big lumber era by the early 1900s. Fortunately, Vermont now has strict guidelines for harvesting trees, and you will seldom see a clear-cut hillside. Forests have grown back and it is only the old roads, built to transport logs from the woods, that attest to the logging that was once so rampant here. The good news is, these former logging roads make for excellent mountain biking, and several of the rides described in this book make use of them. In some locations, small logging operations are still in progress today. I have noted these spots in the individual ride descriptions.

In tandem with logging, farming has created the landscape we see and ride today. During the 1820s, Vermont farmers began raising sheep to supply the woolen mills in southern New England. By 1840, Vermont ranked second in American wool production. At one point, the number of sheep in Vermont totaled 1,700,000, or 6 sheep for every resident. Eventually, however, competition from imported products and sheep ranches in the western United States caused the Vermont wool industry to dwindle. By 1870, dairy farming had replaced sheep farming.

Vermont dairy farming peaked in 1938 with nearly 280,000 cows on 13,000 farms. But dairy farming has also seen the effects of modern economics. In recent years, most Vermont farmers have been forced to sell their land, and now only about 1,800 dairy farms with some 155,000 cows remain in production.

This long farming tradition explains the abundance of stone walls that still stand throughout the state. They mark the boundaries of old pastures, as well as the roads that farmers built to drive their carriages between towns. If you find yourself biking a trail between two stone walls, you can bet you are riding on what was once a carriage road. My experience shows that these roads are more abundant in southern Vermont; many are still Class 4 town roads, even though they are impassable by motor vehicles. These abandoned farm roads make excellent mountain bike trails.

I am especially fond of riding overgrown trails between two stone walls. It is astounding that so many stone walls were built and that so many remain today. And it is awe inspiring to think that Vermont farmers were filled with such drive and determination. In my opinion, the ultimate mountain bike ride includes several miles on a trail flanked by stone walls—and one surprise cemetery. I found many tombstones dated in the 1800s while researching this book; I still hope to discover a marker dated in the 1700s.

RATING THE RIDES

I am a good rider. I am not great. I am slow on the climbs and a wimp on the descents. But I will ride till the cows come home because I enjoy pedaling my bike, being outdoors, moving down the trail, and discovering what's around the next corner. This book is about exploring Vermont, going places and seeing things you probably would otherwise miss on your own. It is about travel and outdoor adventure over the endless miles of remarkable mountain biking on Vermont's legal roads and trails.

As I researched the rides for this book, I plotted new routes and also reviewed well-established ones. I stopped often to orient myself, take photos, and jot down notes. A ride that took me three hours the first time might only have taken two, had I been familiar with the territory. But most rides were new experiences for me, and they took longer to do than usual. This is exactly the situation you will be in when you try one of my rides for the first time. You will stop occasionally to read directions and orient yourself with the map; take a photo or two, perhaps; and, on a long ride, replenish your food supply. I doubt you will take notes, but I am sure you will have as much fun exploring Vermont as I did.

In general, it is difficult to rate rides according to ability: What is hard for one person may be easy for another. However, it is helpful to have some idea of the difficulty of an unknown ride before embarking on it. When deciding how to categorize each ride, I considered its distance, amount of climbing, and amount of technical terrain. I rated the rides in this book in relation to one another, solely from my own perspective. (As I stated earlier, I am a good rider, but I am not great. I often chose to walk my bike on scary sections. On the other hand, I frequently surprised myself by "cleaning" sections I didn't think I could make.)

Here is a key to my ride ratings:

Easy: Less than 10 miles, minimal climbing, dirt and paved roads, no technical terrain.

Easy intermediate: 10 to 15 miles, one or two short climbs, dirt roads, no technical terrain.

Intermediate: 10 to 15 miles, one or two long climbs, some trail riding with moderately technical terrain. An intermediate ride may be only 10 miles long, but technically rather challenging.

Advanced intermediate: 12 to 18 miles, lots of climbing, some trail riding with sections of challenging technical terrain.

Difficult: 15 to 20 miles, several climbs, lots of trail riding with very challenging technical terrain and the possibility of walking your bike several times.

Very difficult: Over 20 miles, lots of climbing, plenty of technical terrain with the likelihood of walking your bike up as well as down extreme sections.

FAMILY RIDES

Parents who encourage their children to be physically active are helping them establish a foundation for a healthy lifestyle. Fortunately, mountain biking is an activity that the entire family can enjoy together. Anyone can pedal a bike up and down the street in front of the house, but to specifically take a child mountain biking suddenly turns the ride into a big adventure. Try this invitation: "Tomorrow, let's go ride bikes in Groton State Forest. We'll pack a lunch and go for a swim after the ride." What could be more fun?

Several of the rides in this book make excellent choices for family outings, and in fact are also favorable for novice riders of any age. The terrain is reasonably flat and often closed to motor vehicles. Some routes feature optional spurs that add mileage and hills, which help keep groups of riders of varying abilities interested and challenged. For a list of rides appropriate for families with young children and novice riders, see "Ride Recommendations for Special Interests" after the Preface on page xxviii.

MAPS

Throughout this book I refer to two atlases: the *Vermont Atlas and Gazetteer* by DeLorme (ninth edition), P.O. Box 298, Freeport, ME 04032, (207) 865-4171; and the *Vermont Road Atlas and Guide* by Northern Cartographic, Inc. (third edition), 4050 Williston Road, South Burlington, VT 05403, (802) 860-2886. Both atlases are easy to find all over Vermont at bookstores, bike shops, specialty sporting-goods stores, and assorted quick-stop convenience stores. These publications were very helpful on most of my rides and also come in handy for exploring Vermont by car. Of the two, I prefer DeLorme's because I find it easier to read. In the name of simplicity, I refer to these atlases throughout this book as DeLorme's and Northern Cartographic's.

For greater detail, I used United States Geological Survey (USGS) topographical maps in the 7.5 minute series. I always carried topo maps and a compass with me, and recommend that you do, too. Most USGS maps are old, however, and occasionally I discovered an unmapped road. I have noted any such discrepancies in the individual ride descriptions.

The USGS 7.5 minute topo maps can be ordered from the National Survey, Inc., School Street, Chester, VT 05143; (802) 875-2121. Capitol Stationers on Main Street in Montpelier (802-223-2393) also keeps a good inventory in stock.

ROAD AND TRAIL CLASSIFICATIONS

Roads in Vermont are classified as Class 1 through Class 4. Class 1 roads are all paved and are maintained by the state (including both federal and state highways); Class 2 roads are primary paved or dirt routes, maintained by their respective towns; Class 3 encompasses secondary dirt roads, maintained for year-round vehicular travel by their respective towns; Class 4 roads are no longer maintained for year-round travel and provide the most interest for mountain bikers.

In turn, Class 4 roads have four subsets: partially maintained roads (which might not be plowed for winter use but might have some erosion-control structures, such as culverts); unmaintained roads; legal trails; and pent roads. Legal trails are usually aged, overgrown, unmaintained roads. Pent roads pass through farmland whose owners have obtained permission to install unlocked gates at their property lines in order to keep livestock confined. (Be sure to close such gates properly, if you open them.) All four types of Class 4 roads are considered public right-of-ways, and often present ideal opportunities for mountain bike riding. Most of the rides in this book run the gamut of Class 4 roads.

Single-track trails hold a particular mystique for most mountain bikers: Everyone wants to know where to find the best single-track riding. My definition of single-track is a trail that is no wider than your handlebars and has not been altered from its natural condition. There is a great deal of single-track riding in Vermont, as well as plenty of double-track riding, where two people can ride side by side on the equivalent of parallel single-track trails. On the other hand, many, many Vermont trails are rocky, overgrown, steep, and technical—yet as wide as a road. While these do not exactly fit my definition of single-track, because they are wider than your handlebars, these routes are equivalent otherwise. Throughout this book, I refer to such wider trails interchangeably as double-track trails, jeep roads, four-wheel-drive roads, and unmaintained Class 4 roads.

TRAIL SIGNAGE

Vermont has several different trail-user groups, each with its own sign system. The most extensive group is the Vermont Association of Snow Travelers (VAST). This association consists primarily of snowmobilers who have put tremendous effort into developing and maintaining trails, and acquiring permission from private landowners to cross their land. VAST's agreement with the

The Catamount Trail
Association (CTA) and
Vermont Association of
Snow Travelers (VAST)
share trail signage on a
Class 4 road near
Lake Ninevah.

landowners is that when the snow is gone, the use of their land ceases.
However, much of the VAST trail network is on Class 4 town roads, which are
public domain and can be used by anyone, any time of the year. Many of my
rides share VAST trails and are marked specifically with VAST trail signage. I
refer to their signs whenever possible throughout the book; for brevity, I use the
acronym VAST in such references.

The Catamount Trail Association (CTA) maintains a cross-country ski trail
that extends from the Massachusetts border to Canada. Like VAST trails, the
Catamount Trail crosses both public and private land and is signed with its own
symbol: a blue diamond with a black pawprint. A few of my rides share short sections of the Catamount Trail; I refer to its signs whenever appropriate, and to the
club as the CTA. Unfortunately, it is not possible to ride the entire Catamount
Trail from end to end for two reasons: Much of the route covers private property,
and it is only maintained for winter travel. However, some sections are on Class
4 town roads, where mountain bikers are allowed to ride.

The state of Vermont and the Green Mountain National Forest have opened
several trails to mountain bikers on state and national forestland (see the sec-

tion on the Green Mountain National Forest, pages 139–163, and Ride 45, Cotton Brook, page 166). These trails are signed with white arrows and white diamonds with black or green silhouettes of mountain bikers.

EMERGENCY ASSISTANCE

People have long joked about Vermont being behind the times. In some ways it is true, especially when it comes to public phone systems and road signs. For years, Vermonters dialed their town's specific police, ambulance, and fire numbers in case of emergency, and referred to numerous public roads by more than one name. However, all that is changing. As I write this book, Vermont is converting to the emergency 911 telephone system used nationwide. By the time this book is published, the new system should be in place throughout the state. You can also reach the state police from a cellular phone by dialing 911.

For the 911 system to work efficiently, each road serving more than three residences must be named and signed. Because the state was only halfway through the conversion process when I put this manuscript to bed, many street signs will appear where they did not exist at the time I researched the rides. It is also possible that certain road names have changed. Please take these caveats into consideration when comparing my route descriptions to your actual riding experiences.

For nonemergency phone calls, remember that since Vermont is so small, it has only one area code: 802. Often you must dial this area code even though you are calling from within the same area code. For example, a person calling downstate to Brattleboro, Vermont, from Waterbury, Vermont, must use the 802 prefix. However, a person calling Stowe, Vermont, from nearby Waterbury, Vermont, need not use it. If you are not sure that the prefix is required, dial it anyway, and a recorded message will tell you to redial without the prefix as needed.

HUNTING SEASONS

Hunting for big and small game is a popular sport in Vermont. Unfortunately, this poses a serious problem for mountain bikers who may choose to share the backcountry with hunters during certain seasons. In my opinion, backcountry users need only be concerned with deer season—and only rifle season, at that—because this is when most hunters take to the woods and the possibilities are greatest that one might mistake you for his or her game animal. Many people are more conservative than I and will not venture into the woods at all during the entire fall hunting season. I find this abstinence unacceptable because it means the mountain biking season ends around September 1—just when some of the best riding begins.

I do ride in the woods during small-game season, because I do not expect to be mistaken for a rabbit or a grouse. I also ride during archery and muzzleloader deer and bear seasons, because the hunter must be very close to the target to make a shot, and I trust that I will not be mistaken for a deer or a bear at that range.

Archery season lasts for most of the month of October and resumes during the first or second week in December, which is shared with muzzleloaders. Most small-game seasons extend from October through the end of December, except for gray squirrel which begins on September 1. Rifle deer season is held during the last two weeks of November, beginning on a Saturday. The precise dates vary each year, but I stay out of the woods then. Besides, it is usually too cold by mid-November to enjoy mountain bike riding in Vermont.

If you choose to ride in the woods during hunting seasons, wear fluorescent clothing—safety orange is best. And be sure to avoid white or beige, which may suggest a deer in flight. Remember also to make a lot of noise. I tie bells under my saddle, which can sound annoying at first, but I get used to them. And those screeching brake pads, which otherwise would drive you crazy, are perfect noisemakers.

For a current copy of Vermont's hunting season dates, write to the Vermont Fish and Wildlife Department, 103 South Main Street, 10 South, Waterbury, VT 05676-9985; (802) 241-3700.

Vermont has a mountain bike organization that was founded in December 1997. Vermont Mountain Bike Advocates (VMBA) calls itself "the voice of mountain biking in Vermont." The group's primary objective is to develop and preserve trail riding in Vermont and to represent mountain biking before state, federal, and private land managers. Other VMBA goals include demonstrating the economic value of the mountain bike industry in Vermont, lobbying for legislation beneficial to mountain bikers, developing community and statewide trail systems, inculcating safe and responsible trail riding, and fostering membership growth.

Anyone interested in the future of mountain biking in Vermont should join VMBA. For more information write to VMBA, P.O. Box 563, Waterbury, VT 05676.

Kate Carter

Wildlife Viewing

1 Heartwellville
2 Harriman Reservoir
3 Prospect Mountain Ski Area
10 Ball Mountain Dam
13 Ninevah Road
14 Shrewsbury
18 Chittenden Reservoir
31 Woodbury Mountain Road
38 Natural Turnpike and Steammill Roads
41 Pine Brook Trail

42 Ash Hill Trail
43 Contest Trail
44 Michigan Road
45 Cotton Brook
47 Old County Road
48 Mount Mansfield
56 Wild Branch
57 Willoughby
59 Victory Bog
60 Fred Mold Memorial Ride

Climbers' Delights

5 Mount Snow's World Cup Cross-Country Course
20 South Hill
29 Mount Cushman
30 West Brookfield (Broken Bike Ride)

37 Snake Mountain
45 Cotton Brook
48 Mount Mansfield
58 Kirby Mountain
60 Fred Mold Memorial Ride

Fishing and Biking

2 Harriman Reservoir
3 Prospect Mountain Ski Area
4 Somerset Reservoir
13 Ninevah Road
18 Chittenden Reservoir

21 Silver Lake
27 Floating Bridge Loop
57 Willoughby
61 Groton State Forest

Short and Sweet

14 Shrewsbury
21 Silver Lake
40 Hogback Mountain

41 Pine Brook Trail
46 Nebraska Valley

Rail Trails

2 Harriman Reservoir
19 Delaware and Hudson Rail Trail
53 Missisquoi Valley Rail Trail

Entry Level Single-track

2 Harriman Reservoir
3 Prospect Mountain Ski Area
11 Stratton Mountain's Sun Bowl
18 Chittenden Reservoir
34 Outdoor Experience at Catamount

35 Shelburne Farms
39 Leicester Hollow Trail
40 Hogback Mountain
41 Pine Brook Trail

(continued)

Family

Technical Single- and Double-track

On Top of the World

Downhillers' Delight

MOUNTAIN BIKE!

Vermont

INTRODUCTION

TRAIL DESCRIPTION OUTLINE

Each trail in this book begins with key information that includes length, configuration, aerobic and technical difficulty, trail conditions, scenery, and special comments. Additional description is contained in 11 individual categories. The following will help you to understand all of the information provided.

Trail name: Trail names are as designated on United States Geological Survey (USGS) or Forest Service or other maps, and/or by local custom.

At a Glance Information

Length/configuration: The overall length of a trail is described in miles, unless stated otherwise. The configuration is a description of the shape of each trail—whether the trail is a loop, out-and-back (that is, along the same route), figure eight, trapezoid, isosceles triangle, decahedron . . . (just kidding), or if it connects with another trail described in the book. See the Glossary for definitions of *point-to-point* and *combination*.

Aerobic difficulty: This provides a description of the degree of physical exertion required to complete the ride.

Technical difficulty: This provides a description of the technical skill required to pedal a ride. Trails are often described here in terms of being paved, unpaved, sandy, hard-packed, washboarded, two- or four-wheel-drive, single-track or double-track. All terms that might be unfamiliar to the first-time mountain biker are defined in the Glossary.

    Note: For both the aerobic and technial difficulty categories, authors were asked to keep in mind the fact that all riders are not equal, and thus to gauge the trail in terms of how the middle-of-the-road rider—someone between the newcomer and Ned Overend—could handle the route. Comments about the trail's length, condition, and elevation change will also assist you in determining the difficulty of any trail relative to your own abilities.

Overall rating: This provides an overall estimate of the difficulty of each ride. For further explanation see "Rating the Rides" in the Preface on page xxi.

Scenery: Here you will find a general description of the natural surroundings during the seasons most riders pedal the trail, and a suggestion of what is to be found at special times (like great fall foliage or cactus in bloom).

Special comments: Unique elements of the ride are mentioned.

Category Information

General location: This category describes where the trail is located in reference to a nearby town or other landmark.

Elevation change: Unless stated otherwise, the figure provided is the total gain and loss of elevation along the trail. In regions where the elevation variation is not extreme, the route is simply described as flat, rolling, or possessing short steep climbs or descents.

Season: This is the best time of year to pedal the route, taking into account trail conditions (for example, when it will not be muddy), riding comfort (when the weather is too hot, cold, or wet), and local hunting seasons.

Note: Because the exact opening and closing dates of deer, elk, moose, and antelope seasons often change from year to year, riders should check with the local fish and game department or call a sporting goods store (or any place that sells hunting licenses) in a nearby town before heading out. Wear bright clothes in fall, and don't wear suede jackets while in the saddle. Hunter's-orange tape on the helmet is also a good idea.

Services: This category is of primary importance in guides for paved-road tourers, but is far less crucial to most mountain bike trail descriptions because there are usually no services whatsoever to be found. Authors have noted when water is available on desert or long mountain routes and have listed the availability of food, lodging, campgrounds, and bike shops. If all these services are present, you will find only the words "All services available in . . ."

Hazards: Special hazards like steep cliffs, great amounts of deadfall, or barbed-wire fences very close to the trail are noted here.

Rescue index: Determining how far one is from help on any particular trail can be difficult due to the backcountry nature of most mountain bike rides. Authors therefore state the proximity of homes or Forest Service outposts, nearby roads where one might hitch a ride, or the likelihood of other bikers being encountered on the trail. Phone numbers of local sheriff departments or hospitals are hardly ever provided because phones are usually not available. If you are able to reach a phone, the local operator will connect you with emergency services.

Land status: This category provides information regarding whether the trail crosses land operated by the Forest Service; Bureau of Land Management; a city, state, or national park; whether it crosses private land whose owner (at the time the author did the research) has allowed mountain bikers right of passage; and so on.

Note: Authors have been extremely careful to offer only those routes that are open to bikers and are legal to ride. However, because land ownership changes over time, and because the land-use controversy created by mountain bikes still has not completely subsided, it is the duty of each cyclist to look for and to heed signs warning against trail use. Don't expect this book to get you off the hook when you're facing some small-town judge for pedaling past a Biking Prohibited sign erected the day before you arrived. Look for these signs, read them, and heed the advice. And remember there's always another trail.

Maps: The maps in this book have been produced with great care and, in conjunction with the trail-following suggestions, will help you stay on course. But as every experienced mountain biker knows, things can get tricky in the backcountry. It is therefore strongly suggested that you avail yourself of the detailed information found in the 7.5 minute series USGS (United States Geological Survey) topographic maps. In some cases, authors have found that specific Forest Service or other maps may be more useful than the USGS quads and tell how to obtain them.

Finding the trail: Detailed information on how to reach the trailhead and where to park your car is provided here.

Sources of additional information: Here you will find the address and/or phone number of a bike shop, governmental agency, or other source from which trail information can be obtained.

Notes on the trail: This is where you are guided carefully through any portions of the trail that are particularly difficult to follow. The author also may add information about the route that does not fit easily in the other categories. This category will not be present for those rides where the route is easy to follow.

ABBREVIATIONS

The following road-designation abbreviations are used in *Mountain Bike! Vermont:*

FR	Forest Service Road
I-	Interstate
TH	Town Highway
US	United States highway

State highways are designated with the appropriate two-letter state abbreviation, followed by the road number. Example: VT 100 = Vermont State Highway 100.

Postal Service two-letter state codes:

AL	Alabama	MT	Montana
AK	Alaska	NE	Nebraska
AZ	Arizona	NV	Nevada
AR	Arkansas	NH	New Hampshire
CA	California	NJ	New Jersey
CO	Colorado	NM	New Mexico
CT	Connecticut	NY	New York
DE	Delaware	NC	North Carolina
DC	District of Columbia	ND	North Dakota
FL	Florida	OH	Ohio
GA	Georgia	OK	Oklahoma
HI	Hawaii	OR	Oregon
ID	Idaho	PA	Pennsylvania
IL	Illinois	RI	Rhode Island
IN	Indiana	SC	South Carolina
IA	Iowa	SD	South Dakota
KS	Kansas	TN	Tennessee
KY	Kentucky	TX	Texas
LA	Louisiana	UT	Utah
ME	Maine	VT	Vermont
MD	Maryland	VA	Virginia
MA	Massachusetts	WA	Washington
MI	Michigan	WV	West Virginia
MN	Minnesota	WI	Wisconsin
MS	Mississippi	WY	Wyoming
MO	Missouri		

RIDE CONFIGURATIONS

Combination: This type of route may combine two or more configurations. For example, a point-to-point route may integrate a scenic loop or an out-and-back spur midway through the ride. Likewise, an out-and-back may have a loop at its farthest point (this configuration looks like a cherry with a stem attached; the stem is the out-and back, the fruit is the terminus loop). Or a loop route may have multiple out-and-back spurs and/or loops to the side. Mileage for a combination route is for the total distance to complete the ride.

Loop: This route configuration is characterized by riding from the designated trailhead to a distant point, then returning to the trailhead via a different route (or simply continuing on the same in a circle route) without doubling back. You always move forward across new terrain, but return to the starting point when finished. Mileage is for the entire loop from the trailhead back to trailhead.

Out-and-back: A ride where you will return on the same trail you pedaled out. While this might sound far more boring than a loop route, many trails look very different when pedaled in the opposite direction.

Point-to-point: A vehicle shuttle (or similar assistance) is required for this type of route, which is ridden from the designated trailhead to a distant location, or endpoint, where the route ends. Total mileage is for the one-way trip from the trailhead to endpoint.

Spur: A road or trail that intersects the main trail you're following.

TOPOGRAPHIC MAPS

The maps in this book, when used in conjunction with the route directions present in each chapter, will in most instances be sufficient to get you to the trail and keep you on it. However, you will find superior detail and valuable information in the 7.5 minute series United States Geological Survey (USGS) topographic maps. Recognizing how indispensable these are to bikers and hikers alike, many bike shops and sporting goods stores now carry topos of the local area.

But if you're brand new to mountain biking you might be wondering "What's a topographic map?" In short, these differ from standard "flat" maps in that they indicate not only linear distance, but elevation as well. One glance at a topo will show you the difference, for "contour lines" are spread across the map like dozens of intricate spider webs. Each contour line represents a particular elevation, and at the base of each topo a particular "contour interval" designation is given. Yes, it sounds confusing if you're new to the lingo, but it truly is a simple and wonderfully helpful system. Keep reading.

Let's assume that the 7.5 minute series topo before us says "Contour Interval 40 feet," that the short trail we'll be pedaling is two inches in length on the map, and that it crosses five contour lines from its beginning to end. What do we know? Well, because the linear scale of this series is 2,000 feet to the inch (roughly 2 3/4 inches representing 1 mile), we know our trail is approximately 4/5 of a mile long (2 inches × 2,000 feet). But we also know we'll be climbing or descending 200 vertical feet (5 contour lines × 40 feet each) over that distance. And the elevation designations written on occasional contour lines will tell us if we're heading up or down.

The authors of this series warn their readers of upcoming terrain, but only a detailed topo gives you the information you need to pinpoint your position exactly on a map, steer yourself toward optional trails and roads nearby, plus let you know at a glance if you'll be pedaling hard to take them. It's a lot of information for a very low cost. In fact, the only drawback with topos is their size — several feet square. I've tried rolling them into tubes, folding them carefully, even cutting them into blocks and photocopying the pieces. Any of these systems is a pain, but no matter how you pack the maps you'll be happy they're along. And you'll be even happier if you pack a compass as well.

In addition to local bike shops and sporting goods stores, you'll find topos at major universities and some public libraries where you might try photocopying the ones you need to avoid the cost of buying them. But if you want your own and can't find them locally, write to:

USGS Map Sales
Box 25286
Denver, CO 80225

Ask for an index while you're at it, plus a price list and a copy of the booklet *Topographic Maps*. In minutes you'll be reading them like a pro.

A second excellent series of maps available to mountain bikers is that put out by the United States Forest Service. If your trail runs through an area designated as a national forest, look in the phone book (white pages) under the United States Government listings, find the Department of Agriculture heading, and then run you finger down that section until you find the Forest Service. Give them a call and they'll provide the address of the regional Forest Service office, from which you can obtain the appropriate map.

TRAIL ETIQUETTE

Pick up almost any mountain bike magazine these days and you'll find articles and letters to the editor about trail conflict. For example, you'll find hikers' tales of being blindsided by speeding mountain bikers, complaints from mountain bikers about being blamed for trail damage that was really caused by horse or cattle traffic, and cries from bikers about those "kamikaze" riders who through their antics threaten to close even more trails to all of us.

The authors of this series have been very careful to guide you to only those trails that are open to mountain biking (or at least were open at the time of their research), and without exception have warned of the damage done to our sport through injudicious riding. My personal views on this matter appear in the Afterword, but all of us can benefit from glancing over the following International Mountain Bicycling Association (IMBA) Rules of the Trail before saddling up.

1. *Ride on open trails only.* Respect trail and road closures (ask if not sure), avoid possible trespass on private land, obtain permits and authorization as may be required. Federal and state wilderness areas are closed to cycling.

2. *Leave no trace.* Be sensitive to the dirt beneath you. Even on open trails, you should not ride under conditions where you will leave evidence of your passing, such as on certain soils shortly after rain. Observe the different types of soils and trail construction; practice low-impact cycling. This also means staying on the trail and not creating any new ones. Be sure to pack out at least as much as you pack in.

3. *Control your bicycle!* Inattention for even a second can cause disaster. Excessive speed can maim and threaten people; there is no excuse for it!

4. *Always yield the trail.* Make known your approach well in advance. A friendly greeting (or a bell) is considerate and works well; startling someone may cause loss of trail access. Show your respect when passing others by slowing to a walk or even stopping. Anticipate that other trail users may be around corners or in blind spots.

5. *Never spook animals.* All animals are startled by an unannounced approach, a sudden movement, or a loud noise. This can be dangerous for you, for others, and for the animals. Give animals extra room and time to adjust to you. In passing, use special care and follow the directions of horseback riders (ask if uncertain). Running cattle and disturbing wild animals is a serious offense. Leave gates as you found them, or as marked.

6. *Plan ahead.* Know your equipment, your ability, and the area in which you are riding—and prepare accordingly. Be self-sufficient at all times. Wear a helmet, keep your machine in good condition, and carry necessary supplies for changes in weather or other conditions. A well-executed trip is a satisfaction to you and not a burden or offense to others.

For more information, contact IMBA, P.O. Box 7578, Boulder, CO 80306; (303) 545-9011.

HITTING THE TRAIL

Once again, because this is a "where-to," not a "how-to" guide, the following will be brief. If you're a veteran trail rider these suggestions might serve to remind you of something you've forgotten to pack. If you're a newcomer, they might convince you to think twice before hitting the backcountry unprepared.

Water: I've heard the questions dozens of times. "How much is enough? One bottle? Two? Three?! But think of all that extra weight!" Well, one simple physiological fact should convince you to err on the side of excess when it comes to deciding how much water to pack: a human working hard in 90-degree temperature needs approximately ten quarts of fluids every day. Ten quarts. That's two and a half gallons—12 large water bottles, or 16 small ones. And, with water weighing in at approximately eight pounds per gallon, a one-day supply comes to a whopping 20 pounds.

In other words, pack along two or three bottles even for short rides. And make sure you can purify the water found along the trail on longer routes. When writing of those routes where this could be of critical importance, each author has provided information on where water can be found near the trail—if it can be found at all. But drink it untreated and you run the risk of disease. (See *Giardia* in the Glossary.)

One sure way to kill the protozoans, bacteria, and viruses in water is to boil it. Right. That's just how you want to spend your time on a bike ride. Besides, who wants to carry a stove, or denude the countryside stoking bonfires to boil water?

Luckily, there is a better way. Many riders pack along the inexpensive and only slightly distasteful tetraglycine hydroperiodide tablets (sold under the names Potable Aqua, Globaline, and Coughlan's, among others). Some invest in portable, lightweight purifiers that filter out the crud. Unfortunately, both iodine *and* filtering are now required to be absolutely sure you've killed all the nasties you can't see. Tablets or iodine drops by themselves will knock off the well-known *Giardia*, once called "beaver fever" for its transmission to the water through the feces of infected beavers. One to four weeks after ingestion, *Giardia* will have you bloated, vomiting, shivering with chills, and living in the bathroom. (Though you won't care while you're suffering, beavers are getting a bum rap, for other animals are carriers also.)

But now there's another parasite we must worry about—*Cryptosporidium*. "Crypto" brings on symptoms very similar to *Giardia*, but unlike that fellow protozoan it's equipped with a shell sufficiently strong to protect it against the chemical killers that stop *Giardia* cold. This means we're either back to boiling or on to using a water filter to screen out both *Giardia* and crypto, plus the iodine to knock off viruses. All of which sounds like a time-consuming pain, but really isn't. Some water filters come equipped with an iodine chamber, to guarantee full protection. Or you can simply add a pill or drops to the water you've just filtered (if you aren't allergic to iodine, of course). The pleasures of backcountry biking—and the displeasure of getting sick—make this relatively minor effort worth every one of the few minutes involved.

Tools: Ever since my first cross-country tour in 1965 I've been kidded about the number of tools I pack on the trail. And so I will exit entirely from this discussion by providing a list compiled by two mechanic (and mountain biker) friends of mine. After all, since they make their livings fixing bikes, and get their kicks by riding them, who could be a better source?

These two suggest the following as an absolute minimum:

tire levers
spare tube and patch kit
air pump
Allen wrenches (3, 4, 5, and 6 mm)
six-inch crescent (adjustable-end) wrench
small flat-blade screwdriver
chain rivet tool
spoke wrench

But, while they're on the trail, their personal tool pouches contain these additional items:

channel locks (small)
air gauge
tire valve cap (the metal kind, with a valve-stem remover)
baling wire (ten or so inches, for temporary repairs)
duct tape (small roll for temporary repairs or tire boot)
boot material (small piece of old tire or a large tube patch)
spare chain link
rear derailleur pulley
spare nuts and bolts
paper towel and tube of waterless hand cleaner

First-aid kit: My personal kit contains the following, sealed inside double Ziploc bags:

sunscreen
aspirin
butterfly-closure bandages
Band-Aids
gauze compress pads (a half-dozen 4″ × 4″)
gauze (one roll)
ace bandages or Spenco joint wraps
Benadryl (an antihistamine, in case of allergic reactions)
water purification tablets / water filter (on long rides)
moleskin / Spenco "Second Skin"
hydrogen peroxide, iodine, or Mercurochrome (some kind of antiseptic)
snakebite kit

Final considerations: The authors of this series have done a good job in suggesting that specific items be packed for certain trails—raingear in particular seasons, a hat and gloves for mountain passes, or shades for desert jaunts. Heed their warnings, and think ahead. Good luck.

Dennis Coello

SOUTHERN VERMONT

Northern Vermonters refer to southern Vermont as the Banana Belt because, relatively speaking, winter comes late and spring comes early. It is true that parts of southern Vermont can have as much as a two-week head start on summer over the rest of the state. Trees bud sooner, flowers blossom earlier, and trails dry out quicker. Except at higher, more sheltered elevations, the snow does not linger as long in the south as it does in the north.

The southern hills are nonetheless steep and often seem endless. The land is heavily forested: Windham County, in the southeast corner, is Vermont's second most thickly wooded area after Essex County, in the Northeast Kingdom. As a result, open meadows with views are rather scarce. However, there is an abundance of stone walls and cemeteries, and the mountain bike riding is thoroughly entertaining on town roads as well as trails.

Because it lies so much closer to the metropolises of Boston, Hartford, and New York City, southern Vermont is highly populated with out-of-staters, both tourists and second-home owners. The locals are greatly outnumbered, and you may well count more license plates from other states than from Vermont.

RIDE 1 · Heartwellville (Black Bear Run)

AT A GLANCE
_____

VT

Length/configuration: 10.8-mile loop; option to add another 4.5 miles

Aerobic difficulty: Good aerobic condition a must; many short, steep hills

Technical difficulty: Many challenging climbs and descents on rocky, rooty, often wet jeep roads; not for the timid

Overall rating: Difficult

Scenery: Mostly wooded; dirt or gravel roads and trails; an old cemetery; views of Dutch Hill

Special comments: Saw a black bear and her cub on this ride!

The 10.8-mile Heartwellville loop might not seem long in distance, but it takes more time than you expect. Several sections are quite challenging. Expert riders will most likely complete the 10.8 miles in an hour and a half, while intermediate riders should budget at least two hours. Beginners should not attempt this ride.

The Heartwellville loop begins with a short section on pavement, followed by two substantial climbs on dirt roads that work their way deep into the backcountry and dwindle into jeep roads. A smooth jeep road covered with pine needles soon changes to a rugged, rocky descent to be ridden with care. The trail then passes the remote Jewell Cemetery, a true surprise since it lies so far from civilization.

It was just after visiting Jewell Cemetery that my partner David and I had a riding experience we will never forget. I was in front, enjoying a gradual down-hill section, when I heard a very loud noise to my left. I was about to stop when I saw the rear end of a black bear charging off into the woods—thankfully away from me. At the same time, I saw a cub run up a tree. I quickly clicked back into my pedal, began riding as fast as I could, and shouted out to David, "Keep ped-aling!" Meanwhile, he saw the cub run back down the tree and off into the woods, but luckily, he never saw the mother. David's fear—like mine—was that we were riding between the cub and its mom. Our adrenaline was still pumping one-quarter mile later, when we came to a stop and were sure we had put some distance between ourselves and the bears. It was thrilling to see these animals in their natural habitat, yet we were aware of the potential dangers that exist when traveling by bicycle in the backcountry. Most of all, we wondered what the bears must have thought when two people on bicycles appeared out of nowhere.

RIDE 1 • Heartwellville (Black Bear Run)

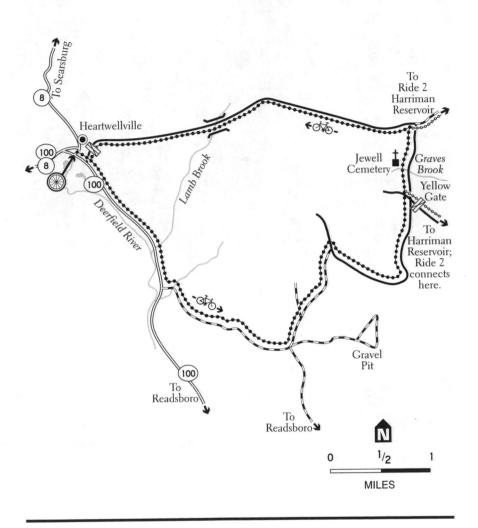

General location: Heartwellville.

Elevation change: There is a 500′ climb at the beginning of the ride, followed by a descent, a 400′ climb at the halfway point, and a final 650′ descent.

Season: June through October.

Services: There are no services in Heartwellville. Readsboro Falls, about 2 miles south of Heartwellville on VT 100, has a general store. Complete services can be found in Wilmington, about 12 miles northeast of Heartwellville at the junction

The obscure Jewell Cemetery has several grave markers dating back to the late 1700s and one dated 1969.

of VT 9 and VT 100. The nearest bike shop is Green Mountain Bikes (802-464-6557), 1 mile north of Wilmington on VT 100.

Hazards: Rough, rocky jeep roads; waterbars on the final descent. Keep an eye out for bears!

Rescue index: This is a remote ride and you are unlikely to see another person (except in winter, when the jeep roads are heavily used). At one point you are 5 miles from a telephone. I do not recommend riding this loop alone, but if you do, be sure to inform someone of your plans and leave them a map of the ride.

Land status: Class 3 and 4 roads.

Maps: This ride appears on DeLorme's and Northern Cartographic's atlases, but the best map is the USGS 7.5 minute quad, Readsboro.

Finding the trail: Heartwellville is situated at the junction of VT 100 and VT 8. Park in the parking lot of the Door of Hope Church, a large white building that was once the Stagecoach Inn for travelers riding by scheduled carriage from Massachusetts to points north in Vermont. The people here are very friendly and do not mind bikers parking in their lot. Your ride begins here.

Sources of additional information: I could not find anyone who could provide me with additional information about this neck of the woods.

Notes on the trail: From the Door of Hope Church, ride south on VT 8 a few hundred feet to the stop sign at the junction of VT 8 and VT 100. Turn left, riding north on VT 100. (The signage here is confusing, because although you are following signs for VT 100 north, you are actually riding due south.)

At 1.4 miles, turn left onto an unmarked dirt road that climbs steeply (the only sign is a stop sign for the traffic coming down the dirt road). Ride up this road, crossing a stream at a sharp right bend in the road. At 3.2 miles, you reach a 4-way junction with a beautiful old barn immediately on your left. Turn left, keeping the barn to your left, and climb steeply and steadily, passing a road to the left. At 4.5 miles is a Y-intersection with a small open area on the left. Take a hard right onto what looks like a driveway. (Do not go straight up the steep gravelly driveway that ends at heavy farm machinery and barking dogs. The man who lives here is very friendly and will point you in the proper direction should you end up here by mistake.)

The hard right driveway is actually a Class 4 jeep road that rolls smoothly through the forest along a stone wall on your left. Begin to descend; the road becomes rougher and rockier the farther down you go. Take care, as this section of trail is very rough and washed out. At the bottom of this hill, at 6.2 miles, is a major 4-way trail junction. The jeep road coming in from the right (yellow gate) is part of Ride 2, Harriman Reservoir. (The two rides share the next .5 mile.)

Turn left and then stay to your right. Cross Graves Brook, pass Jewell Cemetery on the left, and descend to another trail intersection at 6.7 miles where this ride goes left.

To add an additional 4.5 miles to this ride, turn right and follow directions from the 6.5-mile mark in the Ride 2, Harriman Reservoir description. At the bottom of the single-track descent, turn right onto the railroad bed, and follow directions for the spur. The spur is 2 miles long each way, and will bring you back to the Heartwellville loop at the latter's 6.2-mile mark, via the jeep road with the yellow gate. You will then repeat the half-mile section that goes by Jewell Cemetery.

To continue Ride 1, turn left at the trail intersection. You will climb 400′ in the next 2 miles, which are very challenging—lots of ups and downs, rocks, waterbars, and washouts. Pass a nice camp on the right and continue climbing. Eventually, you will begin a gradual descent on rough trail. Cross Lamb Brook on a new, rough-hewn snowmobile bridge. From here, the trail conditions improve and some places are made quite smooth by pine needles. Continue descending to a point where it seems the trail has petered out, at about 9.5 miles. Some 20′ to the right is a gravel road. Take this road and continue descending through several turns until you come to a gate. You must dismount and walk around or lift your bike over the gate. Just ahead is paved VT 100. Turn right, and you immediately reach the junction of VT 100 and VT 8, and the Door of Hope Church where you began this ride. You have pedaled a total of 10.8 very challenging miles (or 15.3 miles with the optional Harriman Reservoir spur).

RIDE 2 · Harriman Reservoir

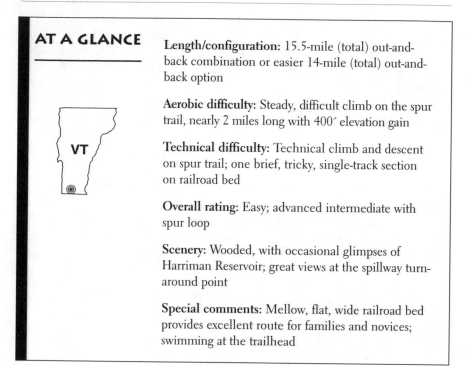

AT A GLANCE

VT

Length/configuration: 15.5-mile (total) out-and-back combination or easier 14-mile (total) out-and-back option

Aerobic difficulty: Steady, difficult climb on the spur trail, nearly 2 miles long with 400′ elevation gain

Technical difficulty: Technical climb and descent on spur trail; one brief, tricky, single-track section on railroad bed

Overall rating: Easy; advanced intermediate with spur loop

Scenery: Wooded, with occasional glimpses of Harriman Reservoir; great views at the spillway turn-around point

Special comments: Mellow, flat, wide railroad bed provides excellent route for families and novices; swimming at the trailhead

A variety of riding conditions makes this 15.5-mile ride fun, interesting, and historically entertaining. You begin by riding on an old railroad bed, skirting the western shore of Harriman Reservoir until you reach the spillway. Remains of trellises evoke another era, when trains were popular for personal travel and for the transport of goods. Now and then, the wooded trail offers glimpses of the reservoir, which dams the Deerfield River. The town of Harriman became deserted over time and now lies at the bottom of the reservoir, after having been flooded when the dam was built.

The railroad bed is wide and flat, with a short section of single-track. Beginners can take the railroad bed south to the spillway, a nice place for a lunch break, and then retrace their steps back to the start for a total of 14 miles. Experienced riders can pick up a side trail on the way back that features a challenging climb and a fun descent on single-track for a total of 15.5 miles. The following directions describe the longer ride.

The longer ride shares a half-mile section of trail with Ride 1, Heartwellville. For an even longer and extremely difficult trip (for experts only—26.3 miles), you can add the entire Heartwellville loop at the 6.5-mile mark of this Harriman Reservoir ride.

General location: Wilmington.

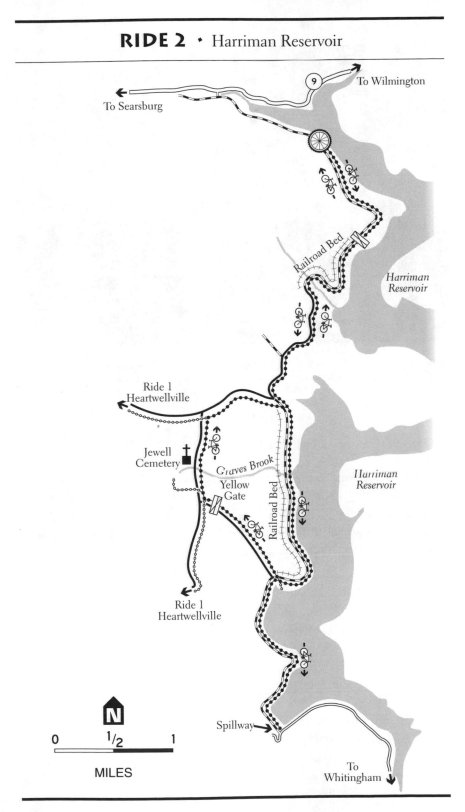

To Wilmington

To Searsburg

Harriman
Reservoir

Railroad Bed

Ride 1
Heartwellville

Jewell
Cemetery

Graves Brook

Harriman
Reservoir

Yellow
Gate

Railroad Bed

Ride 1
Heartwellville

Spillway

To
Whitingham

N

0   1/2   1

MILES

An abandoned railroad bed that runs along the shoreline of Harriman Reservoir is an excellent place for families and novices to spend an afternoon exploring.

Elevation change: One 400´ climb.

Season: You can ride the railroad bed anytime. Try it with studded snow tires in the winter!

Services: All services are available in Wilmington. Green Mountain Bike (802-464-6557) is located on VT 100, about 1 mile north of Wilmington.

Hazards: Nothing unusual. Motor vehicles are not allowed on the railroad bed, except for an occasional NEPCO (New England Power Company) service vehicle.

Rescue index: At the farthest point you are 7 miles from a telephone.

Land status: Class 4 roads and private land owned by NEPCO (parts of the railroad bed). Mountain bikers are welcome.

Maps: The USGS 7.5 minute quad, Readsboro, shows this ride in detail. DeLorme's atlas is also helpful.

Finding the trail: From the traffic light in Wilmington, drive west on VT 9 for 2.6 miles. Turn left on Woods Road, cross a bridge, and go left. Continue for 1 mile and park at the Mount Mills West picnic area in a small cove on the reservoir. You can take a swim here after your ride.

Source of additional information: Check in with Green Mountain Bikes on VT 100, just north of Wilmington.

Notes on the trail: From the picnic area, continue riding on the dirt road you drove in on. After about 1 mile there is a gate, which may be closed. Continue past the gate. You are now on the railroad bed.

After 3 miles, arrive at an open area with several trail options. Stay straight on the trail marked with blue CTA signs (do not take the two trails to the right). Follow this single-track trail through a muddy, narrow channel cut into a rock ledge. Just after the channel, turn right onto a yellow-blazed single-track trail (easy to miss, so keep your eyes open). The trail winds left and downhill, then crosses over a wooden bridge built by the CTA. Come to a trail intersection. (The trail to the right is where you will descend from later in the ride.) Continue straight ahead on the wider trail that skirts the western shore of Harriman Reservoir. Drop down into a gully and shift into your lowest gear for the short, steep climb up the other side.

Come to a major 4-way intersection. The left trail goes to the reservoir and the right trail is the climb you will take later in this ride. For now, continue straight onto a gravelly road surface. It is about 1 mile out to the spillway, where there are great views of the reservoir.

From the spillway, return to the 4-way junction and take the long climb marked with VAST trail signs for 9W, now on your left. This is an unmaintained Class 4 road that gains 400′ in elevation on technically challenging terrain. At the top you will pass through a yellow gate and come to a trail junction. The trail to the left is where Ride 1, Heartwellville, briefly joins this ride.

Turn right, immediately fork right again, and cross Graves Brook. Just as you begin a short climb, look for Jewell Cemetery on your left.

The next section could be rutted and muddy during the spring; otherwise, it is perfectly rideable. Come to a T-intersection. The left is the continuation of the Heartwellville ride. (To add 10.8 very challenging miles, go left here and follow directions for the entire Heartwellville ride, beginning from the 6.7-mile mark.)

To continue this ride, turn right at the T-intersection and descend a fun, technical single-track trail. At the bottom of the descent is the 4-way trail junction you came through earlier in the ride. Turn left and retrace your steps to the start for a total of 15.5 miles.

RIDE 3 · Prospect Mountain Ski Area

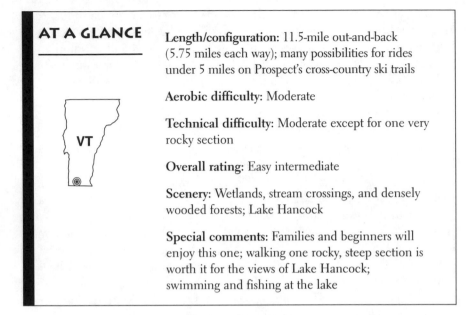

AT A GLANCE

Length/configuration: 11.5-mile out-and-back (5.75 miles each way); many possibilities for rides under 5 miles on Prospect's cross-country ski trails

Aerobic difficulty: Moderate

Technical difficulty: Moderate except for one very rocky section

Overall rating: Easy intermediate

Scenery: Wetlands, stream crossings, and densely wooded forests; Lake Hancock

Special comments: Families and beginners will enjoy this one; walking one rocky, steep section is worth it for the views of Lake Hancock; swimming and fishing at the lake

Prospect Mountain is a defunct downhill ski resort that was resurrected several years ago as a small, intimate cross-country ski center. The lift no longer operates, but the terrain at the base of the mountain is ideal for beginning and intermediate mountain bikers, as well as cross-country skiers. Expert bikers can ride the work road to the top of the mountain for a short (under one mile) yet vigorous aerobic workout.

When I visited Prospect Mountain, it was not yet operating as a mountain bike center. Nevertheless, mountain bikers are welcome on the cross-country ski trails. Some trails are mowed, while others have single-track paths that are used by runners, walkers, and bikers. Plans for the future include opening a bike rental shop at the base area and providing trail maps. Meanwhile, feel free to explore Prospect Mountain's trail system, which is small enough that you are never more than two miles from the base area. Trails are well marked with signs directing you back to the base lodge, so getting lost is nearly impossible.

The following ride makes use of three ski trails—Woodpecker, Round Robbin, and Troll Road—for a total of one mile of trail riding. Troll Road connects to Forest Service Road 273, a curvy, narrow, gravel road that winds for nearly four miles to Lake Hancock in the Stamford Meadows Wildlife Management Area. It is well worth walking your bike over rough sections if necessary, for Hancock is a lovely, small, pristine lake and a good place to take a dip and enjoy a picnic lunch. The shoreline is rocky, so bring a pair of flip-flops or old sneakers if you plan to swim. If you bring a fishing pole, you might catch a smallmouth bass.

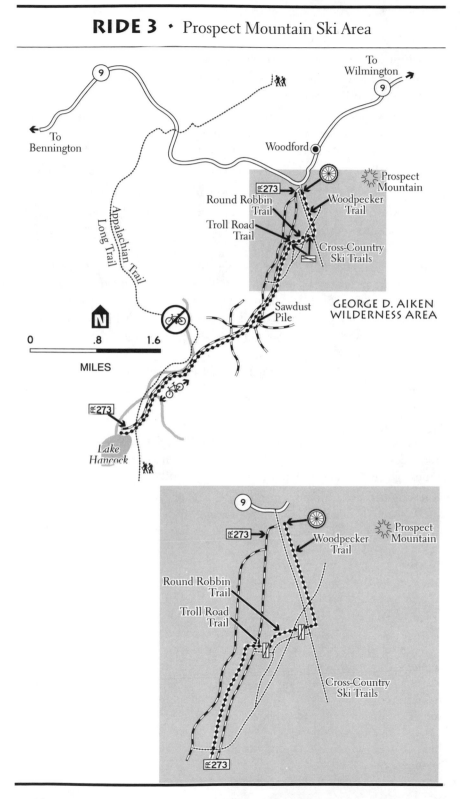

General location: Woodford.

Elevation change: 200´ of elevation is gained very gradually over 5 miles.

Season: Mid-June through mid-November. July and August are the best times for swimming in Lake Hancock.

Services: All services can be found in Woodford. The nearest bike shops are in Bennington: Cutting Edge Mountain Outfitters on Benmont Avenue (802-442-8664) and The Bike Barn on Northside Drive (802-442-4645).

Hazards: FR 273 is a single-lane road shared with an occasional motor vehicle.

Rescue index: Lake Hancock is a remote 5 miles from a telephone.

Land status: Private (Prospect Mountain cross-country ski trails) and public land (Stamford Meadows Wildlife Management Area, managed by the U.S. Forest Service).

Maps: DeLorme's and Northern Cartographic's atlases show the road to Lake Hancock. Maps of the cross-country ski trails are posted along the way, but until Prospect Mountain opens as a bona fide mountain bike center, corresponding handheld maps will not be available. However, it is possible to get a modest trail map at the Greenwood Lodge hostel and campground (802-442-2547), located at the base of the ski area.

Finding the trail: Prospect Mountain ski area is located on VT 9, 10 miles west of Wilmington and 4 miles east of Bennington. Park in the ski area parking lot. The ride begins here.

Sources of additional information: The Greenwood Lodge hostel and campground (802-442-2547) has trail maps and other information on riding in the immediate area. You can also call Prospect Mountain (802-442-2575) and leave a message on the answering machine; someone will call you back.

Notes on the trail: From the parking lot, ride on the gravel road between the gift shop and ski rental building, going toward the defunct ski lift. Turn right just before the restaurant (closed) and immediately left behind the restaurant, riding under a power line. Climb gradually, staying to the right of a small shack on Woodpecker Trail. After a few hundred yards, turn right on Round Robbin Trail, ride around a gate, and cross a small dirt road marked for snowmobiles.

Stay on Round Robbin, which is a grassy, mowed, double-wide trail, until you come to Troll Road. Turn right and descend gradually to a wooden gate. Ride around the gate and arrive at FR 273, having completed 1 mile of trail riding.

Turn left onto FR 273, a curvy, gravel road with several trail and road intersections. Stay on the main road at all times. At 3.5 miles, you reach the former site of a portable saw mill. There is a large mound of sawdust to the left, which has accumulated other forms of garbage. At this point, FR 273 changes to a very rough jeep road for the remaining 2.2 miles to Lake Hancock. For a shorter, easier 7-mile round-trip ride (3.5 miles each way), beginners can turn around here, but I recommend forging ahead and occasionally dismounting at any challenging sections.

Continuing on FR 273 to Lake Hancock, at 4.2 miles pass a small bridge on the right, built by a local ATV club. Continue straight on the rocky road, passing by open wetlands to your right.

Just after the 5-mile mark on this ride, a wooden bridge crosses Stamford Stream. If you pay attention, you might see the Appalachian Trail crossing, marked with white blazes on trees, just beyond the bridge. At 5.7 miles is Lake Hancock. Fork right and ride just a little farther to get to the small camping (and swimming) spots along the lake. From here, retrace your steps gradually downhill (most of the way) back to the start, for a total of 11.5 moderate miles.

RIDE 4 · Somerset Reservoir

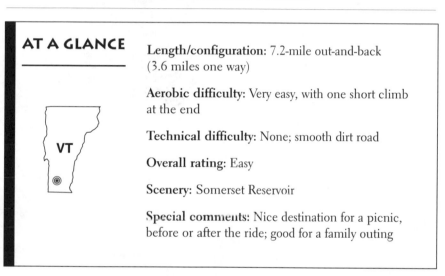

AT A GLANCE

Length/configuration: 7.2-mile out-and-back (3.6 miles one way)

Aerobic difficulty: Very easy, with one short climb at the end

Technical difficulty: None; smooth dirt road

Overall rating: Easy

Scenery: Somerset Reservoir

Special comments: Nice destination for a picnic, before or after the ride; good for a family outing

Somerset Reservoir is a substantial body of water, just shy of 1,600 acres in size, located in the southern half of the Green Mountain National Forest. This 7.2-mile out-and-back ride begins at the reservoir's picnic area and wanders out the road you drove in on, passing by the 1850 Somerset School House and an equally old cemetery. Although the road is shared with traffic, it is fairly quiet except for weekends, when many people come by car to enjoy fishing and boating on the lake. The dirt road is well shaded and the historic landmarks along the way are quite interesting. More ambitious riders can continue on to Kelley Stand Road (an additional 9 miles one way) from the turnaround point.

General location: Somerset Reservoir.

Elevation change: None. This ride is basically flat.

Season: Anytime the roads are free of snow.

RIDE 4 · Somerset Reservoir

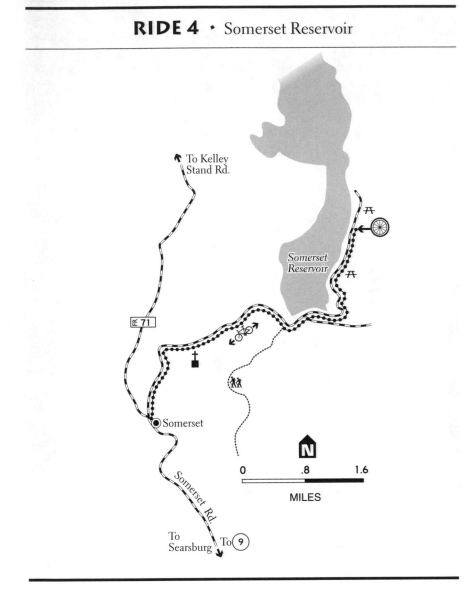

Services: All services are found in Wilmington, 15 miles to the southeast. The nearest bike shop is Green Mountain Bike (802-464-6557), located on VT 100, 1 mile north of Wilmington.

Hazards: The road is shared with motor vehicles.

Rescue index: You are never more than 2 miles from a private residence.

Land status: Class 3 road.

Maps: DeLorme's and Northern Cartographic's atlases are fine.

Somerset Reservoir, with the Green Mountains in the background, is a nice site for a postride picnic.

Finding the trail: From Wilmington, drive west on VT 9 for 6 miles. Turn right onto Somerset Road (Forest Service Road 71). This is a dirt road that passes by Searsburg Reservoir and continues north, parallel to the Deerfield River. After 9 miles, you will come to a fork in the road with signs for Somerset Reservoir. Go right; in 3 miles you arrive at the spillway. Continue up a short, steep pitch to the picnic area. Find a nice spot and park. Your ride begins here.

Source of additional information: For information on the surrounding southern half of the Green Mountain National Forest, call its headquarters in Manchester (802-362-2307).

Notes on the trail: From your picnic area, ride out the same way you drove in. There is a short, steep downhill as you pass by the spillway. At about 2 miles, take a closer look at the Somerset School House. Built in 1850 for 16 students, it is currently being renovated. Just beyond this building is an interesting cemetery.

At 3.6 miles, you come to a **T**-intersection. This is FR 71 and the turnaround point for this ride. To your left is VT 9; to your right is a flat, gravel road that goes past camping areas and several hiking trails, including the Appalachian and Long Trails. At one point, there are beaver meadows and a brief view to the west.

For additional mileage, turn right and follow FR 71 for as long as you want. It is 9 miles from the T-intersection to Kelley Stand Road. At any time, you can turn around and retrace your steps back to the picnic area at Somerset Reservoir.

RIDE 5 · Mount Snow's World Cup Cross-Country Course

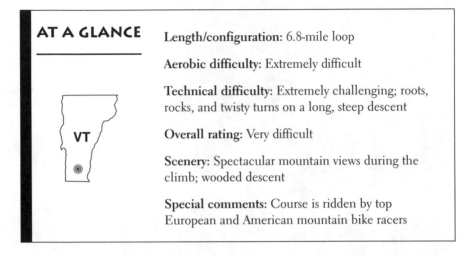

AT A GLANCE

Length/configuration: 6.8-mile loop

Aerobic difficulty: Extremely difficult

Technical difficulty: Extremely challenging; roots, rocks, and twisty turns on a long, steep descent

Overall rating: Very difficult

Scenery: Spectacular mountain views during the climb; wooded descent

Special comments: Course is ridden by top European and American mountain bike racers

Mount Snow is where the concept of mountain biking at downhill ski resorts was first introduced. Dave King, an avid mountain biker and former director of the Mount Snow Ski Patrol, founded the Mount Snow Mountain Bike School in 1988. Since then, many other ski areas have acknowledged the economic value of summer mountain biking.

Mount Snow offers over 140 miles of trails for all ability levels. There is lift-assisted terrain for advanced riders heading down from the 3,600-foot summit; easy riding for beginners at the base area; and the off-resort "Crosstown" trails system that offers something for everyone.

At Mount Snow's base lodge, you will find a complete bike shop with clothing and accessories, retail bike sales, expert repair service, and bike rentals. The mountain bike school offers hourly, half-day, and full-day lessons, as well as guided tours for individuals and groups. Scheduled tours leave the base lodge daily, with different rides for different abilities, or you can pick up a map in the base lodge and go out on your own. Trail passes cost $9 (lifts not included) with special rates for multiday use.

Lift service to the advanced trails at the summit operates daily from mid-June through the October foliage season. Lift passes cost $18 for one ride, $28 for all day (both fees include a trail pass). Multiday rates are available.

Every year during the third weekend in June, the National Off-Road Bicycle Association (NORBA) National Championship Series and the Grundig/UCI World Cup come to Mount Snow. These races feature the world's best mountain

RIDE 5 · Mount Snow's World Cup Cross-Country Course

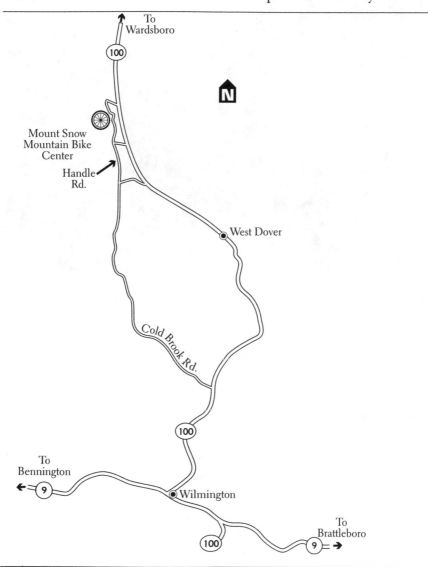

bike riders competing for World Cup points and cash prizes; there are also races for NORBA category racers at the local level. The base area becomes a festival of concessions, booths, demos, and displays by mountain bike manufacturers from across the United States.

Future plans at Mount Snow include a redesigned race course to be used for the NORBA National Championship Series finals. Mount Snow will no longer host the Grundig World Cup, but this former course—your route for Ride 5— will still be marked and available to ride. You can test your fitness by comparing

Mount Snow is one of seven stops in the Grundig World Cup series. John Tomac (bib #2) leads the pack in the grueling cross-country race.

your time for riding this course against the pros, whose times are posted in the mountain bike center.

General location: Mount Snow.

Elevation change: One 1,500′ climb.

Season: Mid-June through mid-October.

Services: All services, including a bike shop, are available at the Mount Snow ski resort and in the nearby town of West Dover.

Hazards: The downhill section of this ride is very steep.

Rescue index: There are emergency aid stations throughout the course; dial four digits: 4578. The mountain bike patrol rides the course regularly.

Land status: The entire ride takes place at the privately owned Mount Snow ski resort.

Maps: The best map is produced by the Mount Snow Mountain Bike School. Pick one up at the mountain bike center in the base lodge.

Finding the trail: From the town of West Dover, drive north on VT 100 for 3 miles. Turn left at the blinking yellow light, then right at the 4-way intersection. Look for the clock tower and park near there. The Mount Snow Mountain Bike Center is located in the base lodge near the clock tower. The ride begins at the clock tower.

Sources of additional information: For information on mountain biking, lodging, and accommodations at Mount Snow, call (800) 245-SNOW; or check out its

Web site at www.mountsnow.com/cgi-bin/mtsnow/menu. For further reading, consult *Mountain Biking the Ski Resorts of the Northeast* by Robert Immler (Woodstock: Countryman Press).

Notes on the trail: Keep in mind that this loop is for intermediate and expert riders only. Riding for beginners can be found at the base area.

From the clock tower at the base area, begin riding toward the ski slopes, bearing right as you go. Look for the red and white arrows with the letters WCXC (World Cup Cross-Country). You will begin climbing immediately on a dirt work road and soon veer sharply to the left. The climb is sustained for approximately 4 miles of dirt road and single-track trails with switchbacks; rocky sections; and short, steep pitches. After about 2.5 miles, there is a short, level break where you can catch your breath before you resume climbing again.

At the crest of the climb (totaling 1,500′), the trail enters the woods for a thrilling, twisting, extremely technical downhill. Be prepared for mud, rocks, tree branches, tree stumps, lots of roots, stream crossings, ledges, and extremely steep pitches on classic Vermont single-track. As you near the bottom, the trail levels out and you finally pop out of the woods with the base area in sight. You can pick up the start of the course and do it again, or proudly call this a day.

RIDE 6 · Oregon Mountain

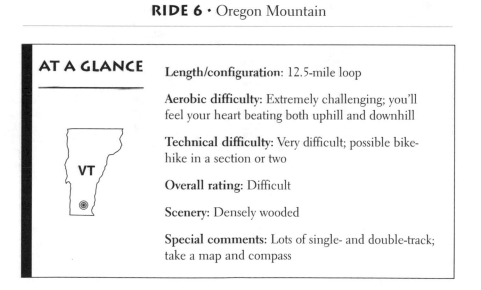

AT A GLANCE

Length/configuration: 12.5-mile loop

Aerobic difficulty: Extremely challenging; you'll feel your heart beating both uphill and downhill

Technical difficulty: Very difficult; possible bike-hike in a section or two

Overall rating: Difficult

Scenery: Densely wooded

Special comments: Lots of single- and double-track; take a map and compass

For some good trail riding in southern Vermont, I looked up my old friend, Dave King. Dave was the founding father of ski-area mountain bike centers. He developed the Mount Snow Mountain Bike School and has consulted with many other ski areas on creating mountain bike trails at their facilities. He is the author of the book *The Mountain Bike Experience,* and has written for numerous

RIDE 6 · Oregon Mountain

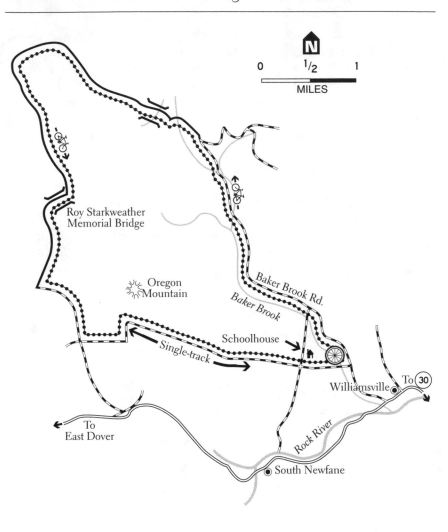

publications about the sport he loves. But the truth about Dave King is, he's a die-hard, single-track woodsman. He loves to ride undeveloped trails—the more challenging, the better. Throw in a few hundred feet of uphill, and he's high on endorphins.

Dave showed me the Oregon Mountain ride, which virtually lies within slingshot of his backyard. (I asked, but he wouldn't let me print directions to his house.) This 12.5-mile loop has a little bit of everything except pavement: dirt road, rugged double-track, cruising double-track, a bit of honest-to-gosh single-track, and some of what Dave calls "hairball descents."

A grassy double-track trail makes up one short section of the otherwise challenging Oregon Mountain loop.

I have a long-haired cat, and I know what a hairball is. But for the life of me, I can't imagine what Dave means by a hairball descent, except that maybe you will want to toss your cookies on the way down. But I didn't think it was so bad. I mean, what the heck: you can always walk. Although this ride is only 12.5 miles long, I rate it for experts.

General location: South Newfane.

Elevation change: About 800´ of elevation is gained in the first 4 miles. There are a few other short climbs throughout the ride.

Season: June through October, with lots of mud in the spring and after heavy rains.

Services: All services are found in Williamsville and South Newfane.

Hazards: Two hairy bridge crossings and some "hairball descents."

Rescue index: At the farthest point you are 3 miles from a private residence.

Land status: Dirt roads, Class 4 roads, double-track and single-track trails.

Maps: DeLorme's atlas comes close to showing most of the trails and topography. Four USGS 7.5 minute quads are also helpful: Newfane, West Dover,

Townsend, and Jamaica, although these maps do not show some of the newer jeep roads.

Finding the trail: From Brattleboro, take VT 30 north. Just after the Maple Valley ski area on the left, turn left onto a paved road, following signs for South Newfane and Dover. In 2 miles, cross a bridge and turn left at the **T**-intersection. Very soon you will see the Lessing Family Store on the right. Take the second right after the store; this is Baker Brook Road (directly opposite the Williamsville post office). Go approximately 1 mile. There is a pullout on the left, just before the bridge that crosses over Baker Brook. Park there.

Sources of additional information: Deane Wilson operates Newfane Off-Road Biking, located behind the general store in Newfane Village. He knows this trail well, can give you a detailed map, and can also provide additional information on riding in the area. Write or call Deane at P.O. Box 111, Newfane, VT 05345; (802) 365-7723. He recently posted trail signs on the Oregon Mountain loop. The signs are crude plaques nailed to trees, handwritten with felt-tip marker.

Notes on the trail: From the parking spot, continue north on Baker Brook Road as it follows the brook, climbing steeply at times, for 3.3 miles. Come to a **T**-intersection and turn left onto a narrow dirt road. Stay left and cross a new wooden-plank bridge, the Roy Starkweather Memorial Bridge. Roy Starkweather was a major player in building the bridge; he died before it was completed. After the bridge, bear right, climbing a washed-out trail that more closely resembles a streambed for 0.5 mile. At times you might choose to walk. (Dave King can ride the whole thing.)

At 4 miles you will come to a trail junction. Veer right and immediately left, following the ATV trail uphill through a stand of pines. This is a very pretty section of trail with lots of ferns and smooth riding. Follow this trail, climbing gradually; eventually, it levels out.

At 5 miles you will come to an area that was recently logged. There is a series of left turns: take the third left, and immediately go left again. The trail narrows. Begin descending and cross a new wooden bridge.

If you can, ride up the washout. (Dave did it; I did half.) At 7 miles, when you reach the top of the climb, turn left onto the double-track jeep trail. Roll and descend to a maintained dirt road, and at 8.6 miles, turn right (there is a red metal gate to your left). Follow this road, and at 9.2 miles, turn left onto another maintained dirt road. At 9.6 miles, take the left onto a third maintained dirt road.

This road ends at a gorgeous old white house with a spectacular view, the only view you will have on this ride. The road becomes a trail at this point, and may be blocked with a wire strung across it. Ignore the wire; this is a public trail. Keeping the house on your right, continue on this trail and pass by a small pond and an opportunity to glimpse the same house from another angle.

At 10.2 miles go straight, following the red arrows. The trail is well marked at this point; just follow the red arrows and tracks.

Climb over the wall and pick up the trail, bearing left as you cross the wall. This is the "hairball descent." It is tough at times, so use caution. The first half mile is very rocky, but conditions improve as you lose elevation. As you get near the bottom, watch out for the big waterbars.

The trail dumps you onto a dirt road just above a 4-way intersection. Go straight through the intersection, keeping the old schoolhouse on your left. Continue downhill to your car, now on the right after you cross Baker Brook.

RIDE 7 · Windmill Hill

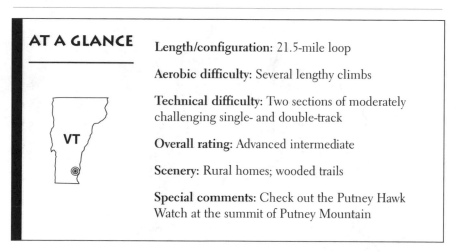

AT A GLANCE

Length/configuration: 21.5-mile loop

Aerobic difficulty: Several lengthy climbs

Technical difficulty: Two sections of moderately challenging single- and double-track

Overall rating: Advanced intermediate

Scenery: Rural homes; wooded trails

Special comments: Check out the Putney Hawk Watch at the summit of Putney Mountain

A few themes prevail throughout this 21.5-mile loop ride: apple orchards, stone walls, and lots of shade. There are not many opportunities for views, but the intimacy created by the narrow, tree-tunneled roads causes you to pay closer attention to the details at hand, such as vegetable and flower gardens, classic old barns, historic stone walls, and unusual dwellings. Around every bend is another source of visual entertainment. And somehow, throughout it all, you climb nearly to the summit of Putney Mountain without even realizing it!

At the top of Putney Mountain is the Putney Hawk Watch viewpoint. The chances of seeing a hawk from here are very good during the spring and fall migrating seasons.

The ride begins and ends at the West Hill Shop, a bicycle and cross-country ski shop that has been a Putney landmark for 20 years. This shop was once located on West Hill, but is now more conveniently located just off the interstate. The West Hill Shop is family operated by Neil and Betsy Quinn; their son, Bevan; and their dog, Woody; along with a staff of slightly macho, yet intellectual and sensitive biker-dudes. Plan on plenty of stimulus when you enter. The only shortcoming is no bathroom; somehow they've managed all this time without one.

General location: Putney.

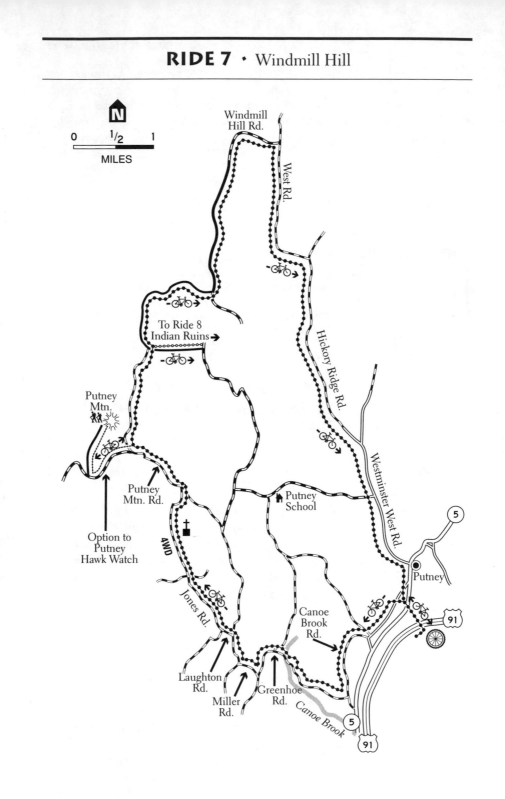

The West Hill Shop in Putney is a complete bicycle shop with sales, service, and rentals. It also has a good selection of maps showing a variety of mountain bike rides in the area.

Elevation change: Most of the 1,000′ of climbing is done on the first half of the ride.

Season: June through mid-November, with lots of mud in the spring.

Services: All services are available in Putney, including the West Hill Shop (802-387-5718). Other bike shops nearby are Specialized Sports (802-257-1017) and the Brattleboro Bike Shop (802-254-8644), both in Brattleboro. The nearest camping is at Bald Mountain Campground in Townshend (802-365-7510), Townshend State Park in Townshend (802-365-7500), and Jamaica State Park in Jamaica (802-874-4660).

Hazards: A few rocky sections on double-track trails.

Rescue index: You are never more than 2 miles from a private dwelling.

Land status: Dirt roads, Class 4 roads, double-track trails.

Maps: Two USGS 7.5 minute quads, Newfane and Townshend, are good. DeLorme's and Northern Cartographic's atlases also show the route. The West Hill Shop has printed an elaborate map of mountain bike rides in the area, including this one.

Finding the trail: The ride begins at the West Hill Shop, just off Exit 4/Putney of Interstate 91.

Source of additional information: The West Hill Shop (802-387-5718) has all the information you need for this ride.

Notes on the trail: From the West Hill Shop, leave the parking lot and turn left onto the paved road. Cross over I-91 and come to a stop sign at US 5. Go directly across US 5, keeping the Putney Coop to your right, and Putney Meadows to your left. Come to another stop sign and turn left onto Old Highway 5.

Pass an apple orchard on your left and take the second right onto gravel Waterman Road. You will climb steadily, but briefly. When the road starts to descend, and just as Waterman Road turns to pavement, turn right onto Canoe Brook Road. The road sign is hidden by tree branches, so look for a nice white house with black trim and a red door. Turn just before the house.

Canoe Brook Road is a blast to ride. It is very narrow, extremely curvy, and in excellent condition. It follows Canoe Brook and eventually comes to Greenhoe Road, where you bear left. Follow Greenhoe to Miller Road and turn right. Miller Road climbs gradually; at the next junction, turn right onto Bunker Road and pass a nice red barn on your left.

Soon you will take a left fork onto Laughton Road. (If you find yourself on pavement, you've gone a mile too far on Bunker Road.) Climb steeply up Laughton, stay right, and look for the sign on the right that says Jones Road. (The left way, which looks like the main road, is a private driveway.)

Stay straight on Jones Road, a double-track jeep trail with 1 mile of single-track. Jones Road runs between 2 parallel stone walls, with pastureland, meadows, and orchards on either side, and has a few challenging, rocky sections. It turns to gravel and comes to a 4-way junction. Jog left and immediately right, reentering Jones Road. Stay on this gravel road until you come to another junction. (Opposite you is a sign that says Leon Road.) Turn left onto Putney Mountain Road and climb gradually for a mile.

At the 8-mile mark, you come to an obvious right turn. There may not be a street sign, but this is Banning Road. At this junction you have an opportunity for a side excursion to the Putney Mountain Hawk Watch. To get to the Hawk Watch, stay on Putney Mountain Road, climbing steadily for 1 mile. On the right is a pullout; there is a 1-mile-long single-track trail, which you can ride out to the viewpoint.

To continue the main ride, take Banning Road and climb gradually. The road becomes narrower as you go. Jog right, then left, and pass by a new brown house with an even newer detached garage. At this point, the road is no longer maintained by the town. Proceed straight onto an unimproved double-track trail. Descend through a rocky section and come to an intersection. Stay left. (Note: The hairpin right is the turn for Ride 8.)

At 10.5 miles, turn right at a **T**-intersection, well marked with a rock pylon. Descend steadily for nearly a mile through rocky washouts. Conditions improve as you go. Come to a gravel road. On the right you will see a small wooden sign with arrows that says Trail and Dodd. Go left here, descending, and at 11.5 miles come abruptly to another **T**-intersection. (There is a road sign that warns you to watch for schoolchildren in the road, off to the right.)

Turn left and climb gradually. Soon the road changes abruptly to an unmaintained double-track trail. Stay straight here and climb through a rocky section;

then roll along a lovely grassy stretch. The road improves as you begin to descend, and soon it becomes gravelly. Pass by a newly built house on your left and continue descending, staying on the main road at all times.

At 14.5 miles come to a **T**-intersection with a road sign indicating that you were just on Windmill Road. Turn right onto a gravel road and descend. Stay on this road, West Road, as indicated by a sign. When you cross the town line from Westminster West to Putney, West Road becomes Hickory Ridge Road. Shortly after Hickory Ridge Road turns to pavement, it joins Westminster West Road. Continue straight, descending all the way into the town of Putney.

At the general store (on your left), turn right onto US 5. Pass by Depot Road on the left. Take the next left, following signs for the Putney Inn. Cross over I-91 and turn right, into the driveway of the West Hill Shop, for a total tour of 21.5 miles.

RIDE 8 · Indian Ruins

AT A GLANCE	**Length/configuration:** 15-mile loop
	Aerobic difficulty: Several climbs; nothing strenuous
	Technical difficulty: Two sections with moderate single- and double-track
VT	**Overall rating:** Intermediate
	Scenery: Rural homes; wooded trails
	Special comments: Shorter version of Ride 7, Windmill Hill; optional 2-mile out-and-back (1 mile each way) to the Putney Mountain Hawk Watch

This 15-mile loop begins exactly like Ride 7, Windmill Hill, but at the 9-mile mark, the Indian Ruins route branches off for a descent past cavelike "ruins" or barrows. The origin of these ruins is unknown and their presence lends mystique to this double-track section of the ride. The Indian Ruins loop includes moderate single- and double-track and a significant amount of climbing, but it is only 15 miles, so I rate it intermediate.

General location: Putney and the countryside to the west.

Elevation change: Most of the 1,000′ of climbing is done on the first half of the ride.

RIDE 8 · Indian Ruins

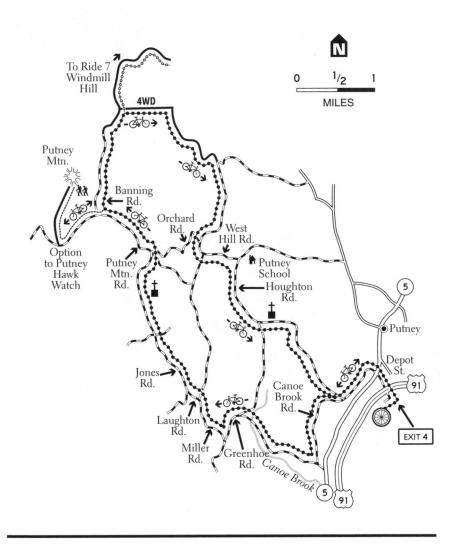

Season: June through mid-November, with lots of mud in the spring.

Services: All services are available in Putney, including the West Hill Shop (802-387-5718). Other bike shops nearby are Specialized Sports (802-257-1017) and the Brattleboro Bike Shop (802-254-8644), both in Brattleboro. The nearest camping is at Bald Mountain Campground in Townshend (802-365-7510), Townshend State Park in Townshend (802-365-7500), and Jamaica State Park in Jamaica (802-874-4660).

Hazards: A few rocky sections on double-track trails.

The curvy, narrow dirt roads of Putney make up the beginning and end of the Indian Ruins ride.

Rescue index: You are never more than 2 miles from a private dwelling.

Land status: Dirt roads, Class 4 roads, double-track trails.

Maps: Two USGS 7.5 minute quads, Newfane and Townshend, are good. DeLorme's and Northern Cartographic's atlases also show the route. The West Hill Shop has printed an elaborate map of mountain bike rides in the area, including this one.

Finding the trail: Begin at the West Hill Shop, just off Exit 4/Putney of Interstate 91.

Source of additional information: The West Hill Shop has all the information you need for this ride.

Notes on the trail: Follow the directions for Ride 7 until you come to the hairpin turn off the double-track trail (after Banning Road). Take the hairpin right turn and begin descending. Look for the cavelike ruins on the left. (Note: At the hairpin right turn, Ride 7, Windmill Hill, continues straight.)

The jeep trail improves as you gradually descend and exit onto Dusty Ridge Road. At this point, all you need is a good pair of brakes because you will be descending all the way back to the start.

At the open meadow on the left, veer sharply right. Pass by Heller Road on your right. Stay with the main road as it winds left. At the next junction there is an old barn and a sign for Dusty Ridge Road. Go right. Descend steadily and come to pavement and the junction of Cory Hill Road. Ride past Orchard Hill Road on the right and immediately turn left onto West Hill Road.

At the next junction, turn sharply right onto Houghton Brook Road. Putney School is on your left. The road alternates between dirt and pavement. Continue this long descent until you come to Old Highway 5. Go left and retrace the first mile of this ride back to the West Hill Shop for a total of 15 miles.

RIDE 9 · Grafton Ponds' Daisy Turner Loop

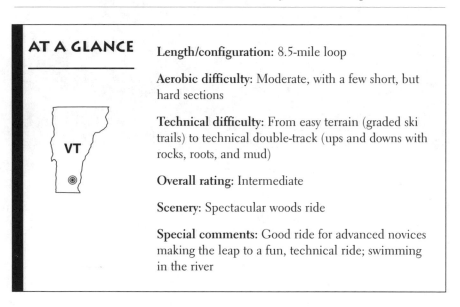

AT A GLANCE

Length/configuration: 8.5-mile loop

Aerobic difficulty: Moderate, with a few short, but hard sections

Technical difficulty: From easy terrain (graded ski trails) to technical double-track (ups and downs with rocks, roots, and mud)

Overall rating: Intermediate

Scenery: Spectacular woods ride

Special comments: Good ride for advanced novices making the leap to a fun, technical ride; swimming in the river

During the winter months, the ski-touring center at Grafton Ponds welcomes cross-country skiers and snowshoers; in the summer, it opens its doors to mountain bikers and hikers. The terrain at Grafton Ponds offers everything from flat, grassy meadows to long climbs and technical single-track. In all, there are 60 miles of riding to explore, about 20 miles each of single-track, double-track, and dirt roads. Riders of all abilities will enjoy the variety of riding at Grafton Ponds.

The 8.5-mile Daisy Turner Loop is named for antislavery activist Daisy Turner, an African-American resident of Grafton who fostered the Underground Railroad and often hid slaves in her home. This well-marked route is fun and challenging, with stone walls, old foundations, and interesting wildlife. A thrilling descent on technical double-track brings you to a Class 4 road and a chance to see the Daisy Turner homestead. The type of geography you encounter on this loop ride is not as important as what you choose to do with it. Ride it slow and cautiously, or hard and fast if you are an expert. Whichever way you ride, you are bound to have a blast.

RIDE 9 · Grafton Ponds' Daisy Turner Loop

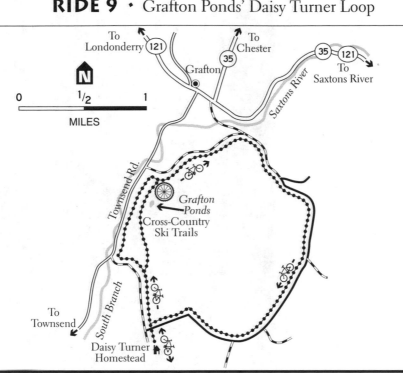

The cozy, rustic base lodge houses a mountain bike center, where you can buy your trail pass, look at assorted maps, and purchase cold drinks. There is a small retail shop with a bike mechanic on hand; Trek mountain bikes stock the rental department. Lessons and guided tours are available for individuals and groups.

The quaint, picturesque town of Grafton is a short ride from the base lodge. There you will find a classic general store, the Old Tavern Inn (dining, drinking, accommodations), and the Grafton Cheese Outlet, where some of Vermont's best sharp cheddar is made.

General location: Grafton.

Elevation change: About 400′ of climbing on the first half of the ride.

Season: Mid-May through mid-November, weather permitting, 9 A.M. to 6 P.M. daily.

Services: All services can be found in Grafton. The mountain bike center at the base lodge is equipped to handle most bike repairs.

Hazards: Some sections of the trail are not maintained.

Rescue index: On the back side of Bear Mountain, you are about 3 miles from a telephone. The Grafton Ponds staff is prepared to assist in emergencies during regular business hours (see "Season" above).

A rider descends a rocky trail on the Daisy Turner loop at the Grafton Ponds Cross-Country & Mountain Bike Center.

Land status: Private land, and Class 3 and 4 roads.

Maps: The USGS 7.5 minute quad, Saxtons River, is helpful, but the best trail map is produced by Grafton Ponds and is available at the base lodge.

Finding the trail: From the village of Grafton, drive south on Townshend Road for 1 mile. Grafton Ponds is on the left. Park in the parking lot; your ride begins here.

Source of additional information: Call Grafton Ponds at (802) 843-2400.

Notes on the trail: From the parking lot, ride away from the base lodge and bear right, following signs for the cross-country ski trails. At first the trail looks like a gravel road, but as you climb and bear left, it starts to resemble a double-track trail. After a mile of gradual climbing, bear right onto a Class 3 road (Kidder Hill Road) to access the Grafton Improvement Association's land behind Bear Mountain. This road provides great views to the left of Grafton village.

Kidder Hill Road climbs for another mile to the crest, where you pass an old stone cabin on your left. Here, at 2 miles, the road turns to a double-track jeep trail. With turn-of-the-century stone walls on either side, cruise along this sweeping double-track trail into a classic Vermont hardwood forest. At 2.2 miles, keep your eyes open and follow the 4-inch red diamonds that mark the loop. (Orange VAST markers are also visible, but remember, you are following the red ones.) For the next 2 miles the trail dips and rolls through old washouts, over exposed ledge, and under a leafy canopy that sometimes tugs at your helmet.

At 3.2 miles the trail forks; stay right. At 5.2 miles, the trail drops hard left and descends through some very technical downhill with exposed rocks, roots, and sweeping drops. This section is a thriller, so keep your eyes open and your body loose. At 5.6 miles you will come out to a Class 4 road (Turner Road). Go left for 0.25 mile to see the old Daisy Turner homestead (private land—please don't wander too close).

To return to Grafton Ponds, retrace your steps back to where you exited from the rugged double-track trail, and continue down Turner Road. At the point where the road drops steeply at a 15% grade, there is an optional single-track jaunt.

To take the single-track, turn right at the 30% dropoff and follow the red markers. This section is about 1 mile long and will bring you to the southernmost point of the well-marked Big Bear cross-country ski trail (part of the Grafton Ponds network). Follow signs back to the base lodge; it is downhill all the way.

If you opt to stay on Turner Road, simply follow the dirt road for 1 mile to pavement, turn right, and ride for 0.5 mile back to Grafton Ponds, where you can enjoy a refreshing swim in the pond or a cold drink at the lodge.

RIDE 10 · Ball Mountain Dam

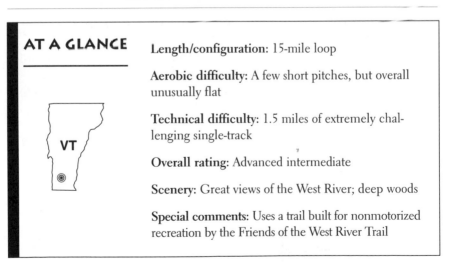

AT A GLANCE

Length/configuration: 15-mile loop

Aerobic difficulty: A few short pitches, but overall unusually flat

Technical difficulty: 1.5 miles of extremely challenging single-track

Overall rating: Advanced intermediate

Scenery: Great views of the West River; deep woods

Special comments: Uses a trail built for nonmotorized recreation by the Friends of the West River Trail

A short section of this ride parallels the West River just north of Ball Mountain Dam. The West River Trail is one link in a proposed 15-mile trail from Townshend Dam to South Londonderry, and is meant to be used by hikers, runners, mountain bikers, cross-country skiers, and snowshoers.

RIDE 10 · Ball Mountain Dam

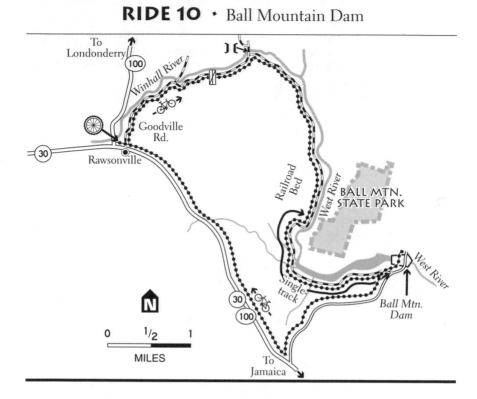

There are no major climbs in this ride, but the West River Trail is very challenging, with many short, technical climbs and several stream crossings. Halfway through the loop, you arrive at Ball Mountain Dam; ride across it for great views of the West River in both directions.

General location: Rawsonville.

Elevation change: No significant changes.

Season: July through October.

Services: All services can be found in Rawsonville, Jamaica, and South Londonderry. The Mountain Riders bike shop (802-297-3138) is in Rawsonville, where the ride begins. Camping can be found close by at Winhall Brook Campground in Rawsonville (802-824-4570), Jamaica State Park in Jamaica (802-874-4600), and Ball Mountain Campground in Townshend (802-365-7510).

Hazards: Typical single-track obstacles; vehicular traffic on VT 100 and VT 30.

Rescue index: The section of single-track trail is deep in the woods and is infrequently traveled. At the farthest point, you are 2 miles from a phone.

Land status: Class 3 and 4 roads, a private trail and some pavement.

Maps: There is no official map of the West River Trail, but the folks at Mountain Riders can give you a hand-drawn map.

A view of Ball Mountain Dam from the West River Trail.

Finding the trail: The ride begins and ends at Mountain Riders, located at the junction of VT 100 and VT 30.

Source of additional information: For information on Friends of the West River Trail, write to P.O. Box 246, Weston, VT 05161.

Notes on the trail: Exit left from the Mountain Riders parking lot, heading south on VT 100 for approximately 100 yards. Turn left onto Goodville Road. Turn right at a brown house, just before a bridge. Ride along the river and pass through a yellow gate. At 2.2 miles, turn right just before a bridge, onto a railroad bed. Stay on this for 2 miles while riding through the Winhall Brook campground.

At 4.2 miles, bear right at a cul-de-sac. Look closely for single-track trails. Take the narrow, right track, and climb steeply. Bear left and cross a stream. Climb to a Trail sign and purple trail markers; this is the West River Trail. Follow the purple markers and you can't go wrong.

The West River Trail dips and winds through the woods, crossing several streams and offering a variety of technical challenges. Eventually, you arrive at a dirt road; go left. You can take the next hairpin turn left and descend to the river for some good views. The main route for this ride goes right and climbs to a paved road. Turn left on the paved road and follow it out to Ball Mountain Dam. Feel free to ride across the dam for more excellent views, and explore the area.

Return to the paved road and follow it out to VT 30. Turn right (north) and ride this busy highway for 2.5 miles back to Rawsonville and the start of the loop.

RIDE 11 · Stratton Mountain's Sun Bowl

AT A GLANCE

VT

Length/configuration: 5-mile total combination (out-and-back with a loop at one end)

Aerobic difficulty: Easy to moderate

Technical difficulty: Easy

Overall rating: Easy

Scenery: Stratton Village; mountain views; intimate woods riding

Special comments: Sun Bowl has something for everybody

Stratton Mountain, one of southern Vermont's prominent ski resorts, has two areas for mountain biking: the main mountain, where intermediate and expert riders can take the gondola to the 3,900-foot summit; and the Sun Bowl area, where beginning and intermediate riders can get a taste of single-track riding on meandering trails maintained for nordic skiing and snowshoeing. The ride described here uses the Sun Bowl trail network; other riding options abound nearby, from country roads to single-track trails.

Stratton Village, located at the base of the mountain, is an alpine-style town center with accommodations, restaurants, and shopping, including the First Run Ski and Bike shop. It provides mountain bike rentals, repairs, and retail sales of bike accessories. Parents can rent bike trailers to tote their toddlers, or the innovative "trail-a-bike" that allows children to "pedal" as they coast behind the adult rider. First Run Ski and Bike is also where you pick up a trail map and purchase a gondola ticket (if you plan to ride the main mountain).

Gondola rides to the summit cost $13 for one ride and $20 for the day, including trail pass. However, a trail pass is not required for the Sun Bowl. You can ride to the Sun Bowl from the main mountain on an easy connecting trail or on the paved access road.

General location: Stratton.

Elevation change: Gently rolling terrain with no substantial climbs.

Season: End of June through mid-October, weather permitting. The gondola runs from 9:30 A.M. to 4:15 P.M. daily.

Services: All services are available in Stratton Village. First Run Ski and Bike (802-294-4321) is there; Mountain Riders bike shop (802-297-3138) is in Rawsonville, about 5 miles from Stratton Village. Camping is nearby at Winhall

RIDE 11 · Stratton Mountain's Sun Bowl

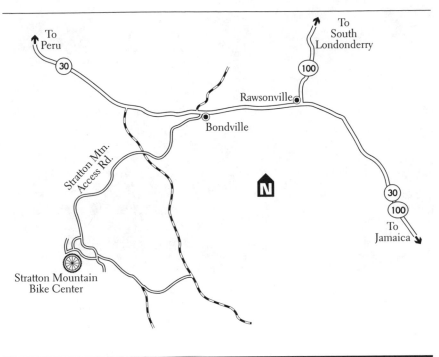

Brook Campground in Rawsonville (802 824 4570), Jamaica State Park in Jamaica (802-874-4600), and Ball Mountain Campground in Townshend (802-365-7510).

Hazards: Automobiles on the access road at the beginning and end of the ride.

Rescue index: You are never more than 1 mile from help. There is a phone at the horse stables in the Sun Bowl base area; in an emergency, call First Run Ski and Bike from this telephone by dialing four digits: 4321. From any other phone, dial 911.

Land status: The Sun Bowl trails are owned and maintained by Stratton Mountain Ski Resort.

Maps: The best one is the Sun Bowl Mountain Biking Trails map, produced by Stratton Mountain and available at First Run Ski and Bike.

Finding the trail: The ride begins at First Run Ski and Bike in Stratton Village. From VT 30 in Rawsonville, take the Stratton Mountain Access Road, which climbs steadily for 3 miles. Turn right into Stratton Village. Park in any public lot. First Run Ski and Bike is located slopeside, to the right of the clock tower.

Sources of additional information: Call 1-800-STRATTON, or check out their Web site at www.stratton.com/stratton/summer/html/biking.htm. Additionally, refer to *Mountain Biking the Ski Resorts of the Northeast* by Robert Immler (Woodstock: Countryman Press).

Explore the mellow Nordic trails of the Sun Bowl area or ride a gondola for a technical, 2,000-foot descent on ski trails and work roads. Photo by Hubert Schriebl.

Notes on the trail: From the First Run Ski and Bike Shop, ride back out through the village to the paved Stratton Mountain Access Road. Turn right, and go approximately 1 mile to the Sun Bowl area. Turn right at the sign for the Sun Bowl, and right again onto a dirt road that takes you to the Sun Bowl base lodge. Continue to the left side of the parking lot and the To Mountain Bike Trails sign. The trail network is well marked.

Ride on Trail 1, an easy, double-wide, grassy surface, passing by Trail 2 on your left. Soon you will come to Old North Cemetery on the right. This small, fenced graveyard probably belonged to a farming family over 100 years ago. Just beyond the cemetery, turn left onto Trail 3, another easy cruise. Trail 3 intersects Trail 2; turn right and follow Trail 2 back to Trail 1. Turn right on Trail 1. You are now back where you first started this ride, going in the opposite direction.

If you are ready to call it a day, retrace your steps on Trail 1, back to the Sun Bowl base lodge. Take the Stratton Mountain Access Road, climbing gradually, back to Stratton Village where you first began, for a total of 5 miles of moderately easy riding.

If you haven't had enough, try Trail 4, which you can pick up just beyond Old North Cemetery, to the right. This loop is a little more challenging than Trails 1, 2, and 3.

The Sun Bowl is a good place for families to ride. There are many other trails, ranging from easy to difficult, including a lot of technical single-track. With something for everyone, you can't go wrong. Best of all, riding at the Sun Bowl is free. Be sure to pick up a trail map first if you choose to explore this area.

RIDE 12 · Danby Road

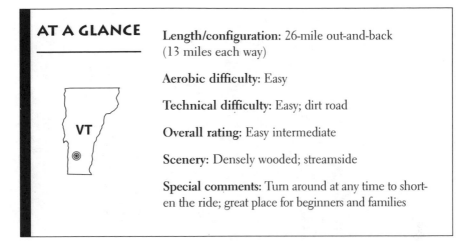

AT A GLANCE

Length/configuration: 26-mile out-and-back (13 miles each way)

Aerobic difficulty: Easy

Technical difficulty: Easy; dirt road

Overall rating: Easy intermediate

Scenery: Densely wooded; streamside

Special comments: Turn around at any time to shorten the ride; great place for beginners and families

The beauty of the Danby Road is not only the sense of being truly in the wilderness, but also the fact that you can make your ride as long as you want. This out-and-back route on Forest Service Road 10 climbs gradually for five miles to White Rocks National Recreation Area in the Green Mountain National Forest. You can turn around here, or continue for another five miles past the Appalachian and Long Trails and down paved switchbacks to US 7 near Danby Four Corners. It is a shady, narrow road that parallels Tabor Brook. There are few opportunities for distant views, but for someone who wants to be intimate with foliage, this is the place to go.

General location: North Landgrove, 2 miles north of Londonderry.

Elevation change: A gradual 600′ climb over 5 miles.

Season: Anytime the road is clear—usually May through mid-November.

Services: All services are available in Londonderry. The nearest bike shops are Mountain Riders, about 10 miles south in Rawsonville (802-297-3138), and Battenkill Sports, about 10 miles west in Manchester (802-362-2734).

Hazards: Occasional motor vehicles.

Rescue index: At the halfway point you are 6.5 miles from a telephone (telephones are in North Landgrove and Danby Four Corners).

Land status: Green Mountain National Forest road.

Maps: DeLorme's and Northern Cartographic's atlases are fine.

Finding the trail: From Londonderry, take VT 11 west. Turn right onto Landgrove Road, following signs for the Village Inn in North Landgrove. Past the Village Inn, bear left at the fork following signs for Danby. Cross a narrow bridge, turn right onto FR 10 and park where appropriate.

RIDE 12 · Danby Road

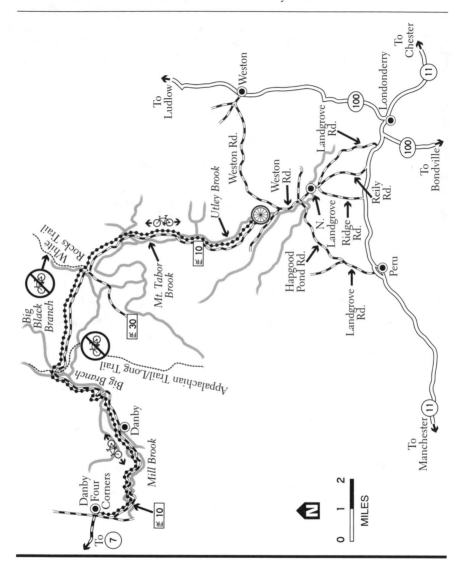

Source of additional information: Green Mountain National Forest, Manchester District, RR1, Box 1940, Manchester Center, VT 05255-9733; (802) 362-2307.

Notes on the trail: Begin by riding north on FR 10, a smooth dirt road. You will cross over Tabor Brook several times. When you reach signs for White Rocks, you have gone 5 miles. At the Appalachian and Long Trails crossing you have ridden 10 miles. If you make it all the way to Danby Four Corners you have gone 13 miles. Turn around any time and retrace your steps—a total of 26 miles if you do the complete route.

CENTRAL VERMONT

Central Vermont is a hotbed for mountain bike riding, from Ludlow north to Montpelier, and from the Connecticut River west to Lake Champlain. The dirt road and trail riding is endless. Rumor has it avid mountain bikers can log 200 miles in one day, never retracing their route, and never rolling their tires on tarmac.

Randolph is the nucleus for trail riding in central Vermont. A group called the White River Valley Trails Association (WRVTA), based in Randolph, is setting a precedent for mountain bike trail organizations in Vermont (see section on Randolph area, page 101). Every year the New England Mountain Bike Festival is held in Randolph on the last weekend in September.

The northern half of the Green Mountain National Forest extends from Chittenden north to Granville. Several experimental trails have been opened to mountain bikers to determine future national forest land use (see section on Green Mountain National Forest, page 139).

Two of my favorite rides, Ninevah Road and Hart Hollow, happen to be in central Vermont. Both have terrain ranging from scenic dirt roads to wooded trails, streams, and classic Vermont farmland. The distances are not too long (18.5 and 13.5 miles, respectively), nor are the climbs, yet when you are done you feel like you have had a good workout. All of this can be said for each ride in the central Vermont section. There is truly remarkable riding here.

RIDE 13 · Ninevah Road

AT A GLANCE

VT

Length/configuration: 18.5-mile "spoon" configuration—the ladle is an 11.5-mile loop; the handle is a 3.5-mile out-and-back

Aerobic difficulty: Many short hills; ride as hard as you want

Technical difficulty: 4 miles of single-track trails with some tricky sections

Overall rating: Advanced intermediate

Scenery: Excellent views of Lake Ninevah and the surrounding countryside

Special comments: This is one of my favorite rides because of the diverse scenery and terrain

This ride's best attribute is its visual entertainment: open meadows, sugar shacks, renovated farmhouses, stone walls, cemeteries, a trailside brook, an antique sleigh, and, of course, Lake Ninevah.

I was introduced first to Lake Ninevah, and shortly afterward to Ninevah Road, with the Great Outdoors Adventure Tours on one of their point-to-point guided tours. I knew immediately that I would return on my own to include Ninevah highlights and some of the nearby double-track trails in this book.

The ride I devised when I returned is shaped like a spoon. You ride up the handle, around the ladel, and back down the handle. Ninevah Road is the handle, which is really good because you get to ride it twice. The spoon has two sections of fast pavement, two sections of fun double-track, and several dirt roads through remarkably beautiful farmland. Lake Ninevah, a one-mile detour from the main ride, is included in the overall loop mileage. The entire ride is 18.5 miles long and has something of everything regarding views and terrain.

General location: Plymouth.

Elevation change: The ride climbs 800´ gradually over the first 5 miles. After that it rolls, with several short, steep climbs.

Season: July through mid-November; the unmaintained trails hold snow late in the season and are quite wet in the spring.

Services: All services are available in Ludlow, including a bike shop, Mountain Cycology (802-228-2722). Other bike shops are First Stop Bike Shop in West Bridgewater (802-422-9050), and Cyclery Plus in West Woodstock, (802-457-3377).

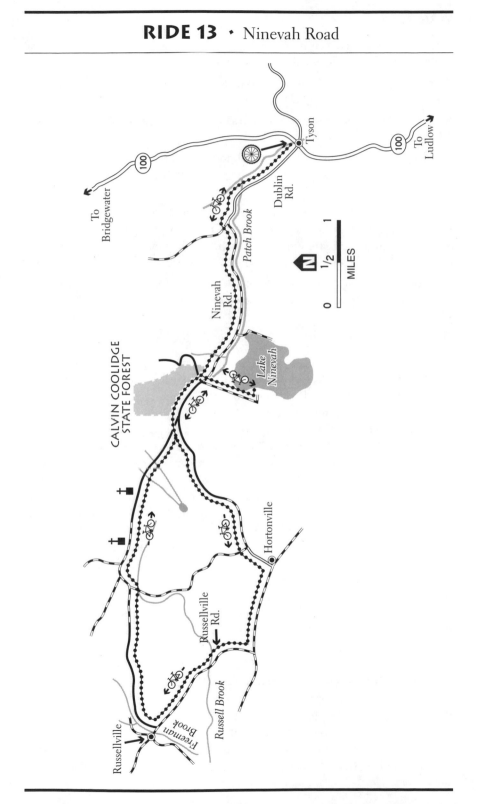

There are no service points along the ride. For information regarding Great Outdoors Adventure Tours, call (800) 345-5182.

Hazards: Any obstacles typical of single-track trail riding, as well as occasional slow-moving farm equipment.

Rescue index: At times you will be at least 2 miles from a private residence and telephone.

Land status: Maintained and unmaintained Class 4 roads and trails with an occasional short stint on pavement. The ride skirts a section of the Plymouth State Forest.

Maps: Two USGS 7.5 minute quads, Ludlow and Mount Holly, are useful. Please note that elevation lines are noted in feet on the Ludlow map and in meters on the Mount Holly map. I did the math (meters × 3.28 = feet) and determined that the elevation gain is a little over 800´.

Finding the trail: Just 5 miles north of Ludlow on VT 100 is a small town called Tyson. Park in the lot next to the Echo Inn at the junction of VT 100 and Dublin Road.

Source of additional information: DeLorme's atlas also shows this route.

Notes on the trail: From the parking lot, begin riding up Dublin Road. It climbs gradually on pavement for 1.25 miles, then turns to dirt. At this point, take the left onto Ninevah Road, a narrow, single-lane road that parallels Patch Brook. The brook and the road hug each other for 1.5 miles until they reach the ride's highest point of land where the road veers away to the right.

At 3.5 miles you will come to a **T**-intersection: the ride continues straight on the unmaintained jeep road, while the jaunt to Lake Ninevah goes left. To get to the lake, go left, climb a short hill, and begin down the other side. The Lake Ninevah access area turn comes quickly, three-quarters of the way down the hill. Turn left for great views of this pristine lake. Return to the **T**-intersection where the ride now goes left onto the jeep road.

Follow this rocky road past an open area where you will see a U.S. Forest Service gate on your right and several signs posted by VAST and CTA to your left. Continue straight on the main trail, riding through a rugged, wet area. At the 6-mile mark you emerge from the forest trail into a grand, open meadow. Pass the VAST trail signs indicating a trail to the left. Continue straight, winding around the big, white farmhouse. The smooth dirt road descends to a **T**-intersection. Go left on the paved road, descending to Hortonville's 4-way intersection.

Turn right onto a gravel road. After 1.5 miles, take the first right onto Russellville Road; there will be a brown house on your left, and a stone wall on your right. Stay left at the **Y**-intersection, and after a mile begin looking on the right for a hidden jeep road. If you miss the jeep road, you'll reach Russellville's 4-way intersection. Turn around at the bridge and ride back the way you came a few hundred yards. Just before the first house on the left, take the jeep trail that climbs steeply on the left. You will have to cross a deep trench to get to it.

At the top of the climb, continue going straight, staying between two houses. The trail is defined by a parallel stone fence. Pass through a wet area and come to a gravel road at the 11-mile mark. Go straight, keeping the big house to your right. In one-half mile the road turns to pavement and hooks to the left.

At the **T**-intersection you will be face-to-face with a beautifully renovated farmhouse. Turn right onto the gravel road. Continue straight past the Dead End sign and working farm. The road becomes less improved and eventually turns into a wide trail. Stay to the right and descend through a rough area (after heavy rains this trail may appear to be a brook). The conditions improve and shortly you reach a **T**-intersection. This is the jeep road you were on earlier, just after visiting Lake Ninevah. Turn left, ride through the wet section, and pass by the U.S. Forest Service gate, now on your left. Come to the 4-way junction, and if you can't resist, pay one last visit to Lake Ninevah. Otherwise, continue straight, descending the entertaining Ninevah Road back to Echo Lake Inn and the start of this ride.

RIDE 14 · Shrewsbury

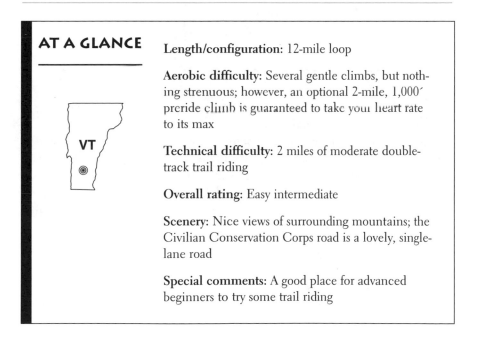

AT A GLANCE

Length/configuration: 12-mile loop

Aerobic difficulty: Several gentle climbs, but nothing strenuous; however, an optional 2-mile, 1,000´ preride climb is guaranteed to take your heart rate to its max

Technical difficulty: 2 miles of moderate double-track trail riding

Overall rating: Easy intermediate

Scenery: Nice views of surrounding mountains; the Civilian Conservation Corps road is a lovely, single-lane road

Special comments: A good place for advanced beginners to try some trail riding

The folks from Great Outdoors Adventure Tours introduced me to the first half of this ride, which they include in one of their guided gourmet mountain bike tours. Their tours are point-to-point, but I made this ride into a 12-mile loop by returning to the start on the Shrewsbury CCC Road. The ride is nestled

RIDE 14 · Shrewsbury

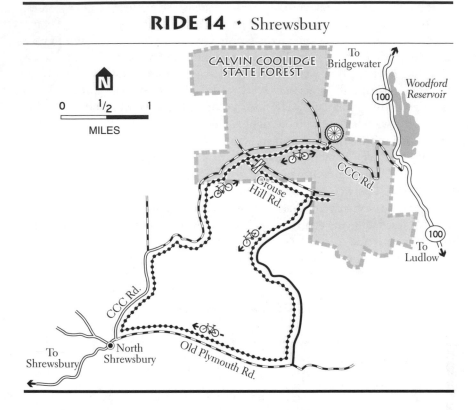

in the southern foothills of the Killington Ski Area, and most of it takes place at 2,000 to 2,200 feet in elevation.

There are no lengthy climbs except for the one you do in the car before the ride begins—hardcore riders can park at the bottom of the CCC Road at Woodbury Reservoir and treat themselves to a 2-mile, 1,000-foot preloop climb. The loop begins with jeep and double-track trails through woods and open vistas, and ends on the CCC Road, a scenic, single-lane road that sees little traffic and is closed to motor vehicles during the winter months.

For an interesting deviation, visit Meadowsweet Herb Farm (802-492-3565) at the halfway point in North Shrewsbury.

General location: North Shrewsbury.

Elevation change: Near the end of the ride, one gradual climb rises 500´ over 3 miles.

Season: Anytime the trails are dry—most likely June through mid-November. October is excellent. The first part of the ride on Grouse Hill is closed during May due to bear habitat, but generally May is too wet to ride in this area anyway.

Services: Most services, including First Stop Bike Shop (802-422-9050) can be found in West Bridgewater, 3.2 miles north of the start of the ride at the junc-

The mellow Shrewsbury loop is a good place for novice riders to try their hand at single-track trail riding.

tion of VT 100 and VT 4. There is a general store halfway through the ride in North Shrewsbury. Killington Resort is about 12 miles north of the start on VT 100 and Ludlow is 13 miles south. Mountain Cycology, a complete bike shop, is in Ludlow (802-228-2722). The Killington Mountain Bike Shop is in the base lodge of Killington Resort (802-422-6232).

Hazards: On the trail you may encounter typical single-track obstacles, and on the CCC Road, which is very narrow, you may encounter a motor vehicle.

Rescue index: At times you may be as far as 4 miles from a telephone, and the chances of someone else coming along are slim. Ride with a friend or, if you choose to ride alone, alert someone of your plan.

Land status: The ride begins with a brief stint in the Calvin Coolidge State Forest. It continues on maintained and unmaintained Class 4 roads and trails and finishes on the CCC Road, a Class 4 road that is closed in the winter. You will also pass by the Plymsbury Wildlife Management Area.

Maps: The USGS 7.5 minute quad, Killington Peak, is the only map you'll need. Most of the ride is indicated on this map.

Finding the trail: The east-west Shrewsbury CCC Road begins on VT 100, 3.2 miles south of West Bridgewater and 13 miles north of Ludlow. Turn onto the CCC Road, climb for 2 miles, and park in the parking area on the right.

Sources of additional information: First Stop Bike Shop and Mountain Cycology have additional information on local riding. Great Outdoors Adventure Tours offers guided gourmet mountain bike tours in this area. For a brochure and schedule of their trips, call (800) 345-5182.

Notes on the trail: Exit the parking area and turn right on the CCC Road, heading due west. After a mile, turn left onto Grouse Hill Road. Ride around the gate. This is easy, relaxing terrain in the Coolidge State Forest and Plymsbury Wildlife Management Area. Snowmobilers use Grouse Hill Road in the winter and it also serves as a section of the Catamount Trail. Follow this dead-end road to an open meadow with views to the south of Burnt Mountain. There are trail markers for skiers to continue south on the Catamount Trail, but bikers must turn around at this point.

Retrace your route for about .5 mile and turn left onto a wide, double-track jeep trail marked for snowmobilers. This is easy trail riding for beginners, with wooded areas, open meadows, and views in all directions. Stay on this trail for about 2 miles until you come to the Old Plymouth Road, an easy-to-spot dirt road open to motor vehicles only in the summer. Turn right and descend steadily for 2.5 miles until you come to a **T**-intersection in North Shrewsbury. There are several dead-end side trails on the Old Plymouth Road for short, fun, single-track exploring. Check them out!

At the **T**-intersection turn right onto the CCC Road, or turn left for a visit to Meadowsweet Herb Farm, .5 mile down the road on the left. The CCC Road is paved for a short distance before it becomes dirt. Climb steadily for about 2 miles before reaching a plateau, then you will have some pleasant riding through hardwoods on a trail edged with stone walls. Pass Grouse Hill Road, now on your right, and make the gentle climb back to your car.

RIDE 15 · Mount Moses Road

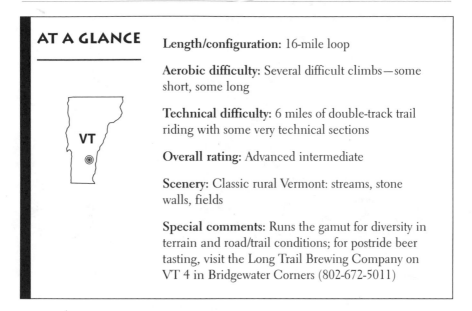

AT A GLANCE

Length/configuration: 16-mile loop

Aerobic difficulty: Several difficult climbs—some short, some long

Technical difficulty: 6 miles of double-track trail riding with some very technical sections

Overall rating: Advanced intermediate

Scenery: Classic rural Vermont: streams, stone walls, fields

Special comments: Runs the gamut for diversity in terrain and road/trail conditions; for postride beer tasting, visit the Long Trail Brewing Company on VT 4 in Bridgewater Corners (802-672-5011)

This 16-mile loop ride starts and finishes just south of Bridgewater Corners at the Topliff Cemetery, where the oldest tombstone I could find was dated 1842 (not really that old by Vermont standards). The ride begins with a gentle climb on Hale Hollow Road to Five Corners, which, though you would never know it today, once boasted a population of 1,500. At Five Corners the ride changes from a tranquil cruise on a mellow country road to a demanding, technically challenging four-wheel-drive road with several stream crossings, washouts, and an 800-foot elevation gain. Welcome to Mount Moses Road!

Lined by stone walls for most of the way, Mount Moses Road rises and plunges through extinct farmland where dilapidated foundations and abandoned fields remind us that men and women once lived off this land. The height of the ride comes at a three-way junction with VAST trail signs. At this point, Mount Moses Road heads directly north, hell-bent for the Ottauquechee River, only to be interrupted by several unexpected, but thankfully brief, climbs. A short single-track section parallel to the Ottauquechee River takes you back to Bridgewater Corners, and a final cool-down on VT 100A returns you to the Topliff Cemetery.

Coolidge State Forest is dedicated to Vermont-born Calvin Coolidge, who became our thirtieth president when President Harding died in 1923. Its 18,500 acres are broken into several parcels of land scattered throughout Woodstock, Ludlow, Plymouth, Bridgewater, and Shrewsbury. Although this ride is geographically located near the birthplace of Calvin Coolidge, none of it actually goes through any part of the Coolidge State Forest.

RIDE 15 · Mount Moses Road

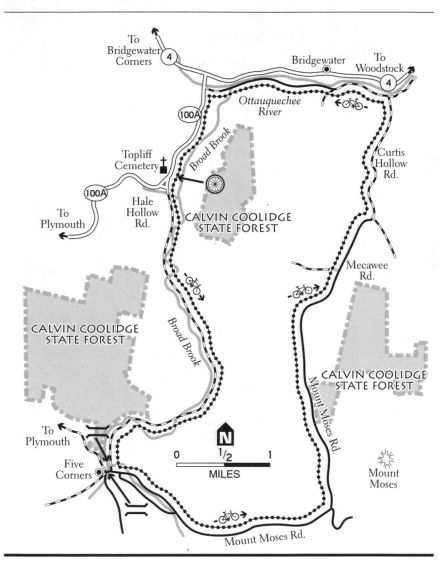

General location: Bridgewater Corners.

Elevation change: 1,200′ of elevation is gained in the first 7.5 miles.

Season: Mid-June through mid-November.

Services: All services can be found in Woodstock, 5 miles east of Bridgewater Corners. Also found along VT 4 to the east and west of Bridgewater Corners are country stores, bed-and-breakfasts, an old mill that has been converted into the

Stone walls and tall trees define Mount Moses Road, an unmaintained Class 4 road near Calvin Coolidge State Forest in Bridgewater.

Bridgewater Mall, and the Long Trail Brewery. Nearby bike shops are Cyclery Plus in West Woodstock (802-457-3377), First Stop Bike Shop in West Bridgewater (802-422-9050), and Mountain Cycology in Ludlow (802-228-2722).

Hazards: The trail is often used by horseback riders; expect to encounter all the usual obstacles found on a double-track trail.

Rescue index: Mount Moses Road is made up of abandoned town trails and roads; at times you may be as far as 3 miles from the nearest telephone. If riding alone, use extra caution and let someone know your route plans.

Land status: Maintained and unmaintained Class 4 roads and trails, VAST trails, and a short section of pavement.

Maps: The best way to go is with the USGS 7.5 minute quads, Plymouth and Woodstock South. DeLorme's and Northern Cartographic's atlases are helpful for overall ride orientation.

Finding the trail: The ride begins at the Topliff Cemetery on VT 100A, 1.5 miles south of Bridgewater Corners at the junction of the Hale Hollow Road. Park on the grassy turf at the entrance to the cemetery.

Source of additional information: Information on the history of the area can be found in nearby Plymouth at the Calvin Coolidge Memorial Foundation, Plymouth Notch Historic District (802-672-3389). This educational organization is devoted to preserving the memory of Calvin Coolidge. On-site resources include a reference library, genealogy materials, photographs, newspaper and magazine articles, postcards, and other memorabilia.

Notes on the trail: From the Topliff Cemetery, take Hale Hollow Road, which runs along the far side of the cemetery. Climb gradually, crossing over Broad Brook and passing interesting old houses mixed in with a few newer dwellings. At 4.5 miles, you will come to Five Corners, an obvious 5-way junction. Cross over the first wooden bridge, but do not go right to cross over the second; rather, take the jeep road to the left.

This abandoned road makes several rocky stream crossings and climbs steadily, alternating between smooth pedaling on dirt to washouts where you will probably have to dismount. At the first fork stay left on what is known locally as the High Road. Stay left again and come to a trail junction well-marked with VAST signs. Continue straight. You are now on the Mount Moses Road, a double-track trail with occasional steep pitches intended to keep you from relaxing.

At a little less than 7.5 miles is a **T**-intersection marked with VAST trail signs indicating Reading and Tyson to the right and South Woodstock to the left. Go left, staying on Mount Moses Road. When the leaves are gone from the trees, you might spot Mount Moses off to the right. The next 3 miles are downhill, but you need to keep your eyes open! The road surface changes erratically from rocky to smooth, down to up, as it skirts the west side of a small parcel of the Calvin Coolidge State Forest.

At just under 10.5 miles a gravel road on the left leads to Mecawee Pond, a small, privately owned club. To the right of this junction you will see a shack and a drive sign marked #506, Torneo. Here you cross the town line into Woodstock, and Mount Moses Road becomes Mecawee Road. Continue descending. Eventually this road joins with Curtis Hollow Road and continues its descent to Bridgewater.

Turn left at the stop sign onto a paved road. Stay straight onto a gravelly road, avoiding the large bridge over the Ottauquechee River to your right. Continue on the gravel road and take the first right after Tarlton Court. Immediately after turning right, and just past a big, white boulder, veer left up an embankment through an opening into the woods. Climb on a steep, grassy, double-track trail to a small meadow. Stay to the right of the fire pit and look for the trail that drops downhill into the woods. Ride this single-track through the woods to an open, grassy mound that is now the landfill. Ride between the left two **J**-vents and down the other side. Pick up the River Road (a.k.a. State Aid 65 Road) at the three large cement blocks and follow that to Bridgewater Corners. Turn left onto paved VT 100A and ride for 1.5 miles back to the starting point.

Celebrate your ride by tasting the excellent ales, lagers, stouts, and porters brewed in Bridgewater Corners at the Long Trail Brewing Company (802-672-5011).

RIDE 16 · Le Tour de Killington

AT A GLANCE

VT

Length/configuration: A 7-mile loop, plus a chair-lift ride on Killington's famed Skyeship (lift ride not included in mileage)

Aerobic difficulty: Easy to moderate; most of the elevation is gained on the Skyeship

Technical difficulty: Several single-track sections require good bike-handling skills

Overall rating: Advanced intermediate

Scenery: Skye Peak (elevation: 3,800´), Killington Peak (elevation: 4,241´), and Bear Mountain (elevation: 3,295´)—the views are spectacular in all directions

Special comments: Killington Mountain Bike Center is so big and the riding so expansive, I recommend starting with a guided tour

Killington Resort, Vermont's largest ski area, opens its slopes during the summer to mountain bike riding on 35 miles of single-track trails and work roads. This ride, le Tour de Killington, begins at the Killington base lodge where you purchase your trail pass and lift ticket. Also located at the lodge are the bike shop, rentals, deli, first aid, maps, riding instruction, guide service, and rest rooms. From there, le Tour works its way for one mile on work roads and single-track trails to Skye Peak, where you and your bike load onto the Skyeship chairlift for a quick lift to Skye Peak's summit. After disembarking from the Skyeship, a gradual climb on a single-track trail takes you to the summit of Killington Peak. From there, it's five miles of downhill on single-track trails and work roads back to the Killington base lodge.

Killington is open to mountain bikers from Memorial Day weekend through mid-October, weather permitting. The trails are open from 9 A.M. to 6 P.M. daily, and the Skyeship lift runs from 9 A.M. to 4 P.M. daily (in fall the lower half of the Skyeship is also open). Trail passes are $8; one-time chairlift ride with trail pass is $20; unlimited chairlift rides with trail pass is $25. Special rates apply for juniors and multiple-day use.

General location: Killington Resort.

Elevation change: About 1,500´ are gained while riding in the Skyeship chairlift.

RIDE 16 • Le Tour de Killington

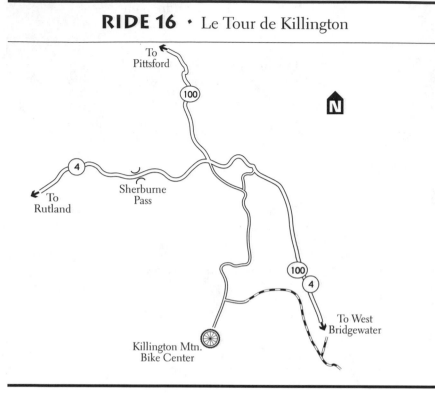

A 400′ gradual climb takes you from the summit of Skye Peak to the summit of Killington Peak. From there it is a 1,700′ descent back to the start.

Season: Memorial Day weekend through mid-October. July and August are the driest months.

Services: All services are found at Killington Resort. For a brochure, information, and trail map, call (800) 621-MTNS. The Killington Mountain Bike Shop offers a good selection of clothing and accessories, repairs, and a rental fleet of Gary Fisher mountain bikes, including the full-suspension Joshua. Guide service is available through the bike shop (802-422-6232).

Hazards: The work roads and some of the single-track trails have waterbars. You may encounter an occasional maintenance vehicle.

Rescue index: Killington Mountain Bike Center has an on-site mountain bike patrol. Its many emergency telephones are indicated on the trail map.

Land status: The trails are all on land owned and operated by Killington Resort.

Maps: The best map is the one produced by the Killington Mountain Bike Center. It is free and can be found at the Killington base lodge and Killington Mountain Bike Shop. The trails are well signed and easy to follow.

Finding the trail: From the junction of VT 100 and VT 4 in Sherburne (look for Bill's Country Store), take the Killington Road for approximately 4 miles to the base lodge. Killington Road is lined with many shops, restaurants, delicatessens, gas stations, convenience stores, and specialty food stores. Just after you pass the Snow Shed lodge on the left, the road hooks to the right. Parking for mountain bikers is on the right, and the Killington Mountain Bike Center is on the left. The ride begins at the center.

Sources of additional information: All information can be found at the Mountain Bike Center (802-422-6232). Visit their Web site at www.killington.com. Amtrak's Ethan Allen Express offers daily express rail service from New York City to Rutland with a special mountain bike package. For information and reservations on Amtrak, call (800) 621-MTNS. Suggested reading: *Mountain Biking the Ski Resorts of the Northeast* by Robert Immler (Woodstock: Countryman Press).

Notes on the trail: Exit left from the Killington Mountain Bike Shop, keeping the ski slopes on your right. Ride a work road briefly to Trail 16, Edgemont Single Track. This fun trail snakes through the woods and tests your single-track skills. If you can handle this section you will have no problem with the rest of the ride.

Very soon you will come to a trail junction on your right. Take Trail 22, Jon's Jaunt, which connects you back to Trail 16. Exit left from Trail 16 onto Trail 1, Easy Way, a work road, and follow this for about a quarter mile, riding gradually downhill to the loading ramp for the Skyeship chairlift. Give your bike to an attendant, who will load it on the back of the cabin as you climb inside. At the top, another attendant will unload your bike and hand it to you.

From the top of Skye Peak, begin riding uphill directly away from the chairlift. On your left is "Woodhenge," two seats made from rocks where skiers bask in the sun on warm, spring days. Just past Woodhenge, the road forks. Take Trail 4, Skye Peak Loop, which branches to the right. This mellow single-track trail climbs gradually and winds its way under the Killington chairlift. Fork right on Trail 2, Off the Top, a short work road that climbs—steeply at times—to the summit of Killington Peak, the highest point on this ride (elevation: 4,241´).

From the summit, take Trail 1, Easy Way, for a mile of easy downhill that alternates between single-track and work roads. The best views are seen from the work roads. Where the trail levels out and offers views of Bear Mountain to the right, begin looking for Trail 6, Single Track Fun, on your right. Take Trail 6 to the summit of Bear Mountain. Views from here are of Mount Ascutney to the southeast and New Hampshire to the east.

Follow signs for Trail 1, which is a work road for the rest of the way down the mountain. Pass under the Skyeship chairlift and continue descending through two switchbacks. Soon you will be on the section of Trail 1 that you rode in the reverse direction at the beginning of this ride. Stay on Trail 1 all the way back to the base lodge for a total of 7 miles of riding.

RIDE 17 · Wheelerville Road

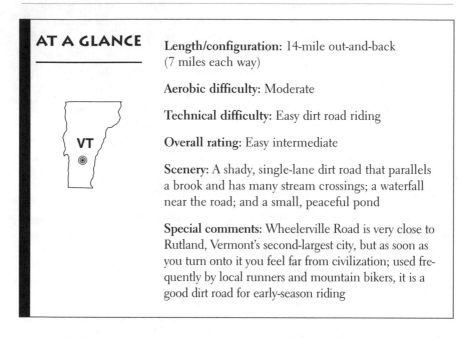

AT A GLANCE

Length/configuration: 14-mile out-and-back (7 miles each way)

Aerobic difficulty: Moderate

Technical difficulty: Easy dirt road riding

Overall rating: Easy intermediate

Scenery: A shady, single-lane dirt road that parallels a brook and has many stream crossings; a waterfall near the road; and a small, peaceful pond

Special comments: Wheelerville Road is very close to Rutland, Vermont's second-largest city, but as soon as you turn onto it you feel far from civilization; used frequently by local runners and mountain bikers, it is a good dirt road for early-season riding

Wheelerville Road lies in the Rutland City Forest, a 4,000-acre plot of land just to the east of Rutland. It is a narrow, curvy, single-lane dirt road deep in the woods that winds its way across many streams and past an occasional private residence. This 14-mile out-and-back ride (7 miles one way) climbs gently for the first five miles and then rolls for two miles and descends to Notch Road, the turnaround point.

At the five-mile mark is a pullout with a short trail (100 yards) to the head of a waterfall; there are several different points from which to view the falls. For a shorter ride you can turn around here. During early spring and late fall, when there are few leaves on the trees, it is worth continuing beyond the falls for the views of Killington and Mendon Peaks to the left, but you will not have these views during the leafy summer.

General location: Mendon, approximately 4 miles east of Rutland.

Elevation change: A gradual 200′ climb during the first 5 miles.

Season: Mid-April through mid-November when the roads are clear of snow.

Services: All services are available in Rutland. The nearest bike shops are also in Rutland: Green Mountain Cyclery (802-775-6762) is on Strongs Avenue; Great Outdoors Trading (802-775-9989) is on ·Woodstock Avenue; Sports Peddler (802-775-0101) is on Main Street.

Hazards: The road is shared with motor vehicles. It is a narrow, windy road, and visibility is limited by the turns in the road.

RIDE 17 • Wheelerville Road

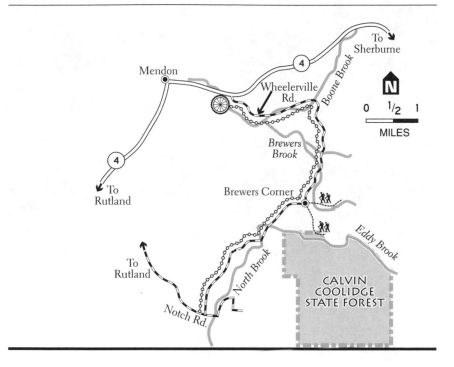

Rescue index: At times you will be 2 miles from a phone.

Land status: Class 3 road in Rutland City Forest.

Maps: The road is shown on DeLorme's and Northern Cartographic's atlases.

Finding the trail: From Rutland, take VT 4 east. Look for the Mendon Country Store on the left. From the store, continue on VT 4 for 1.8 miles, then turn right onto Wheelerville Road. Go 0.3 miles and park in the pull-out on the left. The ride begins here on the Wheelerville Road. From Pico Ski Area, go west for 3 miles on VT 4. Wheelerville Road will be on your left.

Source of additional information: For more information on the Rutland City Forest, contact the City of Rutland, City Hall, North Main Street, Rutland, VT 05701; (802) 773-1800.

Notes on the trail: From the pullout area, begin riding up Wheelerville Road, away from VT 4. On your left will be Boone Brook, which you will cross several times before the road eventually veers to the right and leaves it behind. You will cross another stream, then Brewers Brook, and then will come to Brewers Corner where there is parking for two hiking trailheads (no bikes). Buckland Trail to the left goes to the peak of Bear Mountain, and the trail straight ahead goes to the Mendon Peak Natural Area.

Streamside sculpture along Wheelerville Road.

Wheelerville Road bears sharply right here and continues climbing, more steeply at times. At the 5-mile mark, just before Bridge 15, a pullout on the left leads to a waterfall on the North Branch of Eddy Brook. Ride into the small pullout area and veer to the right on a wide trail. Park your bike and follow the trail for just a few hundred feet to the waterfall. There are several clearings that make nice places for a picnic. For a shorter ride, turn around here and retrace your steps to the start for a 10-mile out-and-back ride.

From the waterfall, continue on Wheelerville Road and pass a small pond on your right. During the spring and fall the views to the left are of Killington and Mendon Peaks. Unfortunately there is no open area for an uninterrupted view. Soon you will descend for about .25 mile and reach a **T**-intersection where Wheelerville Road ends. This is Notch Road, the 7-mile mark and the turn-around point for the ride. Retrace your steps back to the start for a total of 14 miles.

RIDE 18 · Chittenden Reservoir

AT A GLANCE

Length/configuration: 10.5-mile loop

Aerobic difficulty: Moderate; but ride hard for an excellent workout

Technical difficulty: 4 miles of double- and single-track trails are very challenging for beginners

Overall rating: Intermediate

Scenery: Mostly wooded, with views of Chittenden Reservoir and Pico Peak at the beginning and end of the ride

Special comments: A good loop for anyone new to trail riding

Chittenden Reservoir sits high in the Green Mountain National Forest at an elevation of 1,500 feet. This moderately challenging 10.5-mile loop circumnavigates the reservoir, beginning and ending at Chittenden Dam. Part of the ride is on national forest roads and another section rolls through dense forest on cross-country ski trails that are part of the Mountain Top Ski Touring Center trail network. There are no long climbs, but several challenging sections of double-track trails make this a little more than a beginner ride.

Tom Cook, a teacher at the Barstow School in Chittenden who showed me this loop, brings his young students here to ride. When not teaching, Tom operates a small bike shop, Wheels & Weights, out of his home in Proctor (802-459-2749). He rides in this area frequently and has seen moose, wild turkeys, geese, and a bald eagle. To the south are great views of Blue Ridge Mountain and Pico Peak, and to the east you can see the ridge where the Long Trail passes through.

General location: Chittenden Reservoir, north of Rutland.

Elevation change: No significant elevation changes throughout the ride.

Season: June through October; muddy sections will follow any heavy rain. The snow comes early and leaves late at this elevation.

Services: All services, including three bike shops and a hospital, can be found in Rutland. The bike shops are Green Mountain Cyclery (802-775-6762) on Strongs Avenue; Great Outdoors Trading (802-775-9989) on Woodstock Avenue; and Sports Peddler (802-775-0101) on Main Street. There is camping nearby in the Green Mountain National Forest (802-747-6700).

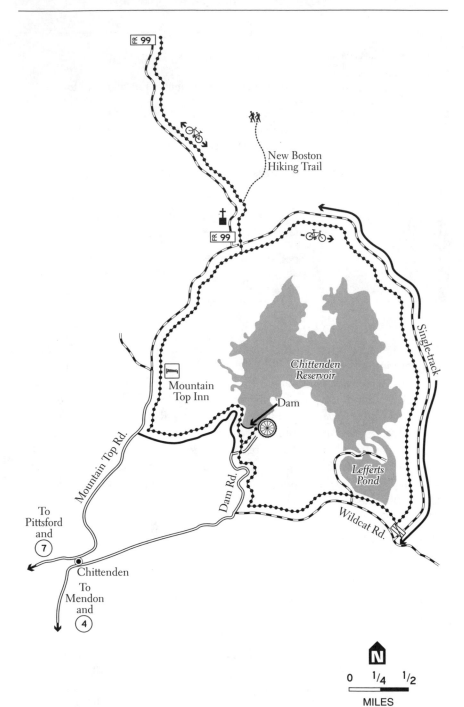

FR 99

New Boston
Hiking Trail

FR 99

Single-track

Chittenden
Reservoir

Mountain
Top Inn

Dam

Mountain Top Rd.

Dam Rd.

Lefferts
Pond

To
Pittsford
and
(7)

Chittenden

Wildcat Rd.

To
Mendon
and
(4)

N

0   1/4   1/2

MILES

It's always good to give your bike a bath after a muddy ride, but don't forget to lube your chain! Chittenden Reservoir and Mount Carmel can be seen from the start-finish area of the Chittenden Reservoir loop.

Hazards: Rocky washouts, waterbars, rough bridges, and an occasional deep hole.

Rescue index: You are never more than 3 miles from a private residence.

Land status: National forest roads, cross-country ski trails, dirt roads, and a bit of pavement.

Maps: The USGS 7.5 minute quad, Chittenden, is useful.

Finding the trail: The ride begins and ends at the parking lot for the Chittenden Dam boat launch, north of the small town of Chittenden, on the Dam Road.

Sources of additional information: Check in with the local bike shops about this and other riding in the area.

Notes on the trail: Leave the parking lot the same way you entered by vehicle. Go right on the paved road until you come to several jeep road options. Stay to the right, riding along the waterfront. Take the second right after a gated road, onto a jeep road. You will pass by Mrs. Creed's house on the left (Mr. Creed was the mailman in Chittenden for many years).

Bear right, staying on the main vein. When you reach pavement, turn right, climbing steeply. Soon you will pass the Mountain Top Inn and Cross-Country Touring Center, an excellent bed-and-breakfast in both summer and winter. Stay straight onto a dirt road. Enter the Green Mountain National Forest on Forest Service Road 99, an unimproved road best suited for four-wheel-drive vehicles and mountain bikes. At 3.5 miles, you arrive at a **Y**-intersection.

Optional spur: At this point, you can take a side trip down FR 99. It's a fun, well-graded, smooth road that dead-ends at a camping spot. Along the way you will pass the Wheeler family graveyard where a child's grave marker is dated 1800–1808. You will also pass the trailhead for Old Boston Trail to Mount Carmel. Total down-and-back mileage for the spur is 4 miles.

From the Y-intersection, stay right on a jeep road, leaving FR 99. Descend through a rocky section—you may need to dismount. The road becomes very narrow and eventually turns into the Round Robin single-track trail of the Mountain Top ski trail network. For 3.5 miles, this entertaining trail winds and dips through woods and meadows. At a 4-way trail junction, continue straight, keeping the big tree with orange arrows to your right. Soon the trail turns back into a jeep road. Watch out here for waterbars. Walk around a silver gate and turn right onto Wildcat Road. Descend past Lefferts Pond on the right. When you reach the paved Dam Road, turn right. At the Y-intersection, stay right and climb back to Chittenden Reservoir where the ride began. Total of 10.5 miles (14.5 including the spur on FR 99).

RIDE 19 · Delaware and Hudson Rail Trail

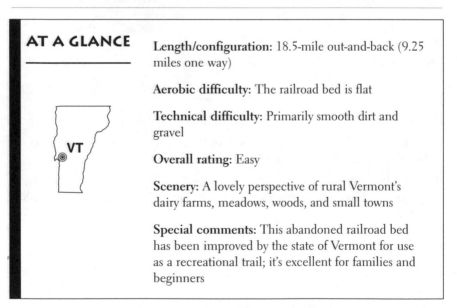

AT A GLANCE

Length/configuration: 18.5-mile out-and-back (9.25 miles one way)

Aerobic difficulty: The railroad bed is flat

Technical difficulty: Primarily smooth dirt and gravel

Overall rating: Easy

Scenery: A lovely perspective of rural Vermont's dairy farms, meadows, woods, and small towns

Special comments: This abandoned railroad bed has been improved by the state of Vermont for use as a recreational trail; it's excellent for families and beginners

This 18.5-mile path was once part of the Delaware and Hudson (D&H) rail system that connected Rutland, Vermont, with Albany, New York. It was built to transport the area's highly sought after slate from Castleton to Eagle Bridge, New York, then to Troy, New York, a port on the Hudson River. Vermont locals referred to the D&H as the "Slate Picker."

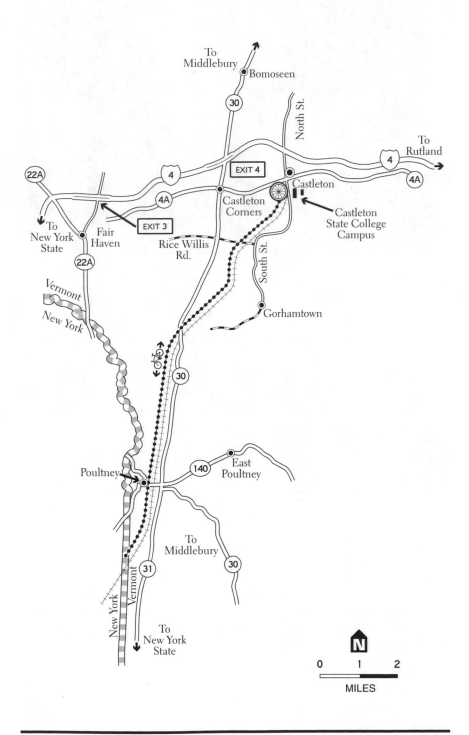

Families and novices will enjoy the easy terrain of the Delaware and Hudson Railroad Bed, which traverses woods and farmland in western Vermont.

Slate quarries boomed in the late 1800s, but eventually the demand declined in the mid-1900s. Trains were still used in western Vermont to transport milk and the occasional quarried products, but soon 18-wheel trucks took over the transport of goods. By the 1960s the use of boxcars to transport freight was nearing its end. D&H service from Castleton to Albany was discontinued in 1983. The state of Vermont was unsuccessful in its attempts to find a short-line operator, so in 1991 the rails and ties were pulled up and the bed upgraded to its current surface of gravel and stone. The original rough ballast can still be found in some short sections.

This 18.5-mile out-and-back ride (9.25 miles each way) makes use of the abandoned D&H railroad bed. It passes through scenic, rural areas of Rutland and Bennington counties, and offers fine views of open farmlands, forests, wetlands, and villages. You will pass old buildings, working farms, and sleepy small towns.

The rail trail is an excellent place for families and beginners to mountain bike. It is flat and smooth, no motor vehicles are allowed, and you can turn around at any point along the ride. I have chosen to describe this route beginning at Castleton State College, but you can get on the railroad bed at any road crossing. You can also do this ride in reverse by starting at the turnaround point at Western Slate Quarry, two miles west of Poultney on the Vermont–New York border.

General location: Castleton.

Elevation change: None.

Season: Anytime there is no snow on the ground—most likely May through November.

Services: All services can be found in Castleton. The nearest bike shops are in Rutland: Green Mountain Cyclery (802-775-6762) is on Strongs Avenue; Great Outdoors Trading (802-775-9989) is on Woodstock Avenue; Sports Peddler (802-775-0101) is on Main Street.

Hazards: The railroad bed has several road crossings, including VT 30, which can be very busy during commuter hours and on Saturdays.

Rescue index: You are never more than 1 mile from a telephone.

Land status: The abandoned railroad bed is now under the jurisdiction of the Vermont Agency of Natural Resources.

Maps: The D&H railroad is clearly depicted on DeLorme's and Northern Cartographic's atlases.

Finding the trail: From Rutland take Interstate 4 west to Exit 6. Take VT 4A west to Castleton State College campus. Turn left on South Street, following signs for the college. Park in the public parking lot behind the Information and Public Safety Building. Ride your bike back to South Street and turn left, keeping the information building on your left. Immediately look for the narrow single-track trail on the right.

Sources of additional information: Vermont Agency of Natural Resources, Department of Forests, Parks and Recreation, RR2, Box 2161, Pittsford, VT 05763; (802) 483-2314. Suggested reading: *Great Rail-Trails of the Northeast* (Amherst: New England Cartographics).

Notes on the trail: Begin by riding southwest from Castleton State College, slightly parallel to South Street. At about 1.5 miles cross over South Street on a pressure-treated bridge. Continue riding through meadows, woods, and wet lands. Pass an area kept extra wet by busy beavers. At about 4 miles cross VT 30; use caution when crossing this busy road. Continue on the railroad bed, passing by open meadows.

After another 2 miles the small town of Poultney will come into view. This is panoramic Vermont at its finest, with barns, silos, and farmlands. Since the railroad bed goes right through town, you can stop for refreshments at the general store. For a shorter ride, this is a good place to turn around and head back.

Or, continue on the railroad bed for a look at two slate quarries still in operation: the Staso/Hampton Quarry and the Western Slate Quarry. On the way you will cross a long bridge spanning the Poultney River. The trail's terminus is at the Western Slate Quarry at the New York State border. Retrace your steps back to Castleton State College for a total of 18.5 flat, easy, and very scenic miles.

RIDE 20 · South Hill

AT A GLANCE

VT

Length/configuration: 9.5-mile loop

Aerobic difficulty: One very long, strenuous climb

Technical difficulty: Extremely challenging; one long, rocky descent seems more like a dry stream bed than a trail

Overall rating: Advanced intermediate

Scenery: Densely wooded

Special comments: Not for the timid; experts can add 9 miles and a 900′ climb by starting at the village green in Pittsfield

The South Hill ride is a wooded, challenging 9.5-mile loop on a combination of rarely used dirt roads and jeep trails impassable by four-wheel-drive vehicles. A one-mile rocky descent in what appears to be a washout will have you yearning for a full-suspension bike. The bone-jarring downhill is followed by the ride's highlight, a shady climb on a winding, single-lane dirt road with a steep drop-off to Fletcher Brook on the left. If you seek solitude, you will like this ride. It is doubtful you will see another person, but you might spot a moose or a family of grouse.

You definitely need to be in good shape for this ride, which I rate as advanced intermediate. The total mileage is only 9.5 miles, but the terrain is very challenging with several short, technical climbs, one long climb along Fletcher Brook, and a one-mile descent that you will most likely walk. Experts can add nine miles and a 900-foot climb by starting at the village green in Pittsfield and climbing South Hill Road to the start of the loop for a total of 18.5 miles.

General location: Pittsfield.

Elevation change: One 900′ climb along Fletcher Brook, halfway into the ride. Experts can add another 900′ climb at the beginning by starting at the village green in Pittsfield and riding up South Hill Road.

Season: June through mid-November, provided there has not been much rain.

Services: Most services are found in Pittsfield. The nearest bike shops are Green Mountain Bicycles (802-767-4464) in Rochester, about 10 miles north of Pittsfield, and Killington Mountain Bike Shop (802-422-6232), about 10 miles south at the Killington Resort base lodge.

Hazards: Typical trail-riding obstacles. Feel free to dismount for the rocky 1-mile descent. I did.

RIDE 20 · South Hill

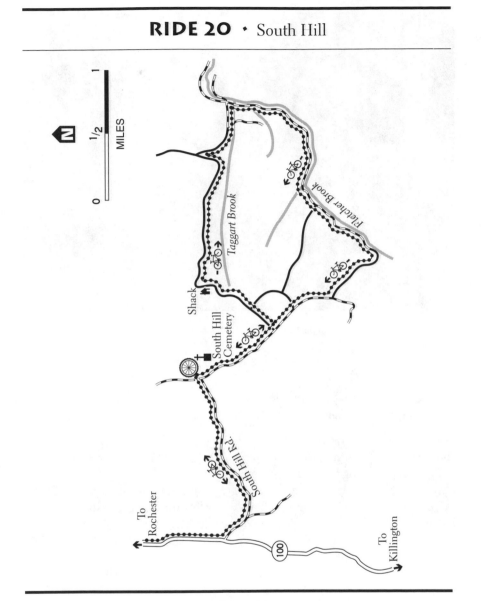

Rescue index: At times you are a rugged 2 miles from a telephone.

Land status: Maintained and unmaintained Class 4 roads.

Maps: Do not go on this ride without a good collection of maps, including two USGS 7.5 minute quads, Pico Peak and Delectable Mountain.

Finding the trail: From Pittsfield, drive south on VT 100 for 2 miles. Turn left onto South Hill Road and climb for 2.3 miles to the top. Park anywhere along the road at the **T**-intersection.

A quiet dirt road takes riders past South Hill Cemetery at the beginning and again at the end of the ride.

Source of additional information: Doon, at Green Mountain Bicycles in Rochester, can comment on this ride (802-767-4464).

Notes on the trail: Begin by turning right and riding south on the gravel road (South Hill Road), immediately passing South Hill Cemetery on your left. After 1 mile, begin looking for a narrow jeep trail on the left. Take the jeep trail, which climbs steeply at first, but becomes more level and easier to ride. Stay with the main vein, ignoring two lesser roads that veer off to the left. Pass a shack on your left and at 2.6 miles come to a fork. Take the washed-out trail/road to the left and begin descending—this is the rocky descent that you will most likely walk. At times you might wonder what you are doing here, but push on, it will soon be over. At 3.5 miles, just after a short, rideable climb, you will come to a dirt road with a brown house on the right. Stay right, keeping the house on your right and arrive at a **T**-intersection. Stay right and continue descending to an intersection of several roads. This is the low point of the loop (in elevation, not mood). Take the sharp right dirt road, keeping Fletcher Brook on your left.

Climb steadily on this road, passing several right-hand options. Stay left at the Road Closed sign. Fletcher Brook should still be on your left. Pass a shack on your right and take the left fork. Pass another shack on your right and take the right, uphill fork. This trail brings you to a **T**-intersection with the "Jones" house directly opposite you. Turn right onto the gravel road.

At 7.8 miles pass a narrow road on your right marked with VAST trail signs for Prior Dam Road and Barnard. Shortly after that, pass Brown Road on your right.

After a fast descent you will pass, on your right, the jeep trail that took you into the woods at the beginning of the ride. From there it is 1 mile back to the start, for a total of 9.5 challenging miles.

RIDE 21 · Silver Lake

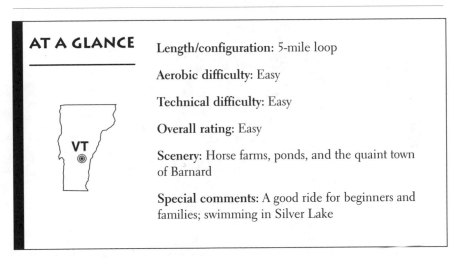

AT A GLANCE

Length/configuration: 5-mile loop

Aerobic difficulty: Easy

Technical difficulty: Easy

Overall rating: Easy

Scenery: Horse farms, ponds, and the quaint town of Barnard

Special comments: A good ride for beginners and families; swimming in Silver Lake

The picturesque town of Barnard is home to Silver Lake and Silver Lake State Park. The region was originally developed as farmland, and many stone walls and meadows remain. This easy, five-mile loop takes you past Silver Lake, Line Pond, and several horse farms. It begins with a mellow trail climb, continues on dirt roads, and finishes on the Barnard-Woodstock Stage Road, which was once the main route between the two towns. The Silver Lake loop is an excellent tour for novice riders, but if you need a greater challenge, check out the many connecting dirt roads.

General location: Barnard.

Elevation change: A 400′ climb at the start and a 500′ gradual climb near the end.

Season: May through mid-November.

Services: Most services are available in Barnard, including a well-stocked general store and a bakery. The closest bike shop is Cyclery Plus, about 13 miles south in West Woodstock (802-457-3377). Camping is available at Silver Lake State Park, Barnard, VT 05031; (802) 234-9451.

Hazards: An occasional motor vehicle.

Rescue index: You are never more than 1 mile from a private residence.

Land status: A town trail, Class 3 roads, and some pavement.

RIDE 21 • Silver Lake

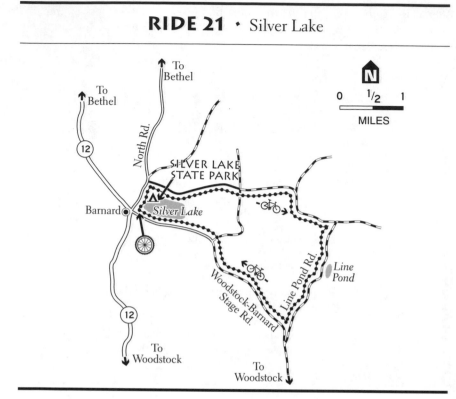

Maps: DeLorme's and Northern Cartographic's atlases both show the route. The USGS 7.5 minute quad, Woodstock North, also shows the route; however, East Road, which is actually a Class 3 road, is shown as a jeep trail.

Finding the trail: The ride begins and ends in Barnard at Silver Lake's public beach on VT 12. There is parking in back of the general store.

Source of additional information: Silver Lake State Park has information on the surrounding area (802-234-9451).

Notes on the trail: From the general store in Barnard, begin by riding toward the entrance to Silver Lake State Park, keeping Silver Lake on your right. Climbing on a paved road, ride past the entrance and look for a tunnel-like trail that drops off to the right. This is an easy trail with a gradual climb. Stay on the main vein for about .5 mile and exit to the right onto a dirt road. Take an immediate left onto East Road, where you will see several spectacular homes.

East Road winds and descends to a T-intersection; go right onto Line Pond Road. Soon you will pass Line Pond on your left, where I spotted a family of Canada geese and a neatly built beaver condominium. Begin a gradual climb that brings you to the Woodstock-Barnard Stage Road. Go right and continue climbing, passing a tiny cemetery on your left. Eventually the dirt road changes to pavement and soon you will see Silver Lake and the starting point.

Who needs a mountain bike? Cross bikes work fine on the Silver Lake ride.

RIDE 22 · Holy Roller

AT A GLANCE

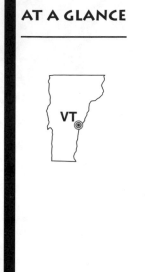

VT

Length/configuration: 22.5-mile "spoon" configuration—the ladle is a 16.5-mile loop; the handle is a 3-mile out-and-back

Aerobic difficulty: This hilly ride is not for the weak-hearted

Technical difficulty: Mostly dirt roads and one 2-mile stretch of moderate double-track

Overall rating: Difficult

Scenery: Beautiful farmland

Special comments: The double-track can be avoided, making this an all–dirt road ride; for a 35-mile ride with more single-track, pick up Ride 23; you can also pick up Ride 24 for a 39-mile ride with more single-track

The Mormon religion, also known as the Church of Jesus Christ of Latter-day Saints, was founded by prophet Joseph Smith, who was born in 1805 in South Royalton, Vermont, where his birthplace is now commemorated in true Mormon fashion. The 360-acre grounds are elaborately landscaped, and the monument, quarried in nearby Barre, is the largest, polished solid shaft of granite in the world. The Visitor Center exhibits paintings, sculptures, and personal possessions that belonged to Joseph Smith and his family. Along the many walking paths on the grounds, a surreal sensation is created by the choral-like music emanating from the woods. The Visitor Center is open daily from 9 A.M. to 5 P.M.; guided tours are free.

Beginning and ending at Joseph Smith's birthplace, this strenuous 22.5-mile loop has many short, steep climbs that will have you gasping in your lowest gear. But it's not just the hills that will leave you breathless: the natural beauty and unaffected diversity of the landscape are spectacular. Ponds, equestrian training centers, historic stone walls (and one new wall made of automobile tires), old cemeteries, and a symphony of babbling brooks add to this ride's roadside entertainment.

At the halfway point you will enter the town of Strafford, where you can visit the home of Justin Morrill, the U.S. Congressman responsible for the Land Grant Acts. Strafford's historic district has approximately 30 late-eighteenth- and nineteenth-century buildings on or near the quintessential village green. The crowning jewel is the Strafford Town Hall, built in 1799.

RIDE 22 · Holy Roller

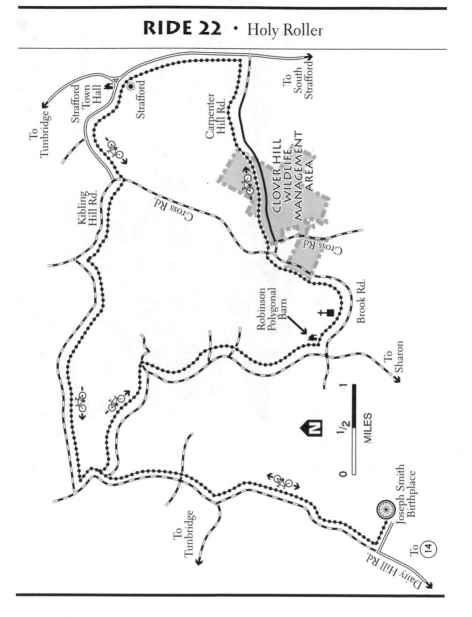

This difficult ride, which consists primarily of narrow, unimproved dirt roads with several sections of unmaintained town roads and single-track trails, will take at least two-and-a-half hours and is not for the faint of heart!

General location: South Royalton and Sharon on VT 14.

Elevation change: You will gain a total of about 2,500´ throughout this loop. The longest ascent is when you leave Strafford and climb steadily and sometimes steeply to the top of Kibling Hill Road, for an elevation gain of 1,300´ in just under 2 miles. From there it is nearly all downhill back to the Joseph Smith birthplace.

This renowned one-piece granite monument can be seen at the Joseph Smith birthplace, where the Holy Roller ride begins and ends.

Season: September and early October are the ideal times to see this area of Vermont because of exceptional fall foliage. However, quick dips in the lakes and ponds along the way make the heat of summer bearable. The first of June is the earliest you could do this ride in its entirety, due to snow that lasts well into spring on the single-track section.

Services: The services closest to the start of the ride are in Sharon. Brooksies' Diner has a great buffet every Sunday. The nearest bicycle shop is Tom Mowatt's, in Lebanon, NH (603-448-5556). At the halfway point, the town of Strafford has a general store and a bicycle shop, Brick Store Bicycles, adjacent to the post office (802-765-4441) .

Hazards: Occasional slow-moving farm machinery.

Rescue index: At times you might think you are in the middle of nowhere, but actually you are never more than 2 miles from a private residence.

Land status: Most roads are narrow town roads or unimproved town roads. One single-track section goes through the Clover Hill Wildlife Management Area.

Maps: The best maps are two USGS 7.5 minute quads, Sharon and South Strafford. Northern Cartographic's and DeLorme's atlases are also good.

The Holy Roller takes riders past the historic Robinson Polygonal Barn.

Finding the trail: Look for the historic landmark sign indicating the Joseph Smith Monument Mormon Prophet's Birthplace at the junction of Dairy Hill Road on VT 14, 2 miles north of Sharon and 1 mile south of South Royalton. Turn right onto Dairy Farm Road and proceed steeply uphill for 2.5 miles. Turn right into the Joseph Smith historical site. Be prepared for a setting so different from Dairy Hill Road you will think you are in a foreign country. There is plenty of parking, as well as great picnic and photo opportunities. McIntosh pond, opposite the entrance to the site, has a picnic and swimming area.

Source of additional information: You can read about the historical sites on this ride in the *Vermont Museums, Galleries & Historic Buildings,* The Museum & Gallery Alliance, c/o Shelburne Museum, P.O. Box 10, Shelburne, VT 05482; (802) 985-3346. The price, $11.45, includes the booklet, postage, and handling.

Notes on the trail: Upon leaving the Mormon monument, turn right (due north) onto Dairy Farm Road, which immediately becomes dirt. Gradually gain elevation on a rarely traveled road. Come to a **T** and bear right, climbing very steeply with your sights on the silo at the top. Descend briefly and pass through a dirt road intersection (right takes you a half mile to the Tunbridge Trout Pond; left takes you 1.5 miles to the Tunbridge Covered Bridge). Continue descending gradually and pass by the Pease family farm, a dairy farm specializing in Guernseys. Come to a junction with a black mailbox #169 on the left; put it in a low gear and take the hairpin right turn which climbs steeply. At the junction, note the road directly ahead, which is where you will come out at the end of the ride.

Regain your composure, shift to a higher gear, and roll along on gentle terrain. A classic, yellow farmhouse on your right will catch your attention as the road sweeps to the left. Stay with the road and immediately begin climbing, very steeply. Recover at the top at a junction where a sign says No Wheeled Vehicles. Stay right and descend past a lake on the left. Continue downhill gradually for 1 mile and pass by a homestead reminiscent of Appalachia. Shortly after this, you will come upon one of the most beautiful polygonal barns in Vermont, the Robinson Barn, built in 1917 and listed on the State Register of Historic Preservation.

The Robinson Barn sits at a **T**-intersection. Directly ahead you will see a sign that reads Sharon 4, Strafford 4. You are headed for Strafford on what is commonly known as the Brook Road. After about 2 miles, turn right onto Cross Road. Stay left and just after the fire warden's house, turn left onto an unmarked, unmaintained double-track trail. Take care on this rocky section as it can be tricky when wet.

Descend gradually for nearly 1 mile and pass through an open meadow with excellent single-track riding. Continue descending; the trail becomes wider and turns into double-track. Come to a junction well marked with VAST trail signs. Stay left, and at the next junction, continue straight. The condition of this road becomes better the farther you descend. Soon you will pass by several houses. To the right are magnificent views of the valley.

The road eventually becomes Carpenter Hill Road (Town Highway 35) and ends at the paved Strafford-Tunbridge Road. Turn left and ride to Strafford on good pavement.

In Strafford, Brick Store Bicycles is on your left, adjacent to the post office. Directly ahead (you can't miss it) is the Strafford Town Hall.

Leaving Strafford, stay to the left of the town hall on Brook Road (TH 5). Begin climbing gradually and stay with the pavement. Turn right onto Kibling Hill Road, which is dirt, and continue climbing. Near the top of Kibling Hill, bear left at the junction with the mailboxes and climb just a little bit more. With all that climbing it seems there should be a view, but there isn't.

Begin descending past old farmhouses and rock walls. At the next junction bear left and continue descending along Farnham Branch brook for nearly 2 miles. You will come to a 4-way intersection with a big brown house dead ahead. Take the left before the brown house (Potash Road goes right; Town Farm Road is the unimproved road straight ahead). After a short climb you will come to a familiar junction. It is the one where you took the hairpin turn to the right, 16 miles ago. Continue straight and retrace your ride back to the Joseph Smith birthplace.

RIDE 23 · Gordo's Loop

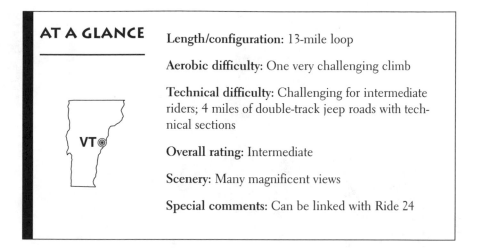

AT A GLANCE

Length/configuration: 13-mile loop

Aerobic difficulty: One very challenging climb

Technical difficulty: Challenging for intermediate riders; 4 miles of double-track jeep roads with technical sections

Overall rating: Intermediate

Scenery: Many magnificent views

Special comments: Can be linked with Ride 24

A serendipitous encounter that occurred while I was researching this loop explains how the ride got its name. My friend, Helene, and I had reached the top of the first long climb and were gawking at a 360-degree panoramic view. Suddenly, we heard the jingling of a bell, and out of the brush bounded a liver-and-white Brittany with what appeared to be a cowbell around his neck. Right behind him was an old English gentleman hunter, fully attired in chaps, chapeau, and tie, carrying a shotgun and a grouse, calling "Hello, Kate!"

It turned out to be Richard, owner of the local bike shop, Brick Store Bicycles, out for a day of bird hunting with his dog, Gordo. The two of them were a handsome and impressive pair, and it was hard to believe we had actually crossed paths in the middle of the countryside, miles from the nearest town. We compared topo maps to figure out who was going where, and from which direction we had come, and finally, when we parted ways, I wasn't sure who was lost and who would make it home. But one thing was for sure: the three of us were having a delightful time outdoors on what we each knew could well be the last great day of the autumn season.

Helene and I continued on our bikes down a breathtaking descent and recommended investigating this ride. Soon we were forced to revise our route when we discovered a trail so overgrown it was impassable. To our ongoing delight, our detour brought us to more scenic vistas, some amazing houses, an angry dog, and a fun descent on a double-track jeep trail.

Gordo's Loop, named in honor of our chance encounter with Gordo and Richard, turned out to be 13 miles long. (Helene suggested we call it 12.75 miles in case anyone reading this is superstitious.) It's an intermediate ride with a few technical sections and some climbing (some of which must be walked due to fallen trees and washouts). The terrain alternates among dirt roads, unmaintained town roads, and town trails. The views are exceptional.

RIDE 23 · Gordo's Loop

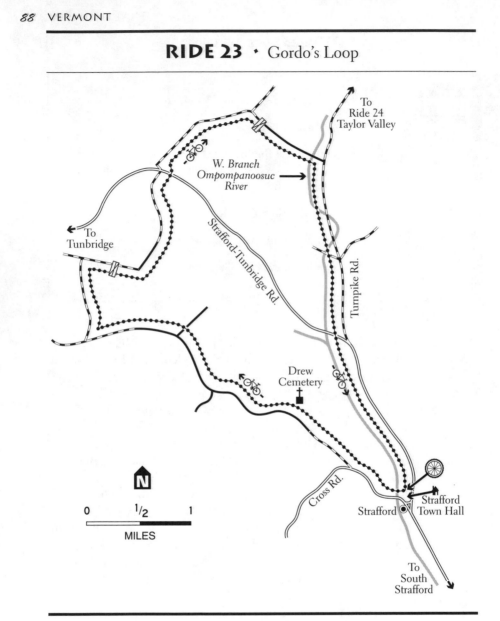

To make the ride longer, at mile 9, pick up Ride 24, Taylor Valley, by going left when this ride joins Taylor Valley Road. Total distance for the combined rides is 25.5 miles.

General location: Strafford.

Elevation change: The elevation of the town of Strafford is approximately 900´. You begin Gordo's Loop by gaining 1,000´ over the first 3 miles.

Season: June through mid-November.

A bike shop owner's day off—Richard Montague and Gordo, of Brick Store Bicycles in Strafford, enjoy grouse hunting on a warm October day.

Services: Strafford has a general store, a post office, a church, and a bike shop, Brick Store Bicycles (802-765-4441). More plentiful services can be found in neighboring villages. Norwich, VT, and Hanover, NH, are within 15 miles.

Hazards: Windfall, rocky sections, washouts, and holes.

Rescue index: It could take a while to find you if you were seriously injured on this ride, so if you go alone, make it a point to let someone know your plan. Give that person a map of Gordo's Loop. Otherwise, a private residence may be up to 3 miles away.

Land status: Class 4 roads.

Maps: Two USGS 7.5 minute quads, Chelsea and Sharon, are useful.

Finding the trail: Gordo's Loop begins and ends in the town of Strafford. To get to Strafford, take the Sharon exit (Exit 2) off Interstate 89 and follow VT 132 east to South Strafford. At the **T**-intersection and stop sign, turn left. It is 2 miles to Strafford. Park at any of the public buildings in town.

Source of additional information: Richard Montague, owner of Brick Store Bicycles (next to the post office), may be able to comment on this ride.

Notes on the trail: From Brick Store Bicycles, pedal toward the Strafford Church, keeping it to your right. Ride on pavement and in less than a mile, turn right onto Wetmore Road. Follow this dirt road, climbing gradually. Pass Drew Cemetery on the right. When the road ends, continue straight onto the unmaintained double-track trail. This section can be steep and rocky at times, and you might have to hike your bike.

At the next trail junction, continue straight, keeping the pond on your left, and climb steeply to the top of a knoll. The trail that leads to the right (there's a sign posted—No Motor Vehicles, Please) takes you to a wide-open area that was probably once a farmer's field; it is still lined with stone walls. This is where Helene and I met Gordo and Richard. It's worth riding out to this area for the views.

From the main trail, continue straight, keeping the No Motor Vehicles, Please sign to your right. The trail conditions improve, and get even better as you descend onto a Class 4 dirt road. Pass through another open area and then stay with the main dirt road as it bends sharply to the right between stone walls where there are great great views.

At approximately 5.25 miles, turn right at the T-intersection. Pass by a beautiful yellow house on the left, where an ugly yellow dog may chase you and nip at your heels.

Ride through a wire gate. If you need to open it, be sure to close it after you pass through. At approximately 6 miles, take the left at the Y-junction, following the yellow-blazed trees. Come to a small pond and farmhouse on the left. The trail turns to a town road and rolls, then climbs to the paved Tunbridge-Strafford Road. Turn left, then immediately turn right onto a dirt road that snakes between several dilapidated and partly burned red buildings. Here are impressive views to the northeast.

Descend quickly, swinging right and then left, winding around a beautiful yellow farmhouse. The road immediately changes to a double-track trail and descends into the woods. Pass by a gate on your left and descend onto an unmaintained town trail. This fun downhill brings you to Taylor Valley Road (where you can go left to join Ride 24, Taylor Valley). Turn right and descend to the paved Tunbridge-Strafford Road. Turn left and ride for 2 miles on a beautiful valley floor. Come to the landmark church in the town of Strafford (on your right) for a total of 13 miles (12.75 for those who are superstitious).

RIDE 24 · Taylor Valley

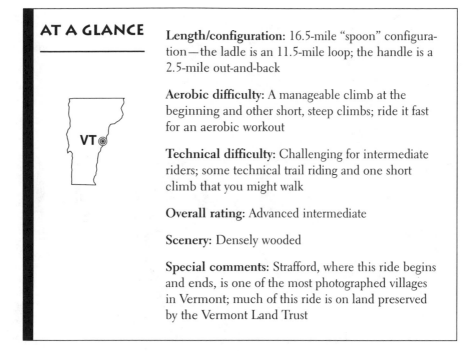

AT A GLANCE

Length/configuration: 16.5-mile "spoon" configuration—the ladle is an 11.5-mile loop; the handle is a 2.5-mile out-and-back

Aerobic difficulty: A manageable climb at the beginning and other short, steep climbs; ride it fast for an aerobic workout

Technical difficulty: Challenging for intermediate riders; some technical trail riding and one short climb that you might walk

Overall rating: Advanced intermediate

Scenery: Densely wooded

Special comments: Strafford, where this ride begins and ends, is one of the most photographed villages in Vermont; much of this ride is on land preserved by the Vermont Land Trust

The west branch of the Ompompanoosuc River carves through Taylor Valley and defines its north-south topography. Running parallel to the river is Turnpike Road, which was once the primary horse-and-buggy thoroughfare from Strafford to Chelsea. This 16.5-mile ride begins by climbing gradually up Turnpike Road for 6 miles to the height of land. It then joins up with a network of trails that lie on 2,200 acres of wooded land owned by John Hemmenway.

Hemmenway managed his land as a model of how he thought forest land ought to be managed in order to preserve it for future generations. The land is currently in the process of being put into a permanent conservation easement with the Vermont Land Trust. The public is welcome to ride mountain bikes on the Hemmenway property provided the land is used with care.

This ride begins and ends in the village of Strafford, which has an historic district with approximately 30 late-eighteenth- and nineteenth-century buildings on or near the village green. The centerpiece of the town is the Strafford Town Hall, built in 1799. You can also visit the home of Justin Morrill, the U.S. Congressman responsible for the Land Grant Acts.

Taylor Valley is an advanced intermediate ride with a few stretches of technical climbing and descending. It can be joined with Ride 23, Gordo's Loop, for a more difficult 25.5-mile ride.

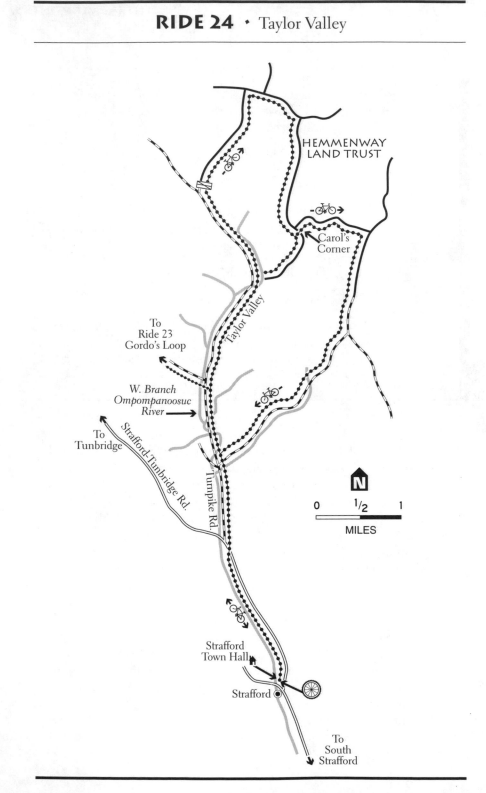

HEMMENWAY
LAND TRUST

Carol's
Corner

To
Ride 23
Gordo's Loop

Taylor Valley

W. Branch
Ompompanoosuc
River →

To
Tunbridge

Strafford-Tunbridge Rd.

Turnpike Rd.

N

0   1/2   1

MILES

Strafford
Town Hall

Strafford ●

To
South
Strafford

The Taylor Valley ride begins and ends at the Town Meeting Hall in Strafford.

General location: Strafford.

Elevation change: 1,000′ are gained in the first 6 miles. The middle section rolls and the last section descends back to the start.

Season: Mid-June through mid-November.

Services: Strafford has a general store, a post office, a church, and a bike shop, Brick Store Bicycles (802-765-4441). More plentiful services can be found in neighboring villages. Norwich, VT, and Hanover, NH, are within 15 miles.

Hazards: The usual obstacles found on trails (roots, holes, rocks, logs), as well as the possibility of a small logging operation.

Rescue index: The trails described in this ride are not frequently traveled, and you are often up to 3 miles from the nearest telephone. If you were injured it could be several days before someone would find you, so if you choose to ride alone, inform a friend of your plan.

Land status: Class 4 roads (maintained and unmaintained) and town trails. A third of the ride takes place on the Hemmenway property, preserved by the Vermont Land Trust.

Maps: Two USGS 7.5 minute quads, Vershire and Chelsea, are helpful.

Finding the trail: To get to Strafford, where the Taylor Valley ride begins and ends, take the Sharon exit (Exit 2) off Interstate 89 and follow VT 132 east to South Strafford. At the **T**-intersection and stop sign, turn left. It is 2 miles to Strafford. Park at any of the public buildings in town.

Source of additional information: Richard Montague, owner of Brick Store Bicycles, showed me this ride. He will be able to point you in the direction of Taylor Valley and provide you with bicycle-related services (802-765-4441).

Notes on the trail: Park at any public parking area near the village green. Begin by riding north on the Strafford-Tunbridge Road, keeping the famous town hall on your left. After 2 miles, fork right onto Turnpike Road, a gravel road that climbs steadily up Taylor Valley and becomes a four-wheel-drive road near the top. At 6.2 miles and the high point of the road, turn right onto an unmarked four-wheel-drive trail and immediately pass under a wire gate. (This is the Hemmenway property.) At the next trail intersection fork right, then fork left.

Soon you will come to a major trail **T**-intersection. Go right and begin climbing a rugged, washed-out section of trail. Pass by a major trail junction, heavily signed with VAST trail signs. Bear right, then left, still climbing.

At the top of the climb, stay left on a gravel road. Come to a dirt road and go right. (At this junction you will see a lot of VAST trail signs.) While on this road, stay left at all trail temptations. At a little over 9 miles you reach the high point of this ride, 2,210'. Continue on this road until you come to Carol's Corner. Go left, passing by the outhouses. (If you go straight, you can take a shortcut back to Turnpike Road where you can go left and descend back down to Strafford.)

Descend to a **T**-intersection of logging roads and take the right through a mucky, muddy area. If you are lucky, you may spot a moose here. Stay on this unmaintained road, descending to a more improved road. At the **Y**-intersection go right, following VAST signs for Strafford. Stay on this gravel road at all times, descending alongside a stream. At mile 14, turn left onto Turnpike Road and keep on going downhill. At the pavement go left and return to your starting point in Strafford.

RIDE 25 · Norwich Turnpike Road

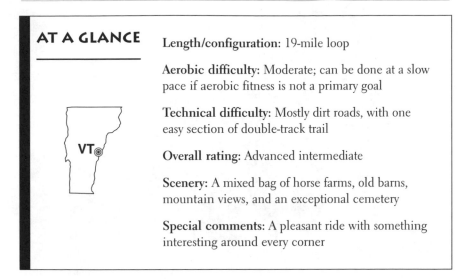

AT A GLANCE

Length/configuration: 19-mile loop

Aerobic difficulty: Moderate; can be done at a slow pace if aerobic fitness is not a primary goal

Technical difficulty: Mostly dirt roads, with one easy section of double-track trail

Overall rating: Advanced intermediate

Scenery: A mixed bag of horse farms, old barns, mountain views, and an exceptional cemetery

Special comments: A pleasant ride with something interesting around every corner

The Turnpike Road was once a stage road that extended from Norwich to Chelsea in the late 1800s. Parts of it are now well-traveled dirt roads and other parts are barely passable by a four-wheel-drive vehicle. This loop ride takes advantage of the Turnpike Road from Norwich to South Strafford. You return to Norwich on the scenic New Boston Road for a total of 19 miles. On the way you will ride by many private homes, some old, some new, through densely wooded forests, and past horse farms with immaculately kept grounds. You will also see several beautiful old barns, and one fascinating cemetery on New Boston Road. (Be sure to check out the dates of birth of two members of the Judd family.)

The ride is mostly dirt roads, plus a two-mile section of double-track, and five miles of pavement at the end. It has one of those long, gradual climbs that make you feel like you are not gaining much elevation, when in fact you are. As a result, you will think this ride is all downhill!

General location: Norwich.

Elevation change: 1,100´ are gained gradually over the first 5 miles. There are several other short, steep climbs.

Season: June through mid-November.

Services: All services are available in Norwich. Omer & Bob's Sport Shop (603-643-3525), across the Connecticut River in Hanover, NH, sells and services bikes. Brick Store Bicycles (802-765-4441) is in Strafford, 2 miles up-valley from the ride's halfway point in South Strafford.

Hazards: Moderate traffic on the dirt roads.

Rescue index: You are never more than 2 miles from a private residence.

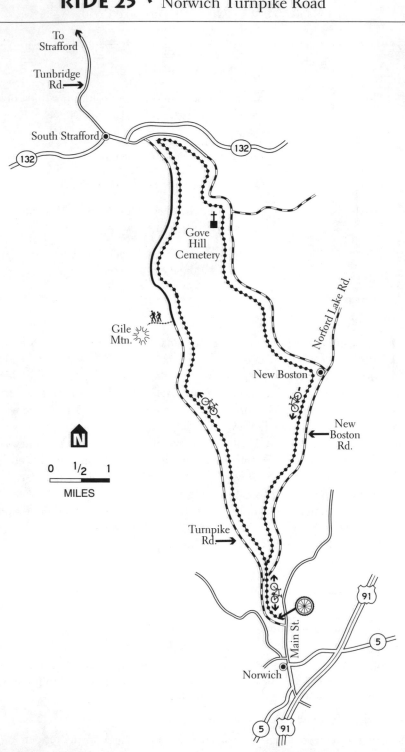

To
Strafford

Tunbridge
Rd.

South Strafford

132

132

Gove
Hill
Cemetery

Norford Lake Rd.

Gile
Mtn.

New Boston

New
Boston
Rd.

N

0   1/2   1
MILES

Turnpike
Rd.

91

Main St.

5

Norwich

5   91

This section of trail on Norwich Turnpike Road was once the stage road from Norwich to Strafford.

Land status: Class 3 and 4 roads, one jeep trail.

Maps: DeLorme's atlas is helpful, as are two USGS 7.5 minute quads, Hanover and South Strafford.

Finding the trail: From the center of Norwich, drive north on Main Street for a half mile. Turn left on Turnpike Road and proceed for .5 mile. Park at the small park on the left. The ride begins here.

Source of additional information: The post office in Strafford has an interesting map of the Turnpike Road mounted on the wall.

Notes on the trail: From the small park, proceed north on paved Turnpike Road. Continue straight at the junction of New Boston Road, where you will come from at the end of the ride.

The Turnpike Road turns into a dirt road and becomes narrower as you gain elevation. Pass the Gile Mountain trailhead on your left and continue straight onto a jeep road. At 6 miles, ride through an open area and pick up the jeep road on the far side. Descend to an improved road (6.5 miles) and stay right. The road continues to improve as you descend.

At about 8 miles, turn sharply right onto paved New Boston Road. You will pass a road sign at the 10.8-mile mark confirming that you are indeed on New Boston Road. Soon the road turns to dirt. Stay right at the next junction. On your right you will pass Grove Hill Cemetery, well worth a visit. New Boston Road rolls and dips but is mostly downhill from this point. At Norford Lake

Road, turn right and descend on pavement for about 4 miles to Turnpike Road. Turn left and retrace your steps to the small park, for a total of 19 miles.

RIDE 26 · Hart Hollow

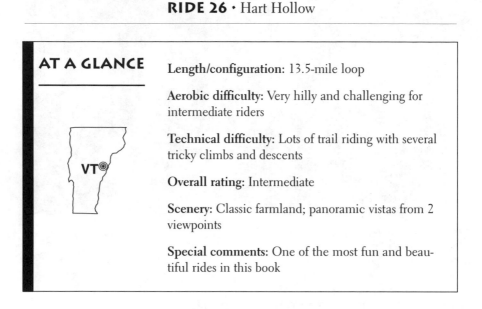

AT A GLANCE

Length/configuration: 13.5-mile loop

Aerobic difficulty: Very hilly and challenging for intermediate riders

Technical difficulty: Lots of trail riding with several tricky climbs and descents

Overall rating: Intermediate

Scenery: Classic farmland; panoramic vistas from 2 viewpoints

Special comments: One of the most fun and beautiful rides in this book

This ride was shown to me by Dirk Anderson, a Chelsea resident who has been riding and skiing the trails in his neck of the woods since his days at Vermont Law School in South Royalton nearly a decade ago. When it was time for me to check out the route, I brought along my eager-to-ride friends, Ernie and Bette, who both agreed that the Hart Hollow loop was the finest ride they'd done all summer long. We lucked out with a supreme fall day full of colorful foliage and with perfect riding temperatures, but then again I'd be happy to do this ride any season of the year, except maybe in winter. Then I'd ski it.

The four of us debated on a title for the ride, tossing around names like "Dirk's Dirty Ride," and "Up and Down with Dirk," and finally settled on Hart Hollow because that is where the most beautiful section of the ride takes place. There is a little of everything on the 13.5-mile Hart Hollow loop: single-track, pavement, and everything in between; a variety of climbs; fun descents; a couple of great viewpoints; and some typical Vermont landscapes where you will think you are riding through an earlier century.

General location: Between the towns of Chelsea and Washington near Washington Heights.

Elevation change: One 800´ climb happens right away over the first 3 miles. A second significant climb of 650´ comes at the 9-mile mark. There are several steep rollers along the way.

RIDE 26 · Hart Hollow

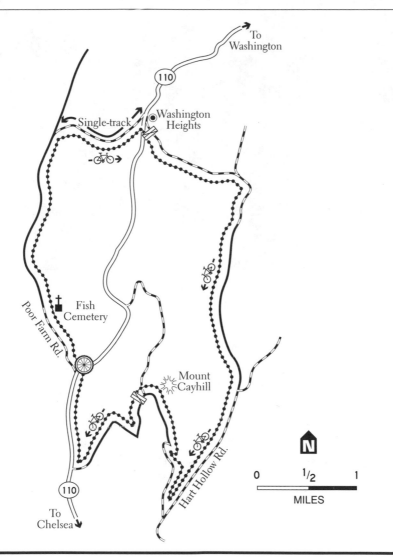

Season: Mid-June through mid-November, but of course fall is the best. We know. We were there.

Services: Chelsea and Washington have general stores. The nearest bike shop is Onion River Sports in Barre (802-476-9750). Brick Store Bicycles is in Strafford (802-765-4441).

Hazards: You may come across an occasional horseback rider, a washed-out bridge, and windfall, all typical of trail riding in Vermont.

King demands bones (Milk Bones) before bikers may pass.

Rescue index: Most of the time you are at least 2 miles from a private residence and telephone.

Land status: Mostly Class 4 roads and trails; some pavement at the end.

Maps: The entire ride can be found on the USGS 7.5 minute quad, Washington.

Finding the trail: Situated halfway between the towns of Chelsea and Washington on the west side of VT 110 is Poor Farm Road, where the ride starts. Look for the pullout on the southwest side of Poor Farm Road where you can park your car.

Sources of additional information: Not many people know about this ride, so your best bet is to go well equipped with this book, a topo map, and a compass.

Notes on the trail: Climb up Poor Farm Road for nearly 3 miles. The road becomes narrow near the top and is not plowed during the winter. At the 3-mile mark, turn right onto a hidden jeep trail. Staying to the right of the field, ride through a series of deep dips and curvy climbs. You will pass apple trees, panoramic views, and old foundations. This trail descends to a dirt road where you turn left. Immediately turn left again onto an improved dirt road, which takes you to paved VT 110.

Turn right on VT 110, then immediately turn left onto a jeep trail. Climb for a bit and pass through an old, wooden gate with a camp to the right. Ride through an open area and descend to a town road. Turn right, then climb steadily. At the top of the climb is a viewpoint in the meadow to the left.

Continue on the dirt road, heading straight at all times. The road turns to trail, and soon you will pass through a muddy stretch with beaver ponds and meadows to the right. This is one of the prettiest sections of the ride; be sure to watch out for a dangerous log bridge.

The trail dumps you out onto Hart Hollow Road, a well-maintained, scenic town road. Turn right and descend. Just after the yellow farmhouse on the right, turn right and immediately right again, crossing over a stream. Climb gradually with a farm, cows, apple trees, and a stream on your left. This is Vermont at its finest.

The road takes a hairpin turn to the right. Just as farm buildings come into view and just before a Drive Very Slowly sign, turn left onto a hidden jeep road (10.5 miles). Climb very steeply with a stone wall on your right and a pond on your left. At 11 miles you will come to an open area at the top of Sky Acres Road. Mount Cayhill is to the right.

Stay left, ride around the chain gate, and continue climbing. At the top of the hill is a 360-degree view. Descend down the other side, taking either trail in the meadow at the Y-intersection. (They come to the same point.)

Enter the woods and come to some old, weathered, wooden structures. Go right between the two buildings onto a jeep road. The road, completely in the woods, climbs a short, steep pitch and bears left. Pass by a stone monument-type gate post and into an open area with views to the left. Just ahead is a clump of trees—continue past the maple tree and take a hard left, descending on a grassy double-track trail toward a red farmhouse and barn.

Just past the red barn turn left. Pick up what appears to be a driveway, bear right, and descend to pavement. This is VT 110. Turn right, and in 1 mile you are back at the starting point after a total of 13.5 miles.

RANDOLPH AREA

Randolph is the nucleus for more than 200 miles of bona fide trail riding in central Vermont. A group called the White River Valley Trails Association (WRVTA) is setting a precedent for mountain bike trail organizations in Vermont and throughout the Northeast. They have located, signed, and mapped approximately 20 rides of varying difficulty in Randolph and neighboring towns. They have also produced an excellent topography map (1:80,000) of the region, the "Randolph Vermont Mtn. Biking Trails," ($4.95), which highlights 240 miles of roads and trails for road biking and mountain biking.

Every year the New England Mountain Bike Festival is held in Randolph on the last weekend in September. For information on the Randolph trail network or the New England Mountain Bike Festival, contact the WRVTA at P.O. Box 219, Randolph Center, VT 05061; (802) 728-4420. You can visit their Web site at www.vermontsite.com.

Rides 27 through 30 are a sampling of what you will find in the Randolph area.

RIDE 27 · Floating Bridge Loop

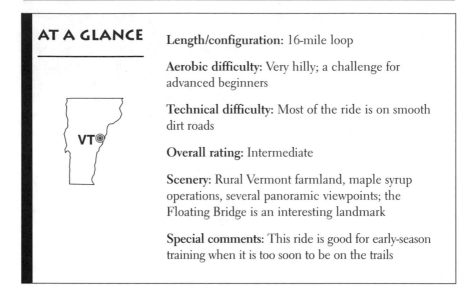

AT A GLANCE

Length/configuration: 16-mile loop

Aerobic difficulty: Very hilly; a challenge for advanced beginners

Technical difficulty: Most of the ride is on smooth dirt roads

Overall rating: Intermediate

Scenery: Rural Vermont farmland, maple syrup operations, several panoramic viewpoints; the Floating Bridge is an interesting landmark

Special comments: This ride is good for early-season training when it is too soon to be on the trails

VT

Brookfield's historic Floating Bridge dates back to 1820, when local towns-people could easily drive horse and sleigh across the frozen lake during winter months. Spring, summer, and fall, however, required a lengthy trip all the way around the lake to the community on the other side. So they devised an ingenious way of crossing it year-round: while the lake was still frozen, they built a bridge of logs on top of the ice. When spring arrived and the ice melted, they were left with their first Floating Bridge.

Periodically, new logs had to be added as old ones became waterlogged and lost their floation. In 1884, a new flotation system was devised using tarred, wooden kerosene barrels. Succeeding bridges kept this basic design until 1978, when the seventh bridge, the one still used today, was built. It is similiar to its predecessors, except this "modern" bridge's wooden barrels were replaced by plastic containers filled with Styrofoam. Its elevated footpath allows pedestrians to cross it without chancing wet feet. Cars, however, may still occasionally cross in water up to their hubcaps.

At the halfway point of this 16-mile loop, you will ride your bike across the Floating Bridge, which connects the east and west shores of Sunset Lake. Don't be surprised if you have to splash through a puddle or two on your way across.

The majority of this ride comprises gently rolling backcountry dirt roads, with panoramic vistas surprising you at nearly every bend. Maple trees, most of them tapped in the spring for their sweet, golden syrup, line many sections of the route, providing shade in the heat of summer and vibrant color in the cool of fall. You will pass several working farms, a bog where wild orchids grow in the spring, and Rood Pond, a little lake with big fish. This is a mellow ride lasting two to two-and-a-half hours, depending on how much time you spend picnicking at the Floating Bridge.

RIDE 27 · Floating Bridge Loop

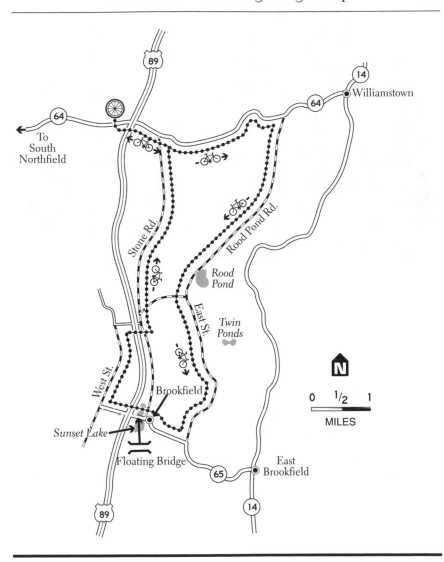

General location: 3 miles west of Williamstown; 4 miles east of Northfield.

Elevation change: The ride begins at a high point and immediately descends 500´ in the first 2.5 miles. The elevation is gained back gradually throughout the ride, with a 0.5-mile climb on a paved road leading into Brookfield, and a short, steep climb just after the Floating Bridge.

Season: Mid-April through the end of October are the best times for this ride; however, it is an excellent ride in March, when the occasional warm days lure you to the outdoors and remind you it's time to get in shape for the upcoming riding season.

The historic Floating Bridge in Brookfield connects the east and west shores of Sunset Lake.

Services: All services can be found in Williamstown, Northfield, and Brookfield.

Hazards: The initial 2.5-mile decent is on paved VT 64. Traffic is moderate and the speed limit is 50 mph. Occasional slow-moving farm equipment may present temporary obstacles.

Rescue index: Private homes are interspersed throughout the ride. You are never more than 2 miles from a phone.

Land status: Old, unpaved town roads and 3 short sections on paved state highways.

Maps: DeLorme's and Northern Cartographic's atlases both show the route.

Finding the trail: Begin on VT 64 at the "park-and-ride," located 500 yards west of Exit 5, off Interstate 89 (heading toward Northfield).

Sources of additional information: Onion River Sports is to the north in Barre (802-476-9750). Green Trails Inn (802-276-3412), in Brookfield across from the Floating Bridge, has trails on its property for its guests to use.

Notes on the trail: Begin by riding east toward Williamstown on VT 64, passing under I-89 and descending for nearly 2 miles. Just as you see the Welcome to Williamstown sign, turn right onto Rood Pond Road, a well-maintained, lightly traveled dirt road. Soon, on the left, you will pass a small bog dotted with wild orchids in the spring and cattails in the fall. After a few more rolling miles you will come to Rood Pond on your left, a deep pond with a state fishing access. Rumor has it that very large trout can be caught here. At a **T**-intersection go left toward the expansive horse stables. Continue on Rood Pond Road, passing several more ponds on the way, until you come to VT 65. Turn right and begin climbing toward the church steeple in the distance, which marks the town of Brookfield.

Once you arrive at the church, the road turns to dirt. Brookfield's historical buildings lie immediately ahead to the right, but the ride bears left and crosses the Floating Bridge which connects VT 65 to the other side of Sunset Lake (another rumor has it that great "crawdaddin'" can be found here). In Brookfield there is a pub, Ariel's, where you can sample beer from local breweries, and the Green Trails Inn, a charming New England bed-and-breakfast.

Ride across the bridge and up a short, very steep, roughly paved section of road. Come to a **T**-intersection and turn right onto maple-lined West Street. At the next **T**-intersection, turn right and immediately pass under I-89. Turn left onto Stone Road, which parallels the interstate briefly and is an excellent example of rural Vermont lying side by side with progressive America. (Note: If you go right on Stone Road you will go back to the town of Brookfield.)

After about 6 miles, Stone Road will bring you back to VT 64 where you had your first big downhill. Turn left onto the pavement, and after a half mile you will arrive back at the park-and-ride where you began.

RIDE 28 · Peth Village Loop

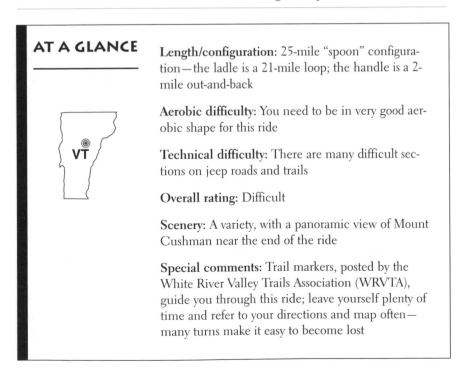

AT A GLANCE

Length/configuration: 25-mile "spoon" configuration—the ladle is a 21-mile loop; the handle is a 2-mile out-and-back

Aerobic difficulty: You need to be in very good aerobic shape for this ride

Technical difficulty: There are many difficult sections on jeep roads and trails

Overall rating: Difficult

Scenery: A variety, with a panoramic view of Mount Cushman near the end of the ride

Special comments: Trail markers, posted by the White River Valley Trails Association (WRVTA), guide you through this ride; leave yourself plenty of time and refer to your directions and map often— many turns make it easy to become lost

RIDE 28 · Peth Village Loop

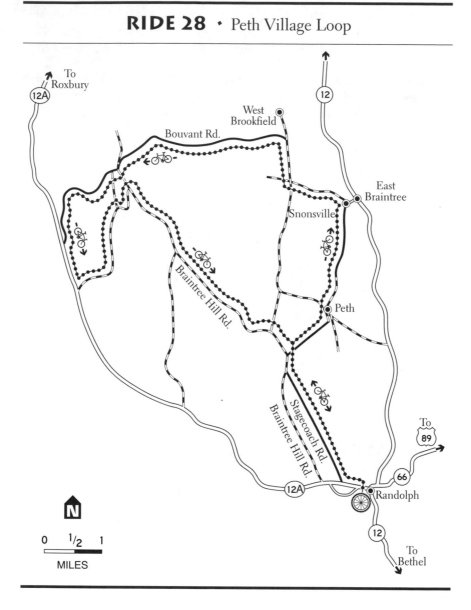

This 25-mile ride is 50% single-track and takes you through the remains of Peth Village, which now consists of a couple of houses. You will begin and end with the Stagecoach Road, an unmaintained Class 4 road that traverses a ridge and was once the main route for horse and buggy between the towns of Randolph and Northfield. Halfway through the ride you will be on Bouvant Road, another overgrown Class 4 road with some challenging single-track descents. The most scenic section of the ride occurs at the end, on Braintree Hill Road, which affords expansive views of the Green Mountains to the west. The

Bette and Ernie Reuter lost among the ferns on the Peth Village ride.

WRVTA has rated this as an intermediate ride, but I would call it a very challenging intermediate ride.

General location: Randolph.

Elevation change: Two big climbs: 900′ in the first mile, half of which is on single-track, and another 900′ at mile 15 on Braintree Hill Road, a Class 2 dirt road. There are also several short, steep climbs throughout the ride.

Season: May through October.

Services: All services are available in Randolph.

Hazards: Windfall, occasional road crossings, and steep, rocky descents. Expect a lot of mud in the spring.

Rescue index: Some of these trails are rarely traveled, so if you were seriously injured, it could take several days for someone to find you. Tell a friend of your plans if you choose to ride alone. You are never more than 3 miles from a phone. Gifford Medical Center is in Randolph.

Land status: Class 2, 3, and 4 roads and legal trails.

Maps: The best map, produced by the WRVTA, can be purchased for $4.95 through the Randolph Chamber of Commerce (802-728-9027). If you join the WRVTA, 15 individual self-guided ride maps are included in the membership fee.

Finding the trail: The ride begins in Randolph at the parking lot behind the New England Land Company, at the junction of VT 12 and VT 12A.

Source of additional information: The White River Valley Trails Association is the best source of information for this ride. Contact them at P.O. Box 219, Randolph Center, VT 05061; (802) 728-4420. You can visit their Web site at www.vermontsite.com.

Notes on the trail: A word of caution—pay attention to where you are and take the time to orient yourself. There are a lot of turns onto hidden trails on this ride.

From the New England Land Company, turn left onto VT 12A. Immediately turn right onto Brigham Hill Road at the **Y**-intersection. Climb on pavement for a half mile. Just after the 30 mph sign, turn right onto a dirt road that looks like a driveway. Go past the house on the right, and just before a clump of trees, turn right onto a barely visible trail that looks more like a mound of dirt and gravel. Immediately turn sharply left and continue parallel to the dirt road you just exited. You will also be riding next to an electric fence. This trail is known as Stagecoach Road.

Stay left at every opportunity and soon you will come to a cornfield. Ride along the edge of the field, heading for the satellite dishes that look like a cat's head. Keep "kittie" to your left and come to a dirt road, Braintree Hill Road. Turn right. Continue a little way on this road, but when it veers obviously to the left, turn right at the huge maple tree. Descend steadily on a legal trail, always staying in the main vein.

Come to a trail junction (the trail to the right is posted with a No Trespassing sign). Head slightly left for the open, mowed field. Once in the field, stay to the right and ride toward the far-right corner, then descend through the woods to a jeep road. Turn right on the road and cross through a barbwire gate. Continue descending on the jeep road to a dirt road. Turn left and ride to a 4-way junction. Go left up the hill, keeping the flower farm on your right. This is Peth Village (mile 4).

Take the next right turn (at the mailbox that says Perry), going up the dirt road. Just before the beautiful red-brick house, take the right at the **Y**-intersection onto a jeep road. Go straight, keeping the beaver pond and log landing area to your left. Reenter the woods and descend to a driveway at a white house. Ride out the driveway to a dirt road and go left. This is the town of Snowsville (mile 6).

Go uphill on this dirt road and continue for about 1 mile to a 4-way intersection. Turn right onto a tree-lined, canopied road. In .5 mile you will cross a small, nondescript bridge. Immediately turn left at the mailboxes and climb steeply up the Class 4 road, known as Bouvant Road. Go uphill along the creek, always staying left on the main trail. Come to a gate and go around it. Soon you will arrive at a nice camp with beautiful views; go left up the grassy trail.

Continue to follow Bouvant Road, which turns into a lovely, fern-lined, single-track trail. Descend, roughly at times, and cross over a rugged snowmobile bridge. Continue downhill and pass another camp on your right. Bouvant Road ends at a **T**-intersection with an old red schoolhouse on the right. Across the road, a rock is painted with the name M Lean in white letters. This is Braintree Hill Road and the junction is called Connecticut Corners (almost mile 11).

Go left and descend. The road turns sharply right and continues descending. When the main road turns sharply left, take the right-hand turn. Ride up this narrow road between a house and a barn. Continue straight up, and when you come upon a fence line, go left, following the main trail. At the VAST sign and 4-way intersection, go left and continue downhill. The more you descend, the more the road conditions improve.

Ride past a camp on the right, and stay right at the next fork. Go by a house on the left. Just after it, you will ride over a bridge and a set of railroad tracks (mile 14.5). Shortly after the tracks you arrive at paved VT 12A. Turn left and after .5 mile start looking for a gray house on the right side of the road. Take the next hairpin left onto a dirt road, just before a concrete bridge. Climb up the dirt road, continuing straight through any intersections. This is, once again, Braintree Hill Road.

When you come to a sharp corner, bear right and ride along the ridge with spectacular views in all directions, but especially to your right. After about 3 miles of this scenic road, you will come to Braintree Church with the Catamount statues on the front lawn (mile 21). Follow the Braintree Hill Road along the ridge, back to the Stagecoach Road and catlike satellite dishes. Descend back down Stagecoach Road, retracing your steps back to the New England Land Company (mile 25).

RIDE 29 · Mount Cushman

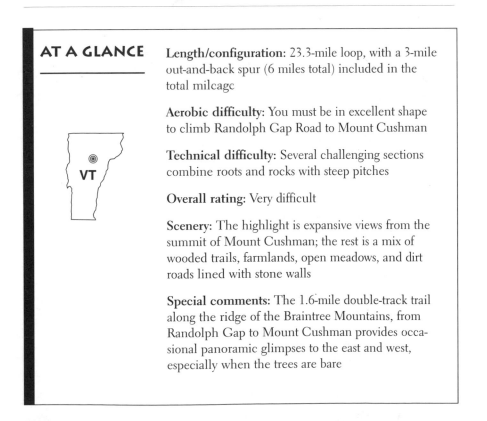

AT A GLANCE

Length/configuration: 23.3-mile loop, with a 3-mile out-and-back spur (6 miles total) included in the total mileage

Aerobic difficulty: You must be in excellent shape to climb Randolph Gap Road to Mount Cushman

Technical difficulty: Several challenging sections combine roots and rocks with steep pitches

Overall rating: Very difficult

Scenery: The highlight is expansive views from the summit of Mount Cushman; the rest is a mix of wooded trails, farmlands, open meadows, and dirt roads lined with stone walls

Special comments: The 1.6-mile double-track trail along the ridge of the Braintree Mountains, from Randolph Gap to Mount Cushman provides occasional panoramic glimpses to the east and west, especially when the trees are bare

RIDE 29 · Mount Cushman

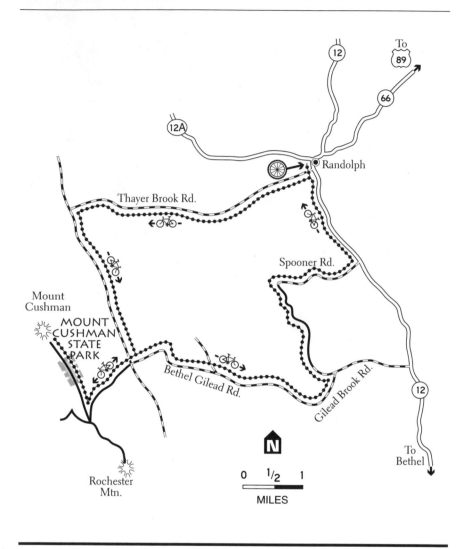

This 23.3-mile ride takes you to the top of Mount Cushman, which has an elevation of 2,750 feet. The ride uses the same Class 4 road built in the late 1800s that a traveling circus once used to cross the Braintree Mountains from Randolph to Rochester through Randolph Gap. The gap goes through a saddle between Mount Cushman and Rochester Mountain. From the saddle the ride takes you on a ridge traverse of the Braintree Mountains, past the footings of a former fire tower, to the summit of Mount Cushman and a clearing that faces west. This clearing was once a popular spot for pilots to launch their hang glid-

A long-standing landmark prepares riders for an upcoming left turn on the Mount Cushman ride.

ers. One can't help but wonder how they made the climb with all that equipment, but when you reach the summit you will see why they made the effort—it is a prime location to launch this type of aircraft.

The first half of the ride is on Class 3 dirt roads that climb gradually through rural farmland to the base of Randolph Gap. Then a steep out-and-back spur takes you to the top of Mount Cushman on a Class 4 double-track jeep road. Back at the base of Randolph Gap, continue on Class 4 roads, descending through more scenic farmland. Just when your legs are about to give out, you climb a double-track jeep road that wanders between old stone walls through deep forests. The final descent brings you to paved VT 12 and an easy cruise back to the start for a total of 23.3 very challenging miles.

The Mount Cushman ride, part of the White River Valley Trails Association (WRVTA) trail network, appears on the WRVTA map, "Randolph Vermont Mtn. Biking Trails" (third edition). I highly recommend purchasing the map before embarking on this or any other rides in the White River Valley. It should be noted that there are slight discrepancies in mileage between the Mount Cushman ride in this book, and the Mount Cushman ride on the WRVTA map. My cyclometer recorded 23.3 miles while their map calls it 22.5. You can purchase the map ($4.95) at Cover to Cover bookstore in Randolph and Onion River Sports in Barre and Montpelier. If you join the WRVTA, the map is included in their dues ($15). Contact WRVTA, P.O. Box 219, Randolph Center, VT 05061; (802) 728-4420. You can also visit its Web site at www.vermontsite.com.

Name that skull! A collection of small animal skulls adorns the side of a barn on the Mount Cushman ride.

The descent from Mount Cushman overlaps a 44.5-mile ride called the Circus Ride, which is featured on the WRVTA's Web site. Expert riders looking for an all-day ride will be challenged by the Circus Ride.

General location: Randolph.

Elevation change: 2,000′ feet in the first half of the ride; a 400′ climb near the end.

Season: June through mid-November. But late October, after the leaves have fallen, is the best time because of the outstanding views from the ridge traverse of the Braintree Mountains that are blocked by leaves in the summer.

Services: All services are available in Randolph.

Hazards: Steep descents with waterbars on Randolph Gap Road.

Rescue index: At the summit of Mount Cushman you are 6 miles from a private residence. If you go on this ride alone, be sure to inform someone of your plans and provide them with a map of the route. If you got hurt on this ride, it would be a long walk out or many days before someone would find you. Gifford Medical Center is in Randolph.

Land status: Class 2, 3, and 4 roads, jeep roads in Mount Cushman State Forest.

Maps: The best map of this ride is published by the WRVTA, P.O. Box 219, Randolph Center, VT 05061; (802) 728-4420. You can purchase the map at Cover to Cover bookstore in Randolph, Onion River Sports in Barre and Montpelier, and other specialty sport shops and bookstores in Vermont.

Finding the trail: The ride begins in the parking lot behind the New England Land Company. There is plenty of parking and a quick-stop convience store across the street.

Source of additional information: The White River Valley Trails Association is the best source of information for this ride. Contact them at P.O. Box 219, Randolph Center, VT 05061; (802) 728-4420.

Notes on the trail: Exit the New England Land Company parking lot and turn right, heading for downtown Randolph. Cross a bridge and turn right onto School Street, just after the big white Bethany Congregational Church. The road is paved to the railroad tracks; after that it is dirt. Once you cross the railroad tracks, the road becomes School Street Extension.

Continue on this road, passing Bailey Tack and Howard's Mill, climbing gradually and steadily. At 4.6 miles is a T-intersection; turn left onto Little Hollow Road. This is a nice, shady cruise between worn-down stone walls and picturesque house sites. Occasionally you have glimpses of the mountains ahead.

At 7.4 miles is a 4-way junction called Four Corners. On the far left corner is a stand of pines. Turn right and ride up an innocent-looking narrow road. Suddenly the road becomes very narrow and very rocky. This is the base of Randolph Gap Road. You have a tough climb of more than 1 mile ahead of you.

The road is very rocky and steep at first, and you might have to walk a section or two, but this rough section is over soon and the road becomes very rideable, although still steep. A few waterbars give you a chance to catch your breath. At 8.8 miles from the start you reach a 4-way trail intersection at the saddle between Rochester Mountain and Mount Cushman. Don't get excited—you are not done climbing! (FYI, it took me 1 hour and 16 minutes from the start to reach the 4-way junction.)

Turn right at the intersection and roll along the ridge on a double-track jeep trail. The trail may be muddy, but you can usually stay clear of the mud by riding around it. There is a steep, short pitch that takes you to the site of a former fire tower. Continue past the site and descend briefly. One more climb takes you to the summit of Mount Cushman, where the views to the west of the Green Mountains are stunning.

Retrace your steps to the 4-way junction and turn left to descend Randolph Gap Road back to Four Corners. Or, for an additional 1,000´ of climbing, go straight through the intersection and climb for 1.5 miles to the summit of Rochester Mountain, which has an elevation of 2,953´. This is a steep, rocky climb for experts only. You are rewarded again, but this time with endless views to the east of the White River Valley and the White Mountains in New Hampshire. Return to the 4-way junction for a total of 3 additional miles not included in this ride's total mileage.

Once you have descended Randolph Gap Road and arrived at Four Corners, continue straight through this 4-way intersection on a rough jeep road, which becomes the Bethel-Gilead Road. At the Y-intersection with a white house on the left, bear right, crossing over a bridge. Continue descending this road until you see a key landmark on the right, an old tractor with a Buffalo Crossing sign attached to the front. Take the left road across from the tractor, immediately past the tan house. Climb steeply to a **Y**-intersection at 17.8 miles from the start. Bear left (not to the right up the driveway posted with a private drive sign). This left turn becomes an overgrown, Class 4, double-track jeep trail. The trail climbs gradually (you will ultimately gain 400´ since the turn at the tractor) and winds through the woods, often between parallel stone walls.

Stay on the main trail at all times. Follow the occasional WRVTA signs that say Rand, pointing the way to Randolph. The jeep trail dumps you out onto a gravel road with a nice house to the right. Follow the road and just after the second house, turn right onto a trail under a power line. The trail does a hairpin right, so you are riding back toward the house. Stay on the main vein, a Class 4 road, which improves the farther you descend. This is Spooner Road, which brings you to VT 12 at 21.3 miles. Turn left on pavement and ride for 2 miles, straight through downtown Randolph and back to the New England Land Company for a total of 23.3 difficult miles.

RIDE 30 · West Brookfield (Broken Bike Ride)

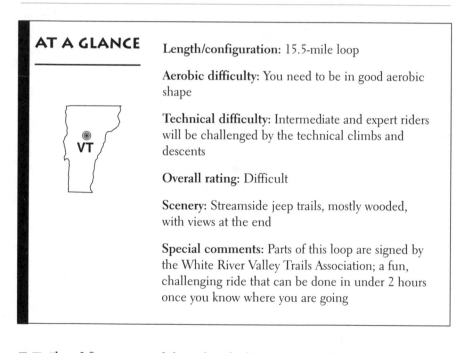

AT A GLANCE

Length/configuration: 15.5-mile loop

Aerobic difficulty: You need to be in good aerobic shape

Technical difficulty: Intermediate and expert riders will be challenged by the technical climbs and descents

Overall rating: Difficult

Scenery: Streamside jeep trails, mostly wooded, with views at the end

Special comments: Parts of this loop are signed by the White River Valley Trails Association; a fun, challenging ride that can be done in under 2 hours once you know where you are going

When I first attempted this ride, I had to turn around at the two-mile mark because suddenly I had no drivetrain. I had stripped the threads on my hub with my freewheel. On the second attempt, my chain broke at the halfway point, on a short climb in Roxbury State Forest. I sure was glad I had my "Cool

RIDE 30 • West Brookfield (Broken Bike Ride)

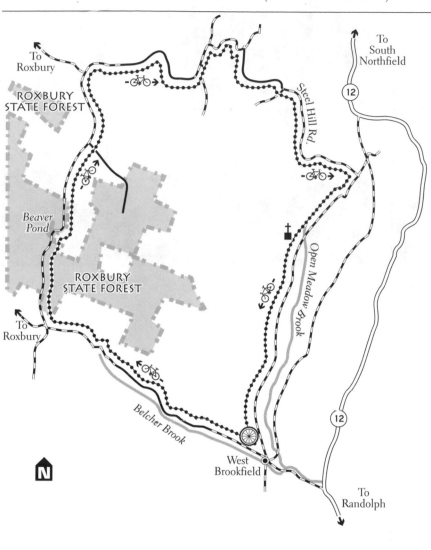

Tool" with me to remove the bad links. Unfortunately, the time it took to repair the chain cost us some daylight hours and we finished the ride in the dark.

Broken Bike Ride is a hilly, 15.5-mile loop that begins and ends in West Brookfield, a town of a dozen houses, a couple farms, and an old church with an equally old post-and-beam carriage barn. Initially it follows scenic Belcher Brook, climbing gradually on an unmaintained and untraveled town road, followed by a technical climb to the height of the land, where you cross over the Roxbury Mountain Range. You then descend on good town roads for one-half mile, pass

The West Brookfield Community Church mascot will ask to be petted at the beginning and end of the ride.

briefly through the Roxbury State Forest, and eventually head east on challenging trails that cross back over the Roxbury mountains. A steady and scenic descent, with expansive views north and east, drops you down to the West Brookfield Valley, where a town road parallels Open Meadow Brook for a gradual descent back to the start.

This ride has some very challenging climbs and one difficult descent. Overall, it is a moderate ride with difficult sections. It is demanding, yet fun, and can be done easily in less than three hours, two if you know the route.

General location: Roxbury lies in the very center of Vermont. The ride begins and ends in West Brookfield, but 98% of it takes place in Roxbury.

Elevation change: There are 2 major climbs. The first, a long, gradual one, is at the start and climbs 900′ in 3 miles. The second rises nearly 1,000′ in half the distance of the first climb.

Season: June through October when the ground is dry.

Services: All services can be found in Northfield, just north of the loop, and in Randolph, to the south. Bicycle Express is on Depot Street in Northfield (802-485-7430). Onion River Sports has two locations: North Main Street in Barre (802-476-7950) and Langdon Street in Montpelier (802-229-9409).

Hazards: Tempting downhills with blind corners and shanty-town dogs.

Rescue index: You are often 2 miles from a private residence. At times, it is unlikely that you will see another person.

Land status: Maintained and unmaintained Class 4 roads and trails.

Maps: This entire ride, amazingly, is contained on just one USGS 7.5 minute quad, Roxbury. DeLorme's and Northern Cartographic's atlases will help you orient yourself within the state. Another good map to have handy is the mountain bike trail map produced by the White River Valley Trails Association (WRVTA). It can be purchased at specialty sport shops and bookstores throughout Vermont or by writing to WRVTA, P.O. Box 219, Randolph Center, VT 05061; (802) 728-4420.

Finding the trail: West Brookfield is about 7 miles south of Northfield, to the west of VT 12. From VT 12, look for the Brookfield Cemetery and a sign for West Brookfield. Turn right and go .5 mile. Park at the church on the left. Your ride begins on a dirt road behind the church.

Source of additional information: The trails and roads in this ride are included in the WRVTA trail system. The WRVTA has put up trail signs and produced a map of roads and trails for mountain bikers in the Randolph and Roxbury areas.

Notes on the trail: Keeping the West Brookfield Church on your left, take the dirt road that heads due west. Immediately veer right onto a narrow dirt road. This is one of the most scenic sections of the ride. It follows Belcher Brook, climbing gradually on a four-wheel-drive road. Come to a **Y**-intersection and stay left, still following the brook. The road becomes more challenging with steep pitches and rocky sections. Cross over a sunken bridge and immediately go right at a WRVTA trail sign. Continue climbing, steeply at times, on a rocky, double-track trail. At the top the road widens and is maintained. Continue straight and soon begin riding downhill.

Descend for .5 mile, pass a few shantylike structures, and take the first right turn onto a well-maintained town road. Stay on this road and ride by Beaver Pond on your left and a man-made pond on your right. A well-marked trail on the right, with a WRVTA trail sign and a Gate Ahead sign, is the 6-mile mark.

At the next **Y**-intersection with a grass median, go right, passing a few primitive structures. Stay right at the Wheeler's gate. Soon the road becomes an unmaintained town road that eventually turns into a difficult downhill trail. When you come to a Class 4 road, turn left. Take the very next right, then shift into low gear and begin climbing. Keep climbing. Bear right, catch your breath, and resume climbing, but not nearly as steeply. At the gate, turn left and go straight onto a trail, still climbing.

The next mile is a really nice section of rolling, grassy trail riding. At the meadow, bear right and continue for .25 mile; at the trail fork, bear left. A short, gradual climb brings you to the top, where it's usually muddy. The trail then descends slightly to a Class 4 road which opens up to a scenic valley. This road intersects Steel Hill Road, another Class 4 road, where you take a right.

Climb very gradually on Steel Hill Road for .5 mile, then descend gently for 3 miles in West Brookfield Valley. Ride along Open Meadow Brook and head back to the West Brookfield Church where you started for a total of 15.5 miles.

RIDE 31 · Woodbury Mountain Road

AT A GLANCE

Length/configuration: 11-mile loop

Aerobic difficulty: You need a good aerobic base to enjoy this ride, although advanced beginners will be okay if they take their time

Technical difficulty: Very technical jeep roads make up half this ride; remains muddy year-round; not for beginners

Overall rating: Intermediate

Scenery: Densely wooded with one outstanding view of the Worcester Range

Special comments: A fun, entertaining ride that can be done in less than 2 hours

Jeep roads impassable by four-wheel-drive vehicles are common throughout Vermont. The Woodbury Mountain Road is a perfect example of an old road so eroded that a mountain bike is the only wheeled machine that could possibly pass through.

This 11-mile loop encircles Hobart Mountain, beginning on the Woodbury Mountain Road and ending on Eagle Ledge Road. You are in the woods most of the time, except for one section that breaks out into an open meadow with stunning views of the Worcester Range to the west.

Both jeep roads are very muddy in places and have several rocky, technically challenging sections. The climb on Woodbury Mountain Road is done at the first half of the ride. This is a good, solid, intermediate ride.

General location: Maple Corners, approximately 10 miles north of Montpelier.

Elevation change: A gradual 400´ climb to the halfway point.

Season: Summer and fall (June through October) are best.

Services: All services are found in Montpelier, including Onion River Sports, a good bike shop on Langdon Street (802-229-9409).

Hazards: Nothing out of the ordinary.

Rescue index: At the farthest point you are nearly 4 miles from a telephone.

Land status: Class 4 roads and jeep roads.

Maps: The best maps are two USGS 7.5 minute quads, Mount Worcester and Woodbury.

RIDE 31 · Woodbury Mountain Road

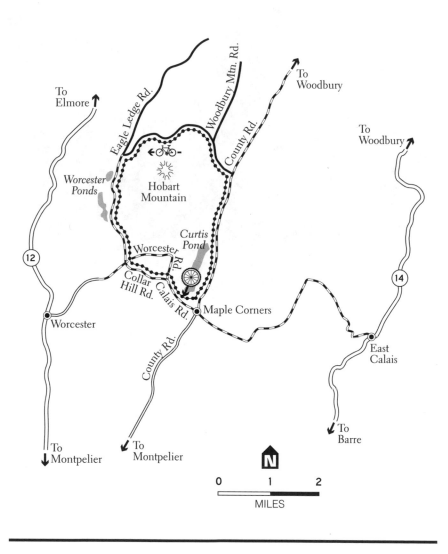

Finding the trail: From Montpelier, drive north on County Road to Maple Four Corners general store. Just past the store, turn left onto Calais Road. Go .5 mile and park at the Curtis Pond fishing access parking lot on the right. The ride begins here.

Source of additional information: You can get information about more riding in this area at Onion River Sports in Montpelier. Ask for Ben, who showed me this ride.

Notes on the trail: From Curtis Pond, ride back to Maple Four Corners and turn left at the 4-way intersection, heading north on County Road. After approximately

A jeep road winds through an open meadow on Woodbury Mountain Road, where riders are treated to exceptional views of Worcester Range to the west.

3 miles, turn left onto Woodbury Mountain Road, a narrow, rocky, jeep road with no street sign. You will know you are on the right road because of a brand new house a little way up on the right. When you come to a fork, take either prong—they rejoin 50 yards later. This rocky section of the road, which has a few tricky sections, is where you do most of the climbing.

At almost 4.5 miles from the start, turn left onto a jeep road that is even more narrow and rocky than Woodbury Mountain Road. This next section through rolling terrain is a lot of fun, with many short technical sections interspersed with large, muddy puddles. Come to an open meadow with a cabin on the left and views of the Worcester Range to the right.

At 7 miles, you will arrive at a **T**-intersection. This is Eagle Ledge Road. Go left (right takes you to Eagle Ledge) and begin descending gradually for 2.5 miles on this rugged dirt road.

At 9.5 miles, go straight through a 4-way intersection to climb steeply on Collar Hill Road. Turn right onto Calais Road and descend to Curtis Pond, now on your left, for a total of 11 miles.

RIDE 32 · Sugarbush's Castlerock Connection

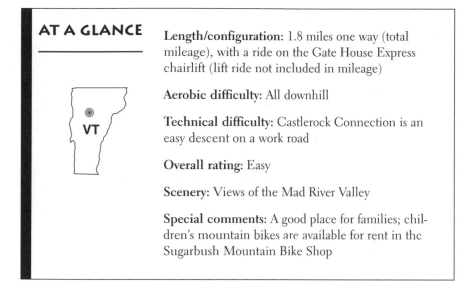

AT A GLANCE

Length/configuration: 1.8 miles one way (total mileage), with a ride on the Gate House Express chairlift (lift ride not included in mileage)

Aerobic difficulty: All downhill

Technical difficulty: Castlerock Connection is an easy descent on a work road

Overall rating: Easy

Scenery: Views of the Mad River Valley

Special comments: A good place for families; children's mountain bikes are available for rent in the Sugarbush Mountain Bike Shop

VT

Castlerock Connection begins at the base of Sugarbush Ski Resort at the Gate House Lodge, where you buy your lift ticket and pick up a trail map. From there it is a few hundred yards to the Gate House Express chairlift where you and your bike are loaded onto a chairlift for a ride to the halfway point on the mountain. The chairlift seats four people and is open to the elements. At the top you will pick up the Castlerock Connection, an all-downhill 1.8-mile work road that terminates at the Gate House Lodge.

Sugarbush Ski Resort is located near Waitsfield in the Mad River Valley. The Sugarbush Mountain Bike Center was Vermont's fifth ski resort to add mountain biking to its agenda of summer activities. The Gate House Express high-speed quad takes riders halfway up the mountain where they can access ski trails and work roads for a variety of descents down the mountain.

Although most of the riding at Sugarbush is easy, one trail—Trail 66 race course loop—will challenge even expert riders. This loop was designed for the Sugarbush stop in the American Ski Company "Trail 66 Series" of mountain bike races held during the summer of 1997 throughout New England. Sugarbush's 3.5-mile Trail 66 course snakes its way across the ski slopes, twisting and turning, climbing and diving, on a relentless trail strewn with roots, rocks, and mud. It is well signed, but extremely difficult and recommended only for experts. Sugarbush also hosts a permanent dual slalom course for downhillers.

Located in the Gate House Lodge, Sugarbush Mountain Bike Center offers guided tours and mountain bike instruction. They have several models of Gary Fisher mountain bikes available for rent, including the full-suspension Joshua,

RIDE 32 • Sugarbush's Castlerock Connection

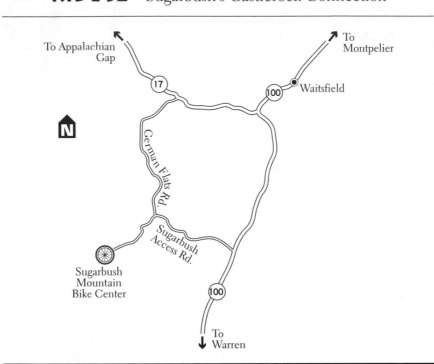

To Appalachian Gap

To Montpelier

17

100 Waitsfield

N

German Flats Rd.

Sugarbush Access Rd.

Sugarbush Mountain Bike Center

100

To Warren

and children's bikes. Hours are from 11 A.M. to 6 P.M., weekends only, from July through mid-October, and also on Fridays from July through the end of August (802-583-2386, ext. 340). A trail pass is $8; a single chairlift ride is $8; an all-day trail and lift pass is $22.

General location: Sugarbush Ski Resort.

Elevation change: One 800′ descent.

Season: July through October.

Services: All services are found on the mountain at Sugarbush Village, including several restaurants, delicatessens, and accommodations. The Sugarbush Mountain Bike Shop is located in the Gate House Lodge where this ride begins (802-496-2386, ext. 340). Many more shops and restaurants can be found in Waitsfield, including The Mad River Bike Shop at the junction of VT 17 and VT 100 (802-496-9500). The Warren Store, in nearby Warren, is an excellent place for gourmet picnic supplies. It is worth stopping in just for the pastries.

Hazards: Waterbars and ski area maintenance vehicles.

Rescue index: At most you are 1.8 miles from the Gate House Lodge and help.

Land status: The trails are all on land owned and operated by the Sugarbush Ski Resort.

At Sugarbush, riders can take the chairlift to access the Castlerock Connection descent that passes by the Trail 66 single-track race course.

Maps: The best map is the one produced by the Sugarbush Mountain Bike Center. It is free and can be found at the Gate House Lodge.

Finding the trail: From the junction of VT 17 and VT 100 in Waitsfield, follow VT 100 south for 3.5 miles. Turn right on the Sugarbush Access Road (look for Black Diamond sportswear on the right corner). Climb steeply on this paved road for 3 miles. It dead-ends at the Sugarbush Ski Resort's Lincoln Peak, where the Gate House Lodge and Mountain Bike Center are located.

Sources of additional information: For complete information on riding at the Sugarbush Mountain Bike Center, as well as lodging information, call (800) 53-SUGAR. Visit its Web site at www.sugarbush.com. Suggested reading: *Mountain Biking the Ski Resorts of the Northeast* by Robert Immler (Woodstock: Countryman Press).

Notes on the trail: From the Gate House Lodge, ride the few hundred yards downhill to the Gate House Express chairlift. Dismount and hand your bike to the attendant. This person will instruct you on how to ride the lift and will load your bike on a chair behind you. The lift ride takes approximately 10 minutes. At the top, another attendant will help you get off the chair and will retrieve your bike for you.

From the top of the chairlift, begin riding directly away from the lift, slightly to the left. Look for trail signs for trail 7, Castlerock Connection, a ski-area work road. Begin descending immediately. The road is dirt and gravel, with a few rocky sections. About halfway down, cross a wide, wooden bridge spanning Clay Brook. Continue descending and soon you will join trail 3, Coffee Run to

Header. This trail change happens automatically, so you probably won't notice it. The road becomes wider as you approach the bottom. Pass under a chairlift and you will see the Gate House Lodge ahead and to the left. Arrive at the Gate House Lodge for a total of 1.8 very easy miles.

RIDE 33 · Huntington Gorge

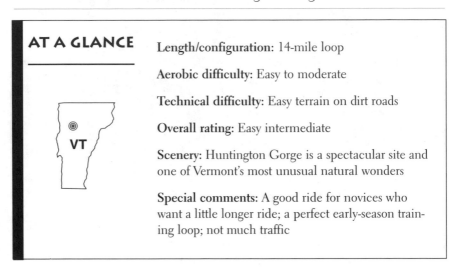

AT A GLANCE

Length/configuration: 14-mile loop

Aerobic difficulty: Easy to moderate

Technical difficulty: Easy terrain on dirt roads

Overall rating: Easy intermediate

Scenery: Huntington Gorge is a spectacular site and one of Vermont's most unusual natural wonders

Special comments: A good ride for novices who want a little longer ride; a perfect early-season training loop; not much traffic

Geography is what makes this 14-mile dirt-road ride so interesting. You will climb gradually along Huntington River and then ride through Huntington Gorge, a steep, narrow cut through the earth where the water flows deep and fast. This is the site of Richmond's first grist mill and electric generating plant. Just downstream is a popular swimming hole. Unfortunately, 15 people have died in Huntington Gorge because they underestimated the power of the current, so use caution if you stop for a swim. Later you will pass by Gillett Pond, a long, narrow pond nestled in the crook between two hillsides. Gillett Pond does not have a reputation as a favorable swimming pond, but in the winter you will always see children and adults playing ice hockey on its frozen surface.

Near the start of the Huntington Gorge ride are two local landmarks: Richmond's historic Old Round Church and Cochran's Ski Area. The 16-sided "round" church was constructed in 1812 to serve five different denominations. It was restored by the Richmond Historical Society and is now considered one of the most important buildings in Vermont. The church is open free of charge, July 4 through Labor Day, 10 A.M. to 4 P.M., daily.

Cochran's Ski Area is one of the few remaining family-owned-and-operated ski hills in Vermont. While other ski resorts have been taken over by large conglomerates, Cochran's continues to operate pretty much as it did 30 years ago

RIDE 33 · Huntington Gorge

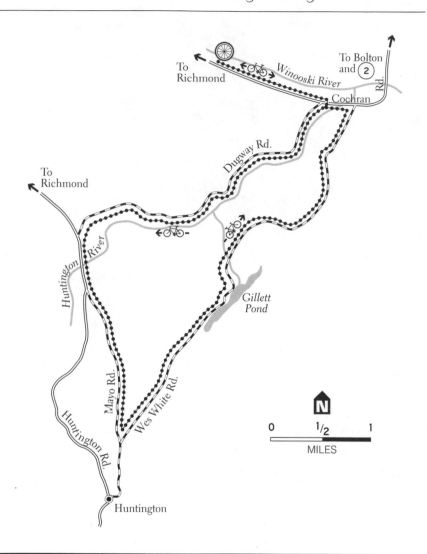

(providing it snows). Olympic medalist Barbara Cochran Siegle, who won a gold medal in slalom at the 1962 Olympics, grew up skiing here.

This scenic, easy ride takes place primarily on dirt roads, is good for novices and early-season riding. To add four miles of pavement to the ride, begin at the Old Round Church in Richmond.

General location: Jonesville and Huntington.

Elevation change: 400′ are gained gradually over the first half of the ride.

Season: Anytime the roads are clear.

November's first snowfall turns Huntington Gorge into a study in black and white.

Services: All services can be found in Richmond.

Hazards: The roads are shared with motor vehicles.

Rescue index: Private residences are always nearby.

Land status: Class 3 and 4 roads.

Maps: The USGS 7.5 minute quad, Huntington, shows the route, as do DeLorme's and Northern Cartographic's atlases.

Finding the trail: From the traffic light in Richmond, head south on Bridge Street, crossing over railroad tracks and an iron bridge. Turn left onto Cochran Road at the historic Old Round Church. Drive 2 miles to a canoe access and parking area on the left. The ride begins here.

Sources of additional information: The nearest bicycle shop is Bret's Village Cyclery at the traffic light in Richmond (802-434-4876). In Williston is Earl's Cyclery (802-864-9197); in Burlington is the Skirack (802-658-3313); in Essex Junction is Essex Junction Bicycles (802-878-1275); and in Winooski is the Winooski Bicycle Shop (802-655-3233).

Notes on the trail: From the canoe access parking area, turn left and ride southeast along Cochran Road. Immediately you will pass a large red barn on your right. Just after an area abundant with blue buildings, turn right onto unpaved Dugway Road. Climb gradually with the Huntington River on your left. Pass by the South Gorge Land Trust Recreation Area, where a narrow path leads to good swimming holes. Shortly beyond the path is Huntington Gorge.

At 4.7 miles from the start, you will come to a paved **T**-intersection—go left. After a half mile turn left onto unpaved Mayo Road. At 7 miles, turn left on Wes White Road, following a sign for Gillett Pond. Gillett Pond will soon appear ahead of you as a notch in the horizon. Continue past Gillett Pond and come to an open area with views of Dugway Road far off to the left. The road turns to pavement and descends very steeply for nearly a mile.

At the bottom of the hill, come to a **T**-intersection and turn left onto Cochran Road. Pass Dugway Road on your left and return to the start for a total of 14 easy miles.

RIDE 34 · Outdoor Experience at Catamount

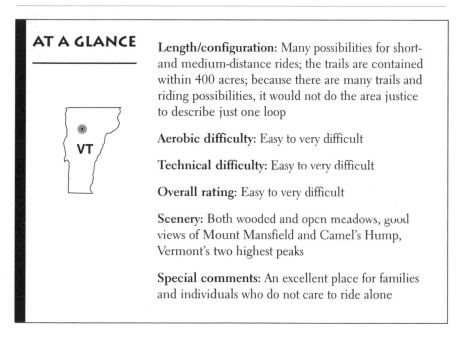

AT A GLANCE

Length/configuration: Many possibilities for short- and medium-distance rides; the trails are contained within 400 acres; because there are many trails and riding possibilities, it would not do the area justice to describe just one loop

Aerobic difficulty: Easy to very difficult

Technical difficulty: Easy to very difficult

Overall rating: Easy to very difficult

Scenery: Both wooded and open meadows, good views of Mount Mansfield and Camel's Hump, Vermont's two highest peaks

Special comments: An excellent place for families and individuals who do not care to ride alone

Located in Williston, not far from the busy metropolis of Burlington, the Outdoor Experience at Catamount Family Center is "good and close," yet its 400 wilderness acres provide a real sense of solitude. The Outdoor Experience is open year-round with activities pertinent to the climate. Nature walks, full-moon snowshoeing, trail running, orienteering, and ice skating are just a few of the sports. During late spring, summer, and fall the trails are buzzing with mountain bikers.

Both beginning and expert riders will find plenty of terrain to suit their needs. Open meadows (some flat and some with hills) and wooded single-track (some smooth and some with roots) will entertain you for hours. There are no sustained

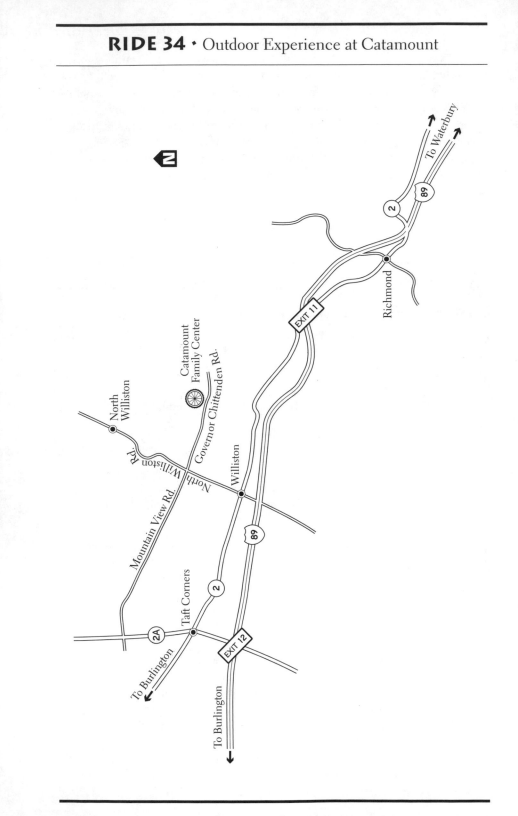

Throughout the summer, the popular Wednesday night training series is an opportunity for riders of all ages to hone their racing skills on the trails at Outdoor Experience at Catamount.

climbs, but plenty of short, steep pitches that will make your heart rate soar. Trails are well marked and maps are available in the center.

Wednesday evenings throughout the summer, the Outdoor Experience is home to a long-standing cross-country mountain bike race series. Over 200 bikers of all ages, male and female, come to ride for recreational fitness and serious training, and also for the social aspect of the event. Thursday evenings are mountain bike clinics for women only, and on weekends there are training rides for different ability levels. Weeklong mountain bike camps are held for juniors, teens, and adults, and there are also special, women-only camps.

The highlight of every summer is the Schwinn/Skirack Eastern Cup held the second weekend in July. This event draws nearly a thousand riders for racing and recreational riding in a festive atmosphere. If you come to the Outdoor Experience at Catamount, be sure to ride the 10-kilometer race loop, even if you only go once around the course. Remember, the expert men and women ride this loop four times as fast as they can during the Eastern Cup race.

Lessons, guided tours, and rentals of a full range of Gary Fisher mountain bikes are available on site. For information on daily use fees, summer memberships, racing, and camp schedules, call the Outdoor Experience at Catamount Family Center (802-879-6001).

RIDE 35 · Shelburne Farms

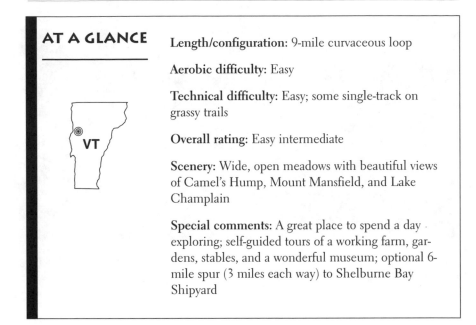

AT A GLANCE

Length/configuration: 9-mile curvaceous loop

Aerobic difficulty: Easy

Technical difficulty: Easy; some single-track on grassy trails

Overall rating: Easy intermediate

Scenery: Wide, open meadows with beautiful views of Camel's Hump, Mount Mansfield, and Lake Champlain

Special comments: A great place to spend a day · exploring; self-guided tours of a working farm, gardens, stables, and a wonderful museum; optional 6-mile spur (3 miles each way) to Shelburne Bay Shipyard

Located on Lake Champlain's beautiful Shelburne Bay, Shelburne Farms is the former estate and working farm of Dr. William Seward Webb and Eliza Vanderbilt Webb. The farms were designed in the late nineteenth century and 1,400 acres remain of the original 4,000. Today the farms are a fine example of stewardship of natural and agricultural resources. Self-guided tours of the property include stops at flower and vegetable gardens, the Dairy Barn, the Breeding Barn, and horse training stables; guided tours include educational programs. Nearby, the Shelburne Museum is packed full of artifacts of daily life in the nineteenth century.

The grounds are interspersed with gravel roads and four-wheel drive roads. There is also a network of walking trails. This 9-mile ride (and optional 6-mile spur to the Shelburne Bay Shipyard) takes advantage of a variety of roads and trails and affords stunning views—Lake Champlain to the west and the Green Mountains to the east—that "car tourists" will never see. The riding is very easy, but plan on lots of stopping and plenty of great photo opportunities. This is an excellent place to ride with children.

General location: Shelburne Bay.

Elevation change: Basically flat.

Season: Anytime there is no snow on the ground.

Services: All services are available in Shelburne.

RIDE 35 • Shelburne Farms

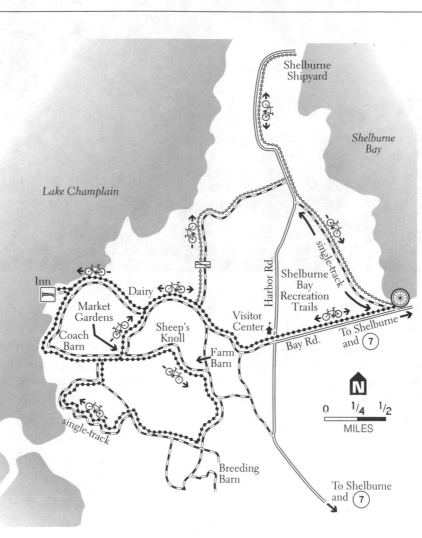

Hazards: Slow-moving motor vehicles.

Rescue index: You are never far from help.

Land status: Roads and trails owned by Shelburne Farms and open to public use, plus a Class 3 road and a single-track trail on the extended 6-mile section.

Maps: The best map is the "Walking Map" published by Shelburne Farms. It can be obtained at the Visitor Center when you first enter the grounds, or by calling (802) 985-8686.

Riders at Shelburne Farms take a break to enjoy the sunset over Lake Champlain and the distant Adirondacks of New York.

Finding the trail: The ride begins in the parking lot of the Shelburne Bay Park and Recreation Area on Bay Road in Shelburne. From the traffic light in the town of Shelburne, proceed north on VT 7 for .5 mile. Turn left onto Bay Road. The recreation area is on your right.

Source of additional information: Shelburne Farms, Shelburne, VT 05482; (802) 985-8686.

Notes on the trail: Leave Shelburne Bay Park and Recreation Area and turn right on Bay Road. Cross Harbor Road and proceed straight through the entrance of Shelburne Farms (cyclists do not need to stop at the entrance kiosk). There is a Visitor Center and gift shop immediately on the right.

Stay on the gravel road and bear right at the first fork, following signs for the Dairy Barn. Fork right again and come to the Dairy Barn, a fully functioning operation that produces all the dairy products used at the farm's inn. After leaving the Dairy Barn, bear left, following signs for Shelburne Inn. When you come to the inn on your right, ride up the circular driveway and check out the gardens on the far side of the building.

Return to the main road and continue riding along the lake (on your right). Ride past the Coach Barn (on your left) and take a hard left onto another gravel road. Soon you will pass by the Market Gardens on the left, where the vegetables used by the inn are grown. Just past the gardens, cross over a gravel road onto a jeep road and climb to Sheep's Knoll viewpoint, which overlooks the Farm Barn and affords remarkable views of Camel's Hump and Mount

Mansfield to the east. Note: As you climb, you will pass walking trails marked with blue-tipped stakes.

Descend on the jeep road to the Farm Barn (rest rooms here), go left and immediately right, riding away from the Farm Barn. Come to pavement and turn right. Climb the paved road and arrive at a major intersection with the Breeding Barn directly ahead. There are plans underway to renovate this monstrous structure and bring it back to operating conditions. To the left is the Old Dairy Barn. The roads that lie ahead lead to private property. This ride turns right on a dirt road and proceeds downhill.

Take the second right off the dirt road, riding around a Do Not Enter sign (the sign is for motor vehicles). Keep your eyes open for the Windmill Hill walking trail, which is marked with blue-tipped stakes, and turn left onto the mowed path that will lead you through the woods. Exit the woods and stay on the nicely mowed path that winds around Windmill Hill. Take the left trail and descend to the lake where there is a great view of the Adirondacks to the west. Climb on the mowed path going away from the lake and come to a dirt road. Go left and come to a **T**-intersection. Turn right, once again passing Market Gardens. Stay on the main road and exit the Farms, retracing your steps to the start for a total of 9 miles.

To take the spur ride to the Shelburne Bay Shipyard proceed as follows: Just prior to exiting the farms, turn left on the first road after you pass the road on the left that is marked with a Private Road sign. Follow this road, which is marked Dead End even though it's a through road. You may be required to lift your bike over or pass it under an electric fence, *which may or may not be turned on.* USE CAUTION! Shortly after the fence, pass through a metal gate, which may or may not be closed. Ignore any discouraging signage: this is a public road that leads to Pheasant Hill.

When you reach a road layered with white stones, turn right, then immediately veer left, avoiding the driveway to the right. Arrive at paved Harbor Road and turn left, exiting Pheasant Hill. Ride to the end of Harbor Road where you will find the historic Shelburne Shipyard.

Retrace your steps and, just beyond the entrance to Pheasant Hill (now on your right), look for a yellow fire hydrant on the left. Just after the fire hydrant turn left onto the Shelburne Bay Recreation Trail. This 3-mile, single-track trail will take you back to the starting point. From this path there are two side trails worth exploring: Clark Trail and Allen Hill Trail. They are both steep and narrow and will challenge your bike handling skills.

Follow the main trail as it weaves through woods and meadows and ends at the Shelburne Bay Park and Recreation Area where you first began this ride. Total mileage including the extended trip to Shelburne Shipyard is 15 miles.

RIDE 36 · Chipman Hill

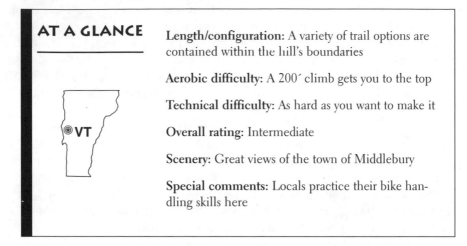

AT A GLANCE
_____

VT

Length/configuration: A variety of trail options are contained within the hill's boundaries

Aerobic difficulty: A 200′ climb gets you to the top

Technical difficulty: As hard as you want to make it

Overall rating: Intermediate

Scenery: Great views of the town of Middlebury

Special comments: Locals practice their bike handling skills here

C hipman Hill is located within walking distance of downtown Middlebury. Skiers and ski jumpers once trained on this hill, and although it is no longer used for skiing, it has become a favorite spot for locals to practice their mountain biking skills. A paved road takes you to the summit (no motor vehicles allowed) where you can choose from many fun trail options. The distances are short, but you can easily spend an afternoon exploring multiple combinations of loops. For those who thrive on the thrill of the downhill, the ski jumps make fun, short descents; hop back on the road, ride to the top, and do it again. Each fall, Middlebury Parks and Recreation holds a cross-country mountain bike race on Chipman Hill, with varying distances for different ability levels.

General location: The north end of the town of Middlebury.

Elevation change: Chipman Hill rises about 200′ over Middlebury.

Season: Anytime the trails are dry.

Services: Everything can be found in Middlebury. Otter Creek Bakery on College Street has yummy treats to satisfy sweet teeth. Stop at Middlebury Natural Food Co-Op and try their gourmet baked pretzels (pesto, roasted pepper, and eggplant).

Hazards: The hill is quite steep. Watch out for endos.

Rescue index: There are private residences at the bottom of the hill. Porter Hospital is on South Street in Middlebury (802-388-4700).

Land status: A Class 3 road and trails on land owned by the town of Middlebury.

Maps: The USGS 7.5 minute quad, Middlebury, will give you a feel for the layout of the terrain.

Finding the trail: From the Grand Union on Washington Street in Middlebury, take High Street to the far end, about .5 mile. Look for the big, yellow road blockade. This is the base of Chipman Hill. (You can see VT 7 from

RIDE 36 · Chipman Hill

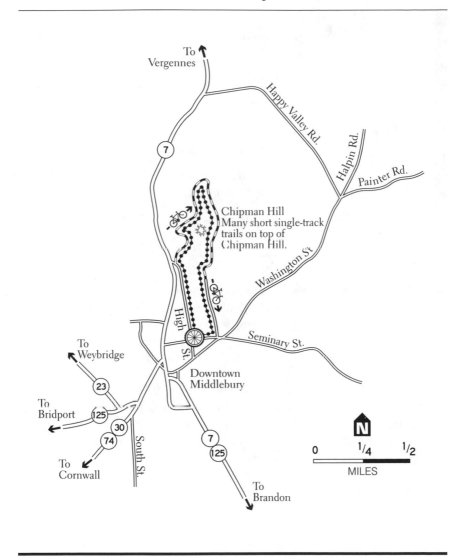

here.) The riding begins at the road barrier, which prevents motor vehicles proceeding up the hill.

Sources of additional information: The staff at the local bike shop, Bike & Ski Touring Center (802-388-6666), can tell you about the riding on Chipman Hill. You can also call Middlebury Parks and Recreation (802-388-4041) for information.

Notes on the trail: The mountain bike riding on Chipman Hill is pretty straightforward. It is obviously contained to the hill, so you can't get lost. Explore and have fun!

RIDE 37 · Snake Mountain

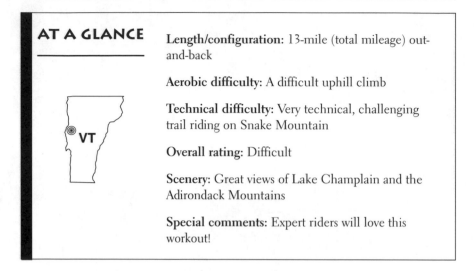

AT A GLANCE

Length/configuration: 13-mile (total mileage) out-and-back

Aerobic difficulty: A difficult uphill climb

Technical difficulty: Very technical, challenging trail riding on Snake Mountain

Overall rating: Difficult

Scenery: Great views of Lake Champlain and the Adirondack Mountains

Special comments: Expert riders will love this workout!

Snake Mountain is a prominent feature of the small towns of Addison and Weybridge, just to the west of Middlebury. It stands by itself and abruptly rises 1,000 feet above the Champlain Valley. A carriage road that served the Grand View Hotel at the turn of the century winds its way for two miles to the summit, where you are treated to spectacular views of Lake Champlain and the Adirondack Mountains in New York.

The Grand View Hotel burned down in the early 1900s, and the property was purchased by a man who began building a home next to the former hotel site. The man died before the house was completed, but the cement foundation remains. Eventually the property was purchased by the state of Vermont. It is now part of the Snake River Wildlife Management Area.

No one knows the exact origins of Snake Mountain's name. Some say it is named for its undulating ridge line as seen from a distance; others claim its rocky ledges once housed rattlesnakes. Neither theory has been verified.

This 13-mile out-and-back ride begins and ends in the tiny town of Bridport. The 4.5-mile approach to Snake Mountain is on flat, dirt roads through apple orchards and dairy farms, a good way to warm up for the climb ahead. The carriage road climbs steadily, and at times steeply, on dirt and rocky terrain. Expert riders will enjoy the challenge of cleaning the trail to the top, while less-seasoned riders may choose to push their bikes at times. Whatever method you use, you will be rewarded for your struggle with breathtaking views at the summit.

Although the mileage is short, the 2-mile climb up Snake Mountain is extremely challenging. I rate this as a difficult ride. Note: You can skip the first 4.5 miles of dirt road riding and start at the trailhead parking lot at the bottom of Snake Mountain, making this a down-and-out hill climb, 2 miles up and 2 miles down.

General location: Addison, 6 miles west of Middlebury.

RIDE 37 · Snake Mountain

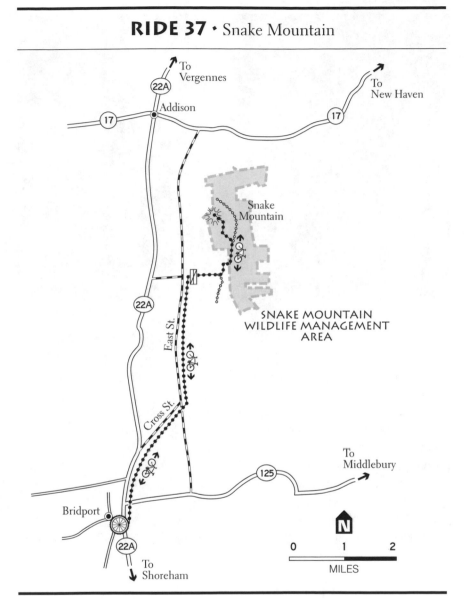

Elevation change: 1,000′ in 2 miles.

Season: June through October.

Services: All services can be found in Middlebury. The Bike & Ski Touring Center is located on Main Street (802-388-6666).

Hazards: Hikers, serious waterbars.

Rescue index: From the top of Snake Mountain you are 2 miles from a telephone. A lot of people use this trail, so you are likely to find help if you need it.

Trailside trillium blooms in July on Snake Mountain.

Land status: Town roads and the Snake Mountain Wildlife Management Area.

Maps: Most of this ride is on the USGS 7.5 minute quad, Port Henry. It is also shown on DeLorme's and Northern Cartographic's atlases. Additional maps showing detail of the surrounding area are available at the Bike & Ski Touring Center in Middlebury.

Finding the trail: The ride begins and ends at the village green in Bridport, slightly south of the junctions of VT 125 and VT 22A. Park next to the Roman Catholic Church.

Source of additional information: The Snake Mountain Wildlife Management Area falls under the jurisdiction of the Vermont Fish and Wildlife Department, 111 West Street, Essex Junction, VT 05452; (802) 878-1564.

Notes on the trail: Begin by riding north for 1 mile on paved VT 22A. Pass Pratt's general store on your left, a good place to stock up on necessities. Turn right on Cross Road, a gravel town road. In a mile, turn left onto paved East Street, which soon turns to gravel. At 4.5 miles you will arrive at the Snake Mountain trailhead, as indicated by a sign. A parking area is just beyond, to the left.

Turn right onto the trail and ride around the orange gate. The trail has the appearance of a jeep road, but no motor vehicles are allowed. Stay on the main trail, which climbs steadily for 2 miles. Many waterbar crossings will test your stamina and agility. You will know you are at the top when you come to an open area with the cement foundation of the unfinished house. This is where the views are best.

Return the way you came, using caution on the waterbars. When you exit the trail, turn left and retrace your steps to the start in Bridport, for a total of 13 miles.

GREEN MOUNTAIN
NATIONAL FOREST

In the Green Mountain National Forest, mountain bikes and motor vehicles are permitted in all the same places except the Contest, Ash Hill, and Pine Brook Trails (see section on Rochester area), and the Leicester Hollow and Silver Lake Trails (see section on Blueberry Hill area), where bikes are welcome and motor vehicles are not. (You are subject to a $100 fine if caught riding on national forest trails posted closed to mountain bikers.)

Several rides described in the following pages are on U.S. Forest Service roads that are smooth, gently graded dirt roads not maintained in the winter. They were originally intended for access to the backcountry by national Forest Service employees, but now they are used mostly to access recreational areas such as hiking trailheads. They receive little vehicular traffic and are usually mellow places to ride. Forest Service roads, also called Forest Roads, are marked with a brown sign and the letters FR in white, followed by a number in white (for example, FR 55).

For information and maps on the northern half of the Green Mountain National Forest, write or call Green Mountain National Forest, Route 7, Middlebury, VT 05753; (802) 388-4362.

RIDE 38 · Natural Turnpike and Steammill Roads

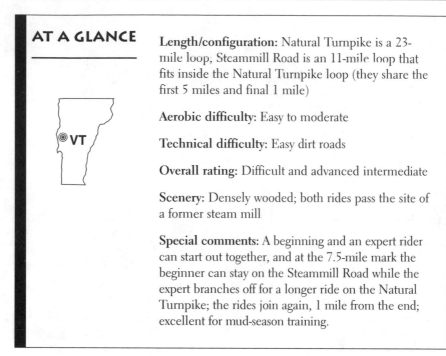

AT A GLANCE

Length/configuration: Natural Turnpike is a 23-mile loop, Steammill Road is an 11-mile loop that fits inside the Natural Turnpike loop (they share the first 5 miles and final 1 mile)

Aerobic difficulty: Easy to moderate

Technical difficulty: Easy dirt roads

Overall rating: Difficult and advanced intermediate

Scenery: Densely wooded; both rides pass the site of a former steam mill

Special comments: A beginning and an expert rider can start out together, and at the 7.5-mile mark the beginner can stay on the Steammill Road while the expert branches off for a longer ride on the Natural Turnpike; the rides join again, 1 mile from the end; excellent for mud-season training.

In the early 1900s the Natural Turnpike was built as a stagecoach road running north-south between South Lincoln and Ripton. Over a period of years, the U.S. government purchased much of the land surrounding the Natural Turnpike for the Green Mountain National Forest. From 1960 through the 1970s the road was upgraded to allow for public travel, recreation, and forest commodity transport. It was also used as a fire road, but its main purpose during that time was for transporting logs from logging operations to the main highway. Some logging is still being done, but the road is now primarily used for recreation and by hikers accessing Vermont's Long Trail.

The Steammill Road, also a Forest Service road (FR 59), takes you from VT 125 to the Natural Turnpike (FR 54), 2.5 miles north of Ripton at the Bread Loaf campus of Middlebury College. On the Steammill Road is the site of a former sawmill which used a steam engine to convert logs to lumber for easier transport out of the forest. Although very little remains of the sawmill, the open meadow attracts wildlife, and therein lies the trailhead to the Skylight Pond hiking trail. The Steammill Road circles back to Ripton and is the shorter ride (11 miles), while the Natural Turnpike spurs off the Steammill Road for a 23-mile ride.

Neither the Natural Turnpike nor the Steammill Road are plowed during the winter, making them excellent places for winter outdoor recreation. As a result, the roads do not suffer from the inevitable potholing that erodes most of

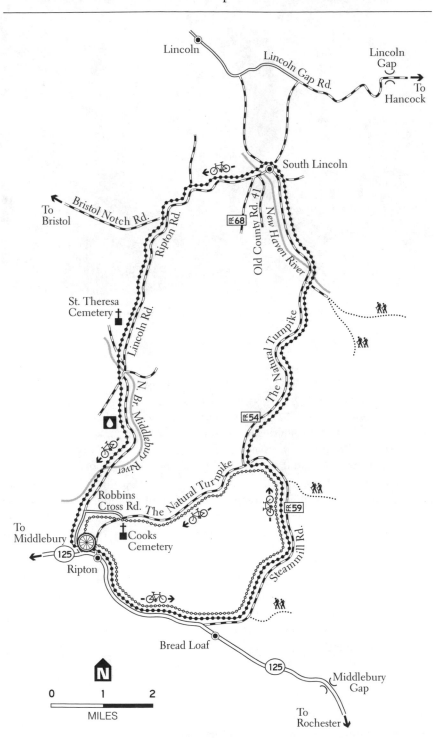

Lincoln

Lincoln Gap Rd.

Lincoln Gap

To Hancock

South Lincoln

Bristol Notch Rd.

To Bristol

Ripton Rd.

FR 68

Old County Rd. 41

New Haven River

The Natural Turnpike

St. Theresa Cemetery

Lincoln Rd.

N. Br. Middlebury River

FR 54

Robbins Cross Rd.

The Natural Turnpike

Cooks Cemetery

FR 59

Steammill Rd.

To Middlebury

125

Ripton

Bread Loaf

125

Middlebury Gap

To Rochester

N

0   1   2
MILES

Moose! The population of these large creatures is on the rise in Vermont.

Vermont's roads during mud season. They remain smooth throughout the spring and are excellent roads for early-season riding.

Beginners will enjoy the Steammill Road loop—the climbs are gently graded and the road surface is smooth, yet the remoteness of the national forest allows for a sense of solitude. The Natural Turnpike is more challenging, mainly because it is twice the distance. Much of the riding on both loops is streamside. Depending on the time of year, you will see a variety of wildlife, including mallards and beavers, and there's even a good chance of spotting a moose. Except for a freshwater spring near the end of the Natural Turnpike ride, there are no places to refill your water bottle along the way, so be sure to carry at least two water bottles on hot days.

General location: The town of Ripton on VT 125, 6 miles east of Middlebury.

Elevation change: Both rides start out by gaining 900′ in elevation during the first 5 miles (1,100′ to 2,000′), but the climbing is gradual since the roads were built to accommodate logging equipment and fire vehicles. For those riding the Steammill Road loop, it's all flat and downhill for the remainder of the ride. For those riding the Natural Turnpike loop, you will climb an additional 200′ before descending 700′ into South Lincoln. From there you will climb steadily for 500′. Your reward is a long, gradual descent back to the start. Total elevation gain on the long ride is 1,600′.

Season: Anytime except winter when the roads are not plowed.

Services: Rudimentary services are in Ripton (general store, phone, bed-and-breakfast). All services can be found in Middlebury, 6 miles west of Ripton. The Bike & Ski Touring Center is located on Main Street in Middlebury (802-388-6666).

Hazards: The possibility exists of encountering an occasional logging truck, but chances are you won't encounter one.

Rescue index: At the farthest point you are 5 miles from the nearest phone.

Land status: Most of this ride is in the Green Mountain National Forest where cyclists are allowed on Forest Service roads but nowhere else.

Maps: You'll need four USGS 7.5 minute quads: Bread Loaf, East Middlebury, South Lincoln, and South Mountain. Northern Cartographic and DeLorme's atlases are also good references. All can be found at the Vermont Book Shop (802-388-2061) on Main Street in Middlebury, 8 miles from Ripton.

Finding the trail: Park at the town hall in Ripton, 8 miles west of Middlebury on VT 125. The ride begins here.

Source of additional information: The best place for information about anything pertaining to the Green Mountain National Forest can be found at the Middlebury District headquarters, 7 miles from Ripton on VT 7, just south of Middlebury. You can write or call Green Mountain National Forest, Middlebury District, Route 7, Box 1260, Middlebury, VT 05753; (802) 388-4362.

Notes on the trail: Steammill Road loop: From the town hall in Ripton, begin by riding east for 2.7 miles on paved VT 125, climbing gradually to Middlebury College's Bread Loaf Campus. You will know you have reached the campus when you see a cluster of yellow buildings. Turn left onto FR 59, a.k.a. Steammill Road, and continue climbing gradually on this smooth, gravel surface with dense woodland on both sides of the road. You are now in the Green Mountain National Forest. Eventually you will come to an opening where the steam engine–driven sawmill once sat; the site is now a small parking area for hikers using the Skylight Pond Trail. Descend gradually until you come to a well-signed junction (7.5 miles into the ride) and turn left, still riding on FR 59.

FR 59 takes you back into Ripton on a gradual descent. Cross over Sparks Brook, and at Cooks Cemetery, bear right on Robbins Cross Road (paved). Ride to a T-intersection and turn left onto Ripton Road (there is no sign) and descend steeply on pavement to VT 125. Turn left and immediately you will see your starting area. Total of 11 miles.

Natural Turnpike loop: Begin with the Steammill Road directions above. To complete the Natural Turnpike loop, go to the junction at the 7.5-mile mark and turn right onto FR 54, the Natural Turnpike. Continue climbing gradually through dense woodland. There are many tempting side trails used for winter recreation, but don't venture onto them; they lie in national forestland where bicycles are not allowed, and anyone caught faces a $100 fine.

Soon you will begin a long descent followed by a mile of flat that affords great views of Mount Abraham (elevation: 4,006'). In South Lincoln (no services) you will come to a 3-way junction—stay to the left and cross over a low bridge. Pass two dirt roads on the left: one has a small white sign that reads Old Country Road 41, the other is FR 68 (both dead ends).

Come to a T-intersection and turn left. This is known locally as the Ripton–South Lincoln Road, or vice-versa, depending on which town you live in. Climb steadily; when you pass a sign on your right for the Bristol Notch Road you have reached the top. Begin a long, gradual descent. Shortly after passing the St. Theresa Cemetery on your right, you will come to a 4-way junction. Bear left (not the hairpin left) onto the Lincoln Road, which parallels the north branch of the Middlebury River. Keep your eyes open for the freshwater spring on the right, a good place to refill your water bottle. Though old, the spring is clearly marked "Compliments of Lucky Seven." The water comes from a pipe and is regularly tested by the Vermont Health Department.

Soon the road turns to pavement. Pass the Robbins Cross Road on your left (this is where the ride rejoins the Steammill Road loop). Descend steeply on pavement to VT 125. Turn left and immediately you will see your starting area. You've just completed a total of 23 miles.

BLUEBERRY HILL AREA

Blueberry Hill Inn was named for the abundance of blueberries growing wild on the south side of Hogback Mountain, ready to be picked in early to mid-August. It is one of Vermont's best cross-country ski centers and is a favorite of classical-style skiers for its narrow trails and carefully set tracks. Tony Clark, owner of the inn, maintains the extensive network of ski trails, composed of old logging roads and jeep trails, on land he leases from the Green Mountain National Forest. Some of these trails are open for mountain biking, providing a wide variety of riding for beginner to expert ability levels, with all trails beginning and ending at the Blueberry Hill Inn.

During the summer, the ski shop is transformed to a bike shop, where mountain bikes are available for rent ($25 per day, $30 per day with suspension). There is no trail fee. A mechanic is on hand to answer questions and perform any necessary repairs. Outside you will find a hose for washing yourself and your bike after your ride, and inside are rest rooms and a changing area.

If you really want to make a day of it, stay for a gourmet dinner at the inn (reservations required). At the very least, have one of Blueberry Hill Inn's famous chocolate chip cookies before you leave. There is enough riding at Blueberry Hill to keep you busy for a few days. I have included just a sampling of what they have to offer—the Leicester Hollow Trail and the Hogback Mountain loop—plus some general-area comments before those specific trails. Many more combinations of trails are available in the area, and it is an excellent place for a bona fide dirt road rider to give single-track a try.

General-Area Comments for Rides 39 and 40

General location: Halfway between Ripton and Goshen on FR 32 (also known as the Goshen-Ripton Road).

Elevation change: Elevation gains range from 300 to 1500´ per ride.

Season: June through October; late July and early August are blueberry picking times.

Services: Rudimentary services are available in Ripton, most at Blueberry Hill Inn; nothing is available in Goshen.

Hazards: The ski trails are well maintained and basically free of natural hazards. The trails in the Green Mountain National Forest are shared with hikers and horses. Keep an eye out for them, share the trail, and respect others.

Rescue index: At times you may be 4 miles from a phone.

Land status: Green Mountain National Forest roads and trails, VAST trails, cross-country ski trails, hiking trails, and dirt roads.

Maps: The best map is the Blueberry Hill Trail Map, which can be purchased at the inn for $2. Other maps depicting the area are USGS 7.5 minute quads, Brandon and East Middlebury, and the locally produced Moosalamoo trail map.

Finding the trails: All rides begin and end at Blueberry Hill Inn, located on the Goshen Road, halfway between Ripton on VT 125 and Goshen on VT 73.

Sources of additional information: For more information on dining, lodging, and mountain bike riding at Blueberry Hill Inn, write or call the Blueberry Hill Inn, Goshen Road, Goshen, VT 05733; (802) 247-6735. Or visit their Web site at www.blueberryhillinn.com. Green Mountain Bikes runs the bike shop and rentals at Blueberry Hill; its complete retail shop is located in Rochester (802-767-4464). There is also a bike shop in Middlebury, Bike & Ski Touring Center (802-388-6666).

RIDE 39 · Leicester Hollow Trail

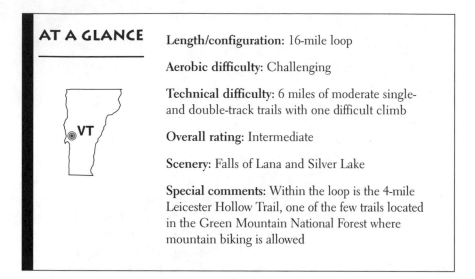

AT A GLANCE

Length/configuration: 16-mile loop

Aerobic difficulty: Challenging

Technical difficulty: 6 miles of moderate single- and double-track trails with one difficult climb

Overall rating: Intermediate

Scenery: Falls of Lana and Silver Lake

Special comments: Within the loop is the 4-mile Leicester Hollow Trail, one of the few trails located in the Green Mountain National Forest where mountain biking is allowed

This 16-mile loop ride takes you first to the Falls of Lana and then onto the four-mile Leicester (pronounced Lester) Hollow Trail for an excellent, mellow, single-track experience. You will pass by peaceful Silver Lake, where no motorized boats are allowed. Much of your time will be spent riding in the Green Mountain National Forest. The first half of the ride descends steadily to the Falls of Lana for a total elevation loss of 800 feet. You must climb 500 feet back up to the Leicester Hollow Trail, and then descend gradually for 4 miles, losing another 500 feet in elevation. You will regain all that elevation as you climb gradually back to the start.

Note: Other category information is presented on page 145.

Notes on the trail: From the bike shop, turn right onto Forest Service Road 32 (FR 32) and ride south on this gravel road for slightly more than a mile. Turn right onto Silver Lake Road (FR 27), following signs for Silver Lake. Stay right on the single-lane gravel road and you will reach the gate at the entrance to Silver Lake Recreation Area in the Green Mountain National Forest. Ride around the gate (closed to motor vehicles) and descend for a mile until you come to a well-marked junction. You will see Silver Lake off to the far left. At this point you can turn left to continue on the Leicester Hollow Trail, or you can turn right to see the Falls of Lana.

Descend steeply through several rocky sections for 1 mile until you come to the falls. This is a fun area to explore by foot, and a nice place for a picnic. The falls are layered in three sections with several good swimming holes. To leave the falls, return the way you came, climbing steeply back up the mile-long trail. Expect to see a lot of hikers as you climb.

Return to the well-marked junction; Silver Lake and the Silver Lake Campground are now on your right. Take the Leicester Hollow Trail, also now on

RIDE 39 · Leicester Hollow Trail

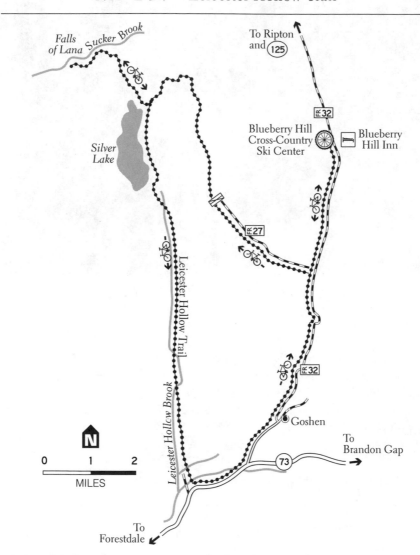

your right, which soon turns into 4 miles of single-track on a gradual descent. This trail is easy to ride and a good place for beginners to get a sense of why single-track is so thrilling. You may have to dismount a few times along the way for fallen trees and a number of unrideable rock slides. You may encounter horseback riders.

Near the end of the trail you will come to a marked trail junction. Stay to the left on the wide, higher trail. Go around a Forest Service gate onto a gravel road and ride to a stop sign at paved VT 73. Go left and climb gradually for about three-quarters of a mile. Take the left turn onto FR 32 following signs for the Blueberry Hill Inn.

The Leicester Hollow Trail is a wonderful single-track trail in Green Mountain National Forest, where mountain biking is allowed.

Come to a junction and go left onto Carlisle Hill Road (FR 32). This intersection is officially the town of Goshen, as you can tell by the small, singular building that houses the town office. The road alternates between gravel and pavement as you climb back to the Blueberry Hill Inn. Pass by Silver Lake Road, now on your left, and return to the start.

RIDE 40 · Hogback Mountain

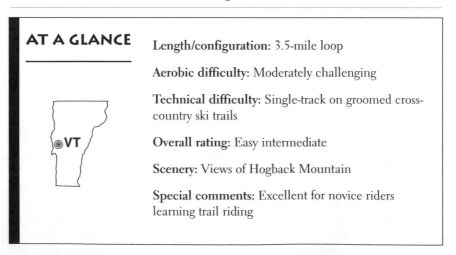

AT A GLANCE

Length/configuration: 3.5-mile loop

Aerobic difficulty: Moderately challenging

Technical difficulty: Single-track on groomed cross-country ski trails

Overall rating: Easy intermediate

Scenery: Views of Hogback Mountain

Special comments: Excellent for novice riders learning trail riding

RIDE 40 • Hogback Mountain

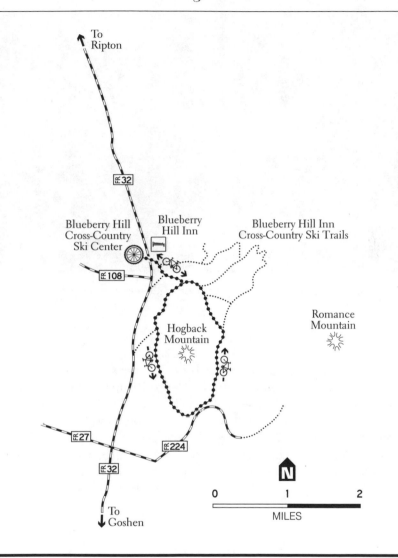

Beginners will love this 3.5-mile ride. It gains only 400 feet in elevation, mostly at the start, which may seem challenging, but hang in there—the rest of the ride is worth it. You will come to an open meadow and the Blueberry Management Area, where wild blueberries grow in abundance. The view to the east, of Romance Mountain, is stunning. The course returns you to the woods and gently back to the start, all on cross-country ski trails.

Note: Other category information is presented on page 145.

Riders will see this view of Hogback Mountain while riding the cross-country trails at Blueberry Hill.

Notes on the trail: Beginning at the bike shop, cross the road and ride to the back of the inn on the left side of the building. Pick up the cross-country ski trail at trail marker 1. Climb the ski trail to trail marker 7 and turn right. Follow this trail, which becomes level, out to the blueberry meadow. Stay on the trail and drop down to a dirt road. You might have to get off your bike to negotiate the trench on the edge of the road. Turn left and follow the road briefly, looking for trail marker 25, where you reenter the woods. Stay left at every opportunity until trail marker 7, where you retrace your steps back to the inn.

ROCHESTER AREA

Pine Brook Trail, Ash Hill Trail, and The Contest Trail, all located within the Green Mountain National Forest, are experimental mountain bike trails established by the U.S. Forest Service in conjunction with the Pico/Killington Cycling Club, a local bike club responsible for maintaining the trails. The purpose of the experiment is to study the impact of mountain bikes on terrain in an area that is shared with wildlife and protected from excessive human impact. The results of the study will be used to determine future possibilities for mountain bike riding within national forest boundaries. The experiment will conclude in the summer of 1998, and, depending on the outcome, the trails may be open to mountain bikes in the future.

Although all three of these rides are rather short, I have listed them separately because they are technically challenging individually.

The Pine Brook Trail is short and sweet, perhaps the sweetest ride in this book. It climbs gradually on Forest Service roads and descends on a well-engineered trail that was once a road but has been closed to vehicular traffic for many years. It is a nine-mile, easy intermediate loop. It can be connected with the Ash Hill Trail for a more challenging 20-mile ride.

The Ash Hill Trail, a point-to-point trail, can be made into a loop if you finish the ride on VT 73 and VT 100. A long, steep descent on the trail can make your hands hurt from using the brakes so much. Total mileage is just under ten miles, making this an intermediate ride. For a more demanding day, connect this trail to the Pine Brook Trail for a total of 20 miles or the Contest Trail for a total of 17.5 miles.

The Contest Trail is also a point-to-point trail that can be made into a loop with the help of Liberty Hill Road (Forest Service Road 223). There are several difficult sections, some easy dirt roads, and a lot of climbing. Total mileage is just under nine miles, but the riding is technical, making this a difficult route. To really challenge yourself, first ride the Contest Trail and continue onto the Ash Hill Trail for a total of 17.5 very difficult miles.

Before riding any of these trails, be sure to stop by the Rochester Ranger Station located a mile north of Rochester on VT 100 to check their status for mountain bike riding, or call the station at (802) 767-4261. They are open Monday through Friday, 8:30 A.M. to 4:30 P.M.

RIDE 41 · Pine Brook Trail

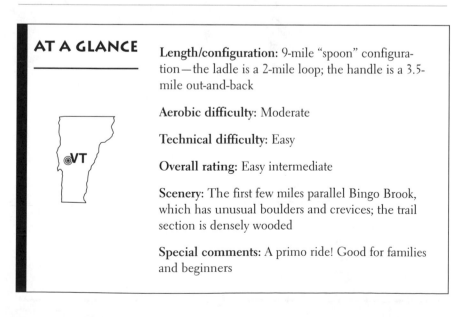

AT A GLANCE

Length/configuration: 9-mile "spoon" configuration—the ladle is a 2-mile loop; the handle is a 3.5-mile out-and-back

Aerobic difficulty: Moderate

Technical difficulty: Easy

Overall rating: Easy intermediate

Scenery: The first few miles parallel Bingo Brook, which has unusual boulders and crevices; the trail section is densely wooded

Special comments: A primo ride! Good for families and beginners

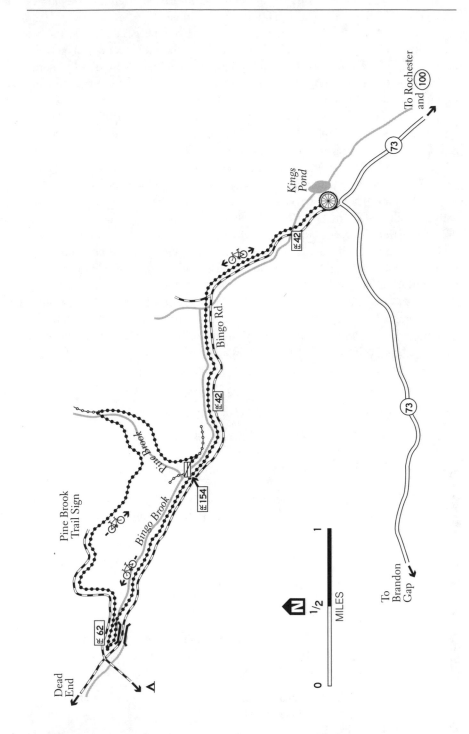

A trail sign welcomes mountain bikers to Pine Brook Trail.

If short and sweet is your style, then this nine-mile loop is for you. It begins with a pleasant, gradual climb on Forest Service Road 42 (a.k.a. Bingo Road), parallel to Bingo Brook, a scenic brook with unusually large boulders. You then climb more steeply on FR 62, which affords scenic views to the south. Eventually you connect with Pine Brook Trail, a grassy, smooth, double-track trail that descends through the woods back to FR 42.

For those not ready for the trail riding on Pine Brook Trail, stay on Bingo Road which dead-ends about one-half mile past the junction of FR 62. Bingo Road is about eight miles out and back. There is a pullout with a picnic table about a mile from the start of Bingo Road. If you begin there, the ride is only six miles round-trip. This is an excellent place for beginners and families.

General location: Rochester.

Elevation change: 500′ are gained gradually over the first half of the ride.

Season: May through mid-November. Pine Brook Trail was engineered as a Forest Service road and has excellent drainage. When other trails are still wet, this one is probably dry.

Services: All services can be found in Rochester, near the start of the ride.

Hazards: An occasional motor vehicle on FR 42 and FR 62, and the gate at the bottom of the descent on Pine Brook Trail.

Rescue index: You are never more than 2 miles from a telephone.

Land status: Green Mountain National Forest roads and trails.

Maps: Three USGS 7.5 minute quads show the entire ride: Breadloaf, Mount Carmel, and Rochester. The Green Mountain National Forest, Rochester Ranger District, also has maps of the trail, including a map of the northern half of the Green Mountain National Forest. Pine Brook Trail is well marked with a trailhead sign, white mountain bike rider signs and white arrows, blue diamonds, and blue arrows.

Finding the trail: One-half mile south of Rochester on VT 100, turn onto VT 73 (a.k.a. Brandon Gap Road). In approximately 2 miles, VT 73 makes a sharp left. Continue going straight onto FR 42, and park anywhere along the road. Your ride begins where you park.

Sources of additional information: The Rochester Ranger Station is the best source for information on this ride (802-767-4261). It is open Monday through Friday, 8:30 A.M. to 4:30 P.M., and are located on VT 100, 1 mile north of Rochester. The Green Mountain Bicycle Shop in Rochester (802-767-4464) also has staff who are knowledgeable about this and other rides in the area.

Notes on the trail: Ride up FR 42 (Bingo Road) for 3.5 miles. Turn right onto FR 62. Climb steadily to the end where you pick up Pine Brook Trail. Look for a small, carved wooden sign, and a small white biker sign. Follow Pine Brook Trail, descending steadily. At any questionable trail junction, pay attention to the signs and you can't go wrong. At the bottom of the descent, dismount and crawl under the Forest Service gate. Go right, still descending. Bear left onto FR 154 and immediately left on FR 42. Retrace your steps to the start.

RIDE 42 · Ash Hill Trail

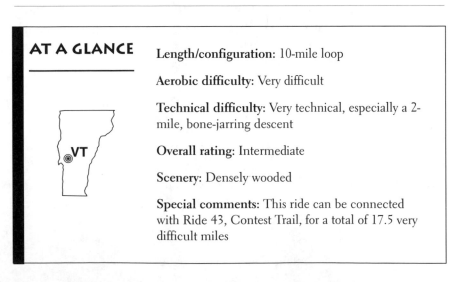

AT A GLANCE

Length/configuration: 10-mile loop

Aerobic difficulty: Very difficult

Technical difficulty: Very technical, especially a 2-mile, bone-jarring descent

Overall rating: Intermediate

Scenery: Densely wooded

Special comments: This ride can be connected with Ride 43, Contest Trail, for a total of 17.5 very difficult miles

RIDE 42 · Ash Hill Trail

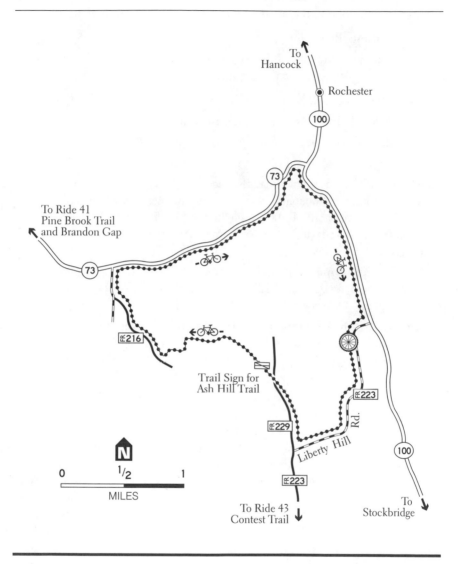

This 10-mile loop is basically a climb followed immediately by a descent. The initial, long climb is on dirt roads and jeep trails. You have about one-half mile of flat terrain at the top to catch your breath before descending a rocky, steep, knuckle-aching, bone-jarring trail. Once you make it to the bottom you can relax and spin your way back to the start on flat pavement. You will have good views of farms and fields as you climb, but once you reach the height of the land you will enter a dense pine and hardwood forest.

I chose to do Ash Hill Trail in the clockwise direction because the climbing is done mostly on dirt roads. For those who love technical, very demanding climbing, try this loop in the opposite direction—you *will* be challenged!

General location: Rochester.

Elevation change: The only climb worth mentioning is the initial one of 900´.

Season: Mid-June through mid-November.

Services: All services can be found in Rochester, near the start of the ride.

Hazards: Ash Hill Trail has an extremely rocky and rugged descent.

Rescue index: You are never more than 2 miles from a telephone.

Land status: Green Mountain National Forest roads and trails.

Maps: One USGS 7.5 minute quad, Rochester, shows the area but not the trail. The Green Mountain National Forest, Rochester Ranger District, office has maps of the trail. It is located on VT 100, 1 mile north of Rochester (802-767-4261). Ash Hill Trail is well marked with a trailhead sign, white mountain bike rider signs, and white arrows.

Finding the trail: A mile south of Rochester on VT 100, turn right onto Liberty Hill Road (Forest Service Road 223). Go .5 mile, cross a concrete bridge and park in the area on the right. Your ride begins where you park.

Sources of additional information: The Rochester Ranger Station is the best source for information on this ride (802-767-4261). It is open Monday through Friday, 8:30 A.M. to 4:30 P.M. The Green Mountain Bicycle Shop in Rochester (802-767-4464) also has staff who are knowledgeable about this and other rides in the area.

Notes on the trail: From the parking area, begin riding on Liberty Hill Road, heading for the big red barn. Liberty Hill Road is gravel and begins climbing right away. You will pass a beautiful white house on the left, followed by another outstanding farmhouse farther up the climb.

After more than 1.5 miles of climbing, you will come to a trail junction marked with VAST signs and small, white mountain bike rider signs. Go right on FR 229, following signs for the Ash Hill Trail. (The Contest Trail ride mentioned above goes to the left.) Stay on FR 229 until you come to a gate marked with Ash Hill Trail signage. Go around the gate and begin some fun, single-track riding, descending gradually. Pass a hunting camp on the right, then at a **T**-intersection go right. Descend, steeply at times, on a rocky double-track trail, a.k.a. FR 216.

At 4.5 miles from the start you will arrive at a small parking area on FR 226, a.k.a. Corporation Road. Stay right and ride out to VT 73. Turn right on pavement and descend gradually to VT 100; turn right and ride for 1.5 miles to Liberty Hill Road. Turn right, cross a bridge, and return to where you started for a total of nearly 10 miles.

This ride can be done in conjunction with Ride 43, Contest Trail, for a total of approximately 17.5 miles of moderate riding with some challenging sections.

RIDE 43 · Contest Trail

AT A GLANCE

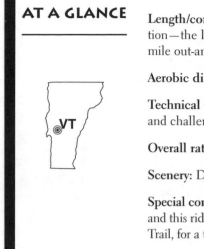

Length/configuration: 9-mile "spoon" configuration—the ladle is a 6-mile loop; the handle is a 1.5-mile out-and-back

Aerobic difficulty: Very difficult

Technical difficulty: Very difficult climbs, tricky and challenging single-track

Overall rating: Difficult

Scenery: Densely wooded; one meadow view

Special comments: The single-track section is a blast, and this ride can be connected to Ride 42, Ash Hill Trail, for a total of 17.5 very difficult miles

It took me two tries to figure out this ride. The first time, I intended to ride it in a clockwise direction, but I missed the left turn from the road onto the trail. By the time I realized my mistake I was so far along it seemed smarter to continue on and pick up the Contest Trail from the farther end, then ride it in a counterclockwise direction. Then, I got confused in the meadow, and after checking out several possible trails, I ran out of time and turned around, retracing my steps back to the start.

The second time out I had better luck finding the Contest Trail at the far end of the meadow, thanks to a bird hunter, who gave me definitive directions. Once I found it, the Contest Trail was a real treat. I sure was glad I rode it counterclockwise because the final descent would have been a killer to climb had I gone the other way.

General location: Rochester.

Elevation change: The climb at the beginning is 900′ and the climb at the halfway point is 600′, a total of 1,500′ elevation gain.

Season: Mid-June through mid-November and any other time the trails are dry.

Services: All services can be found in Rochester, near the start of the ride, or Pittsford, near the halfway point.

Hazards: Unpredictable trail conditions such as windfall, large rocks, sudden drop-offs, potholes, and rocky descents.

Rescue index: You are never more than 2 miles from a telephone.

RIDE 43 · Contest Trail

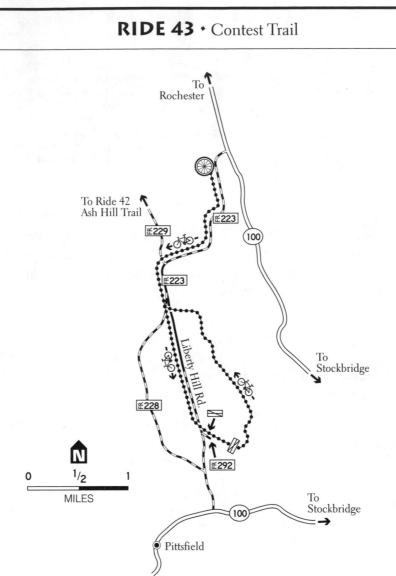

Land status: Green Mountain National Forest roads and trails.

Maps: One USGS 7.5 minute quad, Rochester, shows the area but not the trail. You can pick up a map of the trail at the Green Mountain National Forest, Rochester Ranger District, office (802-767-4261) on VT 100, 1 mile north of Rochester. Contest Trail is marked with a trailhead sign and white mountain bike rider signs, but nonetheless, a map is handy—you never know when a sign might disappear . . .

The Contest Trail gets a thumbs up!

Finding the trail: A mile south of Rochester on VT 100, turn west onto Liberty Hill Road (Forest Service Road 223). Go .5 mile, cross a concrete bridge, and park in the area on the right. Your ride begins where you park.

Sources of additional information: The Rochester Ranger Station (802-767-4261) is the best source for information on this ride (it is closed on weekends). The Green Mountain Bicycle Shop in Rochester (802-767-4464) also has staff who are knowledgeable about this and other rides in the area.

Notes on the trail: From the parking area, begin riding on Liberty Hill Road (FR 223), heading for the big red barn. Begin climbing right away and soon you will pass a beautiful white house on the left; farther up the climb you will pass a beautifully refurbished farmhouse with outbuildings and excellent views to the south.

After more than 1.5 miles of climbing, come to a trail junction marked with VAST trail signs. You will also notice a white mountain biker sign. Stay to the left at this junction and continue climbing. Stay left at the next **Y**-intersection where FR 228 goes off to the right. A quarter mile from this intersection, you will pass the Contest Trail terminus on the left. Don't go that way—clockwise on the Contest Trail is brutal (but not impossible), which is why I have presented this ride in the counterclockwise direction.

This section of Liberty Hill Road is moderately challenging, with rocky and muddy sections along the way. Eventually it descends along a stone road with meadow views ahead and to the right. In 1 mile it turns to a maintained town road. Continue descending and at 3.7 miles turn left onto FR 292. Look for the little, white mountain bike rider sign.

Climb steeply on this double-track trail to a high meadow with great views to the right. Pass through a gate and go left as you enter the meadow. Follow the grassy trail, veering right and passing remnants of stone foundations on your left. Cross the meadow to the far side, then go left on a grassy trail. Ride north on the edge of the meadow, parallel to a stone wall, climbing steadily all the way to the far end of the meadow. Turn right to enter the woods through an opening in the stone wall. Climb a steep pitch to the high point of the ride and begin about 2 miles of fun single-track that is well marked with mountain biker signs and white arrows. This is the Contest Trail.

Following a long descent, the Contest Trail brings you back to Liberty Hill Road. Turn right and retrace your steps back to the start, for a total of 9 moderate miles with a few difficult sections. Or, at the next trail junction, take Ride 42, Ash Hill Trail for a longer ride (17.5 miles).

RIDE 44 · Michigan Road

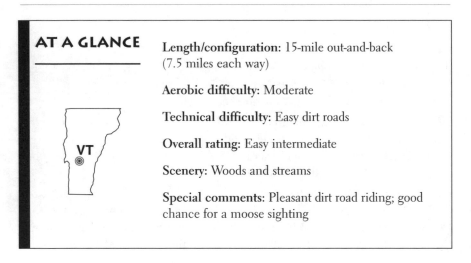

AT A GLANCE

Length/configuration: 15-mile out-and-back (7.5 miles each way)

Aerobic difficulty: Moderate

Technical difficulty: Easy dirt roads

Overall rating: Easy intermediate

Scenery: Woods and streams

Special comments: Pleasant dirt road riding; good chance for a moose sighting

Michigan Road is a Forest Service road that weaves in and out of the Green Mountain National Forest. It lies just west of Pittsfield, a tidy town with simply designed white houses neatly trimmed in green and black. Also known as Forest Service Road 35 (FR 35), Michigan Road parallels the West Branch of Michigan Brook. This 15-mile out-and-back ride climbs gradually on a two-lane dirt road. The farther you go, the more narrow the road becomes, until eventually you are on a single-lane, four-wheel-drive road.

The nicest aspect of Michigan Road is the brook that is with you for most of the ride. Also, you can turn around at any point, making this a good choice for riders of different abilities. In addition, since the road does not go anywhere, there is little to no traffic with which to contend. If you are lucky, like I was, you will see a moose.

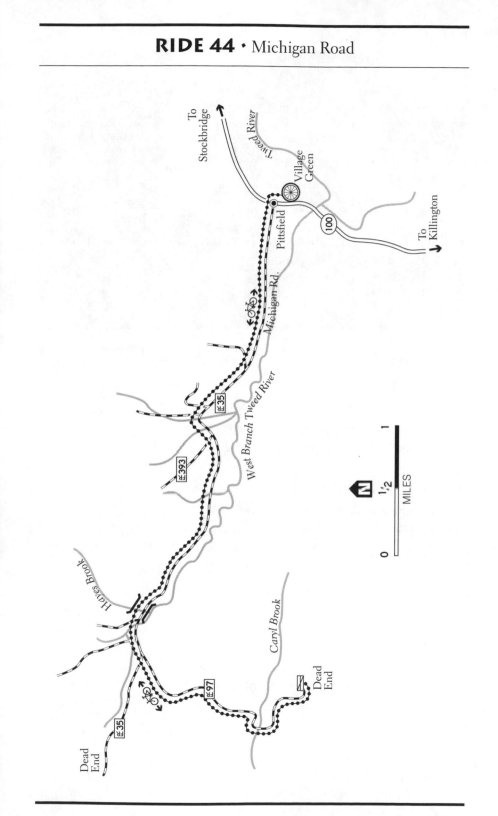

To Stockbridge

Tweed River

Village Green

Pittsfield

100

To Killington

Michigan Rd.

West Branch Tweed River

TH 35

TH 393

Hayes Brook

Caryl Brook

TH 97

TH 35

Dead End

Dead End

N

0   ½   1
MILES

The classic village green of Pittsfield is where the Michigan Road ride begins and ends.

This is an easy-intermediate ride with no technical terrain. Best of all, when you reach the end of the road, it is downhill all the way back. For a shorter ride, park 2.5 miles up Michigan Road at a small parking area. This cuts five miles off the entire ride.

General location: Pittsfield.

Elevation change: You climb 1,100´, very gradually, over 7.5 miles to the turn-around point.

Season: May through mid-November.

Services: All services are available in Pittsfield.

Hazards: Occasionally a logging operation occurs along this road. If so, there will be signs indicating "logging operation ahead."

Rescue index: At the turnaround point you are about 4 miles from a telephone.

Land status: Town roads and Forest Service roads.

Maps: The best map is the Green Mountain National Forest map (north half). You can pick one up at the Green Mountain National Forest, Rochester Ranger District, office on VT 100, 1 mile north of Rochester (802-767-4261). Cost is $4.

Finding the trail: The ride begins at the village green in Pittsfield on VT 100. Park by the town hall. (Behind the town hall is a portable toilet.)

Sources of additional information: The Rochester Ranger Station is a good source for information on this ride. It is open Monday through Friday, 8:30 A.M. to 4:30 P.M.; (802) 767-4261. Green Mountain Bicycles (802-767-4464) in

Rochester, about 10 miles north of Pittsfield, also has staff who are familiar with this and other rides in the area. The Killington Mountain Bike Shop (802-422-6232) is about 10 miles south at the Killington Resort base lodge.

Notes on the trail: From the village green, ride north on VT 100. Immediately turn left at the Pittsfield General Store onto FR 35, a.k.a. Michigan Road. Climb gradually, passing homes on both sides of the road. At 2.5 miles is a parking area on the left. This is a good place to park for a shorter, 10-mile ride.

Cross Hayes Brook (signed) and climb a short, steep pitch. Cross two more brooks. Immediately after the second, at 5 miles, fork left, staying on the better traveled FR 97. AT 7.5 miles you will come to an open area. At the far end is a gate with VAST signs and a sign that indicates this trail is closed to bikers. Although you may be tempted to take this trail because it connects to Lower Michigan Road, you will be trespassing on private property owned by Stanley Tools. Please turn around at this point, and retrace your steps to the start, for a total of 15 fairly easy miles.

NORTHERN VERMONT

Vermont's highest mountains are in the northern part of the state: Mount Mansfield, 4,393 feet; Camel's Hump, 4,083 feet; Mount Hunger, 3,539 feet; Jay Peak, 3,861 feet; and many more. These mountains are 1,000 feet higher than the tallest mountains of southern Vermont. They are rugged, dramatic, and magnificent up close and from a distance.

Northern Vermont was heavily logged at the turn of the century; although clear-cutting was routine then, it is not the standard now. Logging operations now must conform to state regulations designed to protect the land from future devastation. Forests have grown back and the land is no longer barren. Old logging roads, as well as new ones, are commonplace in this region and some of the rides described below make use of these roads. Occasionally, small logging operations are in progress, as noted in individual ride descriptions.

Dairy farms are quite abundant in northern Vermont. Open meadows, four-story barns, silos, farm machinery, cows, and old farmhouses paint the landscape. Many dairy farms supply the milk and cream used by the Ben & Jerry's ice cream plants in Waterbury Center and St. Albans, as well as by the Cabot Cheese Company in Cabot.

The province of Quebec influences the northernmost areas of Vermont, and commerce is strong at the border. Buildings and names reflect Quebecois tradition, and many Canadians come to Vermont for their ski vacations. In the summer, they come for the great mountain biking.

Winter comes early and stays late. It is a distinctly different climate from what is found in southern Vermont. When riding in northern Vermont, it is a good idea to bring an extra layer of clothing.

STOWE AREA (RIDES 45–48)

Stowe is a classic ski town, with a busy village that features excellent restaurants and specialty shopping. The eight-mile Mountain Road, which extends from the town to the Mount Mansfield Ski Resort, is packed with more of the same. The award-winning Stowe Rec Path (paved) parallels the Mountain Road. During the summer it is used by runners, walkers, in-line skaters, baby strollers, and beginning mountain bikers. Experienced riders usually find it too crowded for safe riding and stick to the Mountain Road.

Most of the land in the heart of Stowe is privately owned, but four excellent rides on public land depart from Nebraska Valley, located on the outskirts of Stowe. These four rides, Cotton Brook, Nebraska Valley, Old County Road, and Mount Mansfield, are described here.

RIDE 45 · Cotton Brook

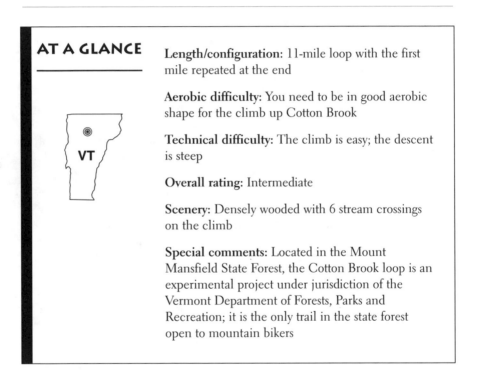

AT A GLANCE
_____

Length/configuration: 11-mile loop with the first mile repeated at the end

Aerobic difficulty: You need to be in good aerobic shape for the climb up Cotton Brook

Technical difficulty: The climb is easy; the descent is steep

Overall rating: Intermediate

Scenery: Densely wooded with 6 stream crossings on the climb

Special comments: Located in the Mount Mansfield State Forest, the Cotton Brook loop is an experimental project under jurisdiction of the Vermont Department of Forests, Parks and Recreation; it is the only trail in the state forest open to mountain bikers

This 11-mile loop is an experimental trail that was constructed under the supervision of the Vermont Department of Forests, Parks and Recreation, and it was subsidized in part by the state's gas tax. It climbs steadily up an old logging road and then suddenly drops on a double-track snowmobile trail to Cotton Brook's basin. The loop, which is used by snowmobilers and cross-country skiers in the winter, is marked with little white signs bearing the silhouette of a mountain biker. During the first two miles of the logging road several well-marked, dipsy-doodle side jaunts take you off and bring you quickly back to the main route. They add an element of challenge to the otherwise flat approach to the climb.

RIDE 45 · Cotton Brook

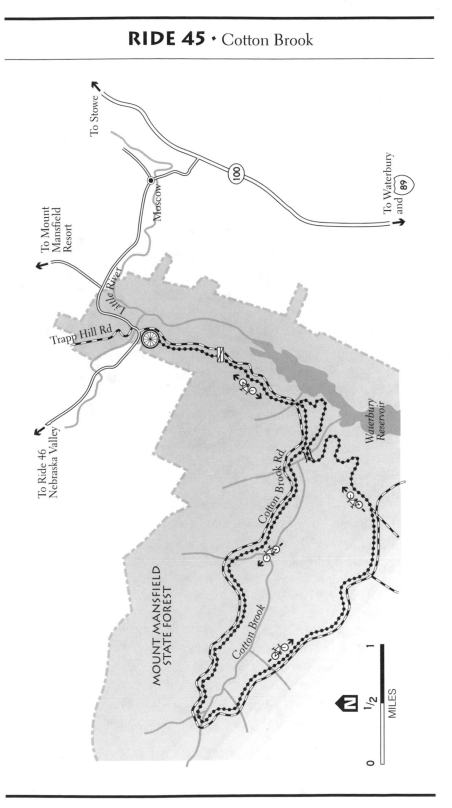

Closed to motor vehicles (except logging trucks), Cotton Brook Road, a logging road in Mount Mansfield State Forest, climbs steadily for seven miles. A single-track trail designed for mountain bike use drops steeply back to the start of the ride.

General location: Near Moscow on the Waterbury Reservoir.

Elevation change: The ride has one 800′ climb.

Season: The 6.7-mile climb takes place on a logging road that can be ridden up and back from May through mid-November, but there is a chance of snow in the spring and fall at the highest elevation (1,500′). The second half of the loop, a renovated double-track snowmobile trail, stays wet in the spring and shouldn't be ridden until late June.

Services: All services are available in Stowe. Two bike shops, The Mountain Bike Shop (802-253-7919) and Stowe Action Outfitters (802-253-7975) are both on the mountain road (VT 108) in Stowe. There is camping at Mount Mansfield State Park.

Hazards: The possibility of a logging truck or a moose. The descent is very steep at times, and a few sections may be washed out. An occasional dismount may be required.

Rescue index: At the summit of the climb you are at least 7 miles from a phone. This means a long walk out if you get hurt, but chances are good that another rider will be along, as Cotton Brook gets a lot of use.

Land status: Old logging roads in the Mount Mansfield State Forest.

Maps: A map of the Cotton Brook loop is posted at the trailhead—the only map in print press time. Note: A sign posted at the trailhead, Trail Closed to Mountain Biking, applies to a different hiking trail, not the Cotton Brook loop.

Finding the trail: From Exit 10 off Interstate 89, proceed north for 8 miles on VT 100. Turn left, following signs for the town of Moscow. Pass by the Moscow General Store and post office on your left and continue for 1.5 miles. Immediately after Trapp Hill Road (on the right), the main road, Nebraska Valley Road, bears sharply right while Cotton Brook Road, a dirt road, lies straight ahead. Take Cotton Brook Road for 100 yards and park in the parking area on the right. This is where the ride begins.

Source of additional information: The staff at the Mountain Bike Shop on the Mountain Road (VT 108) can answer all your questions (802-253-7919). They lead guided tours in the Stowe area by appointment and they host group mountain bike rides on local trails every Tuesday evening from May through October. They also have a good selection of maps.

Notes on the trail: From the parking area, continue up Cotton Brook Road and ride around a gate. The road climbs steadily for 6.7 miles and crosses 6 streams, where the spring runoff can be high and forceful. Expect to see moose tracks on a level stretch near the top. The road crests at an open vista with good views directly ahead and then descends through a cleared area. At the fork take a sharp left onto a trail marked with VAST signs. Descend steeply through several switchbacks and drop abruptly to the valley floor of Cotton Brook. Use caution on the descent—there may be some washouts where you will have to walk. At the bottom, cross a brand new bridge. Follow the stream until the trail bends sharply left. You will come to a short, gut-wrenching climb that brings you back to Cotton Brook Road. Retrace your steps to the start.

RIDE 46 · Nebraska Valley

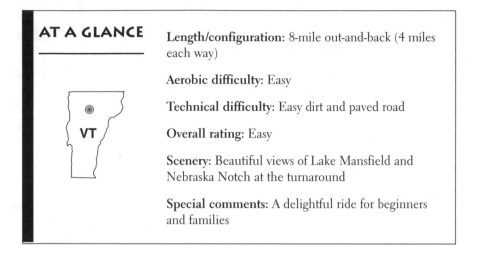

AT A GLANCE

Length/configuration: 8-mile out-and-back (4 miles each way)

Aerobic difficulty: Easy

Technical difficulty: Easy dirt and paved road

Overall rating: Easy

Scenery: Beautiful views of Lake Mansfield and Nebraska Notch at the turnaround

Special comments: A delightful ride for beginners and families

Nebraska Valley Road climbs gradually beside Miller Brook all the way to Lake Mansfield. The beginning and end of the ride are paved and the midsection is gravel. This eight-mile out-and-back course is excellent for beginners and families. It is also a good place for early-season training when trails are too wet to ride. During spring runoff, Miller Brook is filled to the brim and the thundering sound of cascading falls along the way makes conversation nearly impossible at times.

At the farthest point of the ride is pristine Lake Mansfield, fed by many tributaries pouring down from Nebraska Notch. It is home to the private Lake Mansfield Trout Club. There are stunning views here of Nebraska Notch.

General location: 4 miles northwest of Stowe.

Elevation change: Nebraska Road climbs a gradual 400´.

Season: Anytime, but the best times are when the roads are not snow covered.

Services: All services are available in Stowe. Two bike shops, The Mountain Bike Shop (802-253-7919) and Stowe Action Outfitters (802-253-7975) are both on the Mountain Road (VT 108) in Stowe. There is camping at Smugglers Notch State Park on VT 108, 8 miles north of Stowe near Mount Mansfield Ski Resort (802-253-4014).

Hazards: Vehicular traffic.

Rescue index: You are never far from a private residence.

Land status: Class 3 road.

Maps: Northern Cartographic's and DeLorme's atlases are both good maps of the route.

Finding the trail: From Exit 10 off Interstate 89, proceed north for 8 miles on

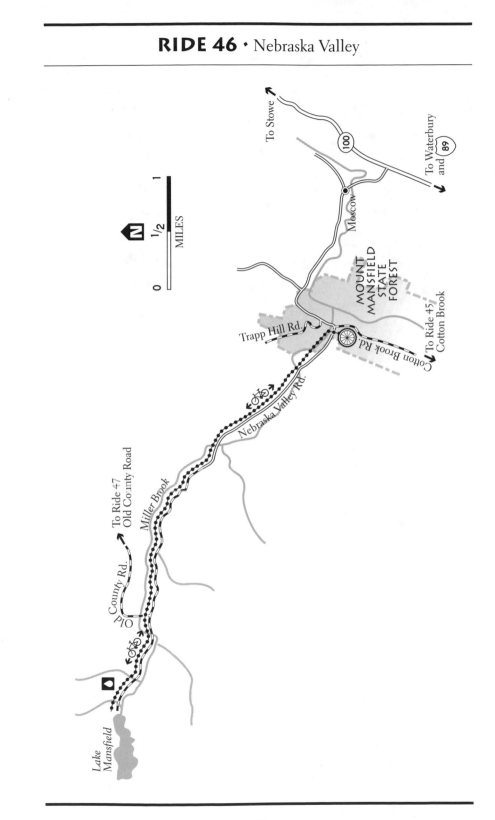

To Stowe

100

To Waterbury and 89

N

0   1/2   1
MILES

Moscow

MOUNT MANSFIELD STATE FOREST

Trapp Hill Rd.

Cotton Brook Rd.

To Ride 45 Cotton Brook

Nebraska Valley Rd.

Miller Brook

To Ride 47 Old County Road

Old County Rd.

Lake Mansfield

Bette fills her water bottle at the fresh spring (pronounced safe by the Vermont Department of Health) near Lake Mansfield.

VT 100. Turn left, following signs for the town of Moscow. Pass by the Moscow General Store and post office on your left and continue for 1.5 miles. Immediately after Trapp Hill Road (on the right), the main road, Nebraska Valley Road, bears sharply right while Cotton Brook Road, a dirt road, lies straight ahead. Take Cotton Brook Road for 100 yards and park in the parking area on the right. This is where the ride begins and ends.

Source of additional information: The staff at the Mountain Bike Shop on the Mountain Road (VT 108) can answer all your questions (802-253-7919). They lead guided tours in the Stowe area by appointment and they host group mountain bike rides on local trails every Tuesday evening from May through October. They also have a good selection of maps.

Notes on the trail: From the parking area in Cotton Brook, ride back out to the paved road and turn left on Nebraska Valley Road. After 2 miles, the road turns to dirt. Continue climbing gradually and eventually you will pass by Old County Road on your right. (This is where Ride 47, Old County Road, and Ride 48, Mount Mansfield, both continue.)

After a short, steep climb you will see a large cement vessel where you can fill your water bottle with fresh spring water from the pipe (tested frequently by the Vermont Department of Health). Note: Depending on rainfall, this well may be dry in the summer. Continue to Lake Mansfield. You must turn around at the Trout Club—the road beyond is private. Retrace your steps for a fun and fast ride back to the start.

RIDE 47 · Old County Road

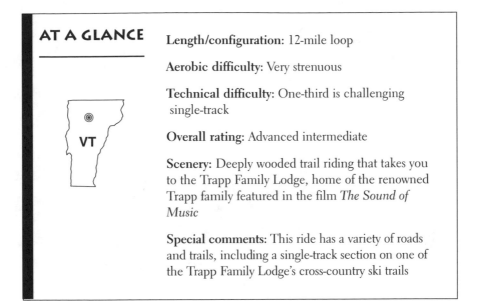

AT A GLANCE

Length/configuration: 12-mile loop

Aerobic difficulty: Very strenuous

Technical difficulty: One-third is challenging single-track

Overall rating: Advanced intermediate

Scenery: Deeply wooded trail riding that takes you to the Trapp Family Lodge, home of the renowned Trapp family featured in the film *The Sound of Music*

Special comments: This ride has a variety of roads and trails, including a single-track section on one of the Trapp Family Lodge's cross-country ski trails

This challenging 12-mile loop begins on Nebraska Valley Road and takes you to the Trapp Family Lodge Cross-Country Ski Center via Old County Road, a bygone Class 4 road. Old County Road has a one-mile climb on a rocky, wet, jeep trail that becomes a cross-country ski trail when it crosses onto the Trapp Family Lodge property. At this point the trail is mellow for a mile and goes through "The Narrows"; then it descends steeply to a paved road that climbs steadily to the Trapp Family Lodge. At Trapp's you have excellent views of the Worcester Range to the left.

The Trapp Family Lodge offers year-round accommodations and dining. If you are a dessert fan, be sure to visit the Tea Room. The gift shop has a good selection of maps and local literature. Besides movie fame, the Trapp Family Lodge is best known for cross-country skiing. The center has more than 90 miles of groomed trails that connect to other cross-country ski areas in Stowe (see Ride 48, Mount Mansfield). Summer guests are welcome to hike on the ski trails, but the only trails open to mountain bikes are Old County Road and Haul Road.

From Trapp's, the ride continues on a dirt road which turns and descends steadily back to the start, for a total of 12 hilly and challenging, but very entertaining, miles.

General location: Nebraska Valley, 4 miles northwest of Stowe.

Elevation change: One 950´ climb with technical single-track on Old County Road. Then a rocky 400´ descent drops you quickly to Luce Hill Road. There is a short, steep climb on pavement, followed by a 1.5-mile, fast descent on a dirt road back to the start.

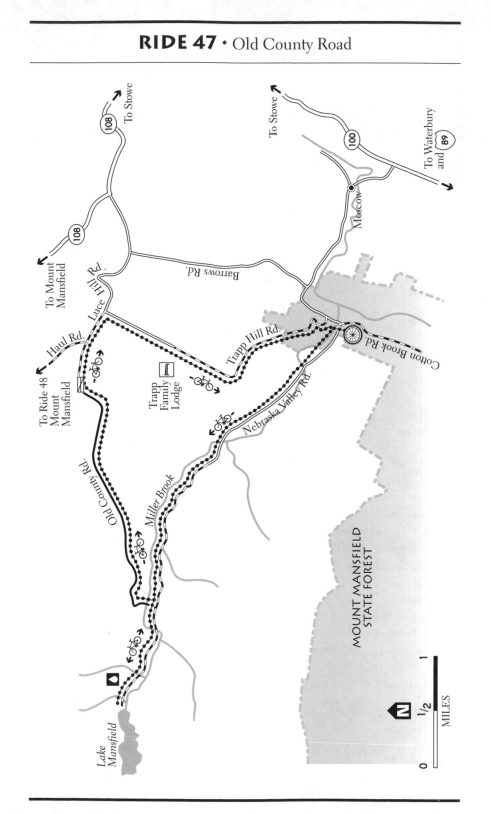

Old County Road is peaceful at first, but soon turns to a rugged jeep trail that climbs to ski trails at Trapp's Cross-Country Ski Resort.

Season: The best riding is from mid-June through October, but if it's a dry season the conditions could be favorable in May. Snow is possible at the higher elevations in May and early October.

Services: All services are available in Stowe. Two bike shops, The Mountain Bike Shop (802-253-7919) and Stowe Action Outfitters (802-253-7975), are both on the Mountain Road (VT 108) in Stowe. There is camping at Smugglers Notch State Park 8 miles north of Stowe on VT 108 near Mount Mansfield Ski Resort (802-253-4014).

Hazards: The terrain is very rocky at times, making descents very tricky. There is the possibility of a logging operation on the descent of Old County Road. Watch out for bottomless holes caused by spring runoff, and keep your eyes open for moose.

Rescue index: Don't ride these trails alone. There are times when you will be several miles from civilization and help. It's a long way out, and it could be several hours, or even days, before another rider came along and found you. If you choose to go alone, inform a friend of your plans. A first-aid kit is a good idea.

Land status: Class 4 roads, logging roads, cross-country ski trails, and some paved sections.

Maps: A combination of maps will give you the complete picture. Two USGS 7.5 minute quads, Stowe and Bolton, show Old County Road as a trail when in fact it is a Class 4 road. Northern Cartographic's is pretty good, but it named Old County Road as Meisler Road (all signs call it Old County Road). All maps can be found at assorted shops in Stowe. Trapp's gift shop also has a good selection of local maps.

Finding the trail: Take Exit 10 off Interstate 89; go north for 8 miles on VT 100. Turn left, following signs for the town of Moscow. Go through Moscow (don't blink) and continue for 1.5 miles past Barrows Road and Trapp Hill Road, both on your right. Immediately after Trapp Hill Road, the main road bears sharply right while Cotton Brook Road, a dirt road, lies straight ahead. Take Cotton Brook Road for 100 yards and park in the parking area on the right. This is where the ride begins and ends.

Sources of additional information: The staff at the Mountain Bike Shop on the Mountain Road (VT 108) can answer all your questions (802-253-7919). They lead guided tours in the Stowe area by appointment and they host group mountain bike rides on local trails every Tuesday evening from May through October. They also have a good selection of maps. For information on the Trapp Family Lodge, call (802) 253-8511.

Notes on the trail: From the parking area go back to the main road and turn left. This is Nebraska Valley Road which parallels Miller Brook. In 2 miles it turns to dirt. Continue climbing gradually to Mansfield Lake, passing Old County Road on your right. (You will return to this road after a brief visit to Mansfield Lake and the Mount Mansfield Trout Club.)

Just before you reach the lake is a spring where you can fill your water bottle with fresh mountain water that comes out of a pipe (tested frequently by the Vermont Department of Health). After checking out the scenery at Mansfield Lake and the Trout Club's interesting log building, return to Old County Road, now on your left.

Take Old County Road, which eventually turns from a dirt road into a jeep trail and then to single-track. The single-track can be quite tricky, especially when wet, but it's completely rideable from bottom to top. Expert riders will enjoy this challenging section.

After about a mile of single-track, you will come to the Trapp Family Lodge Cross-Country Ski Center trail network. Be sure to stay on Old County Road because all other ski trails are on private land. You will know you are on Trapp property when you see the large trail map and trail signs on your left. Continue going straight, still climbing on Old County Road. The trail levels out as you ride through "The Narrows," as it is known by local skiers. At the far end of The Narrows, the trail drops off steeply and descends through a rocky section. Then the pitch becomes less dramatic and eventually you arrive at a well-marked cable suspended across the trail — bear left onto a dirt road, Luce Hill Road, and continue descending until you come to Trapp Hill Road for a total of 9 miles.

Turn right onto paved Trapp Hill Road. Climb to the Trapp Family Lodge Resort. On your left is the Tea Room, open daily for light fare, and on your right is the lodge, restaurant, and gift shop. Across from the gift shop are greenhouses and gardens. As you begin to descend, the road turns to dirt. Look to the right and you will see a stage where outdoor concerts are held. Shortly after that, on the right, look for the herd of Scottish Highland cattle. They are really cute, for a bunch of cows. Continue descending, steeply at times, until you come to a paved road. Turn right and almost immediately you will be back at Cotton Brook Road and your starting point. If you are hungry after all this riding, the Moscow general store has great sandwiches!

RIDE 48 · Mount Mansfield

AT A GLANCE

VT

Length/configuration: 19-mile loop

Aerobic difficulty: Very strenuous

Technical difficulty: 50% trail riding on cross-country ski trails, logging roads, and jeep trails

Overall rating: Difficult

Scenery: Deeply wooded trails, views of Mount Mansfield, and a cruise on the scenic Mountain Road

Special comments: A challenging tour of Stowe's finest cross-country ski areas—Trapp Family Lodge and the Mount Mansfield Resort Cross-Country Center

The first half of this ride takes you through the Trapp Family Lodge Cross-Country Ski Center on two Class 4 roads: Old County Road and Haul Road. The Haul Road takes you to Stowe Mountain Resort Cross-Country Center ski trails at Mount Mansfield, making the ride a lengthy tour of Stowe's foremost Nordic ski areas. These trails are favorites of local bikers for several sections of demanding single-track, both uphill and downhill. Most of the riding is done in dense woods; a better part of the second loop is in the Mount Mansfield State Forest on the Ranch Camp and Burt trails. Both trails were built in the 1920s by the U.S. Army Corp of Engineers, and in recent years were revamped for use by the Stowe Mountain Cross-Country Center.

General location: Nebraska Valley, where the ride starts, is 4 miles northwest of Stowe.

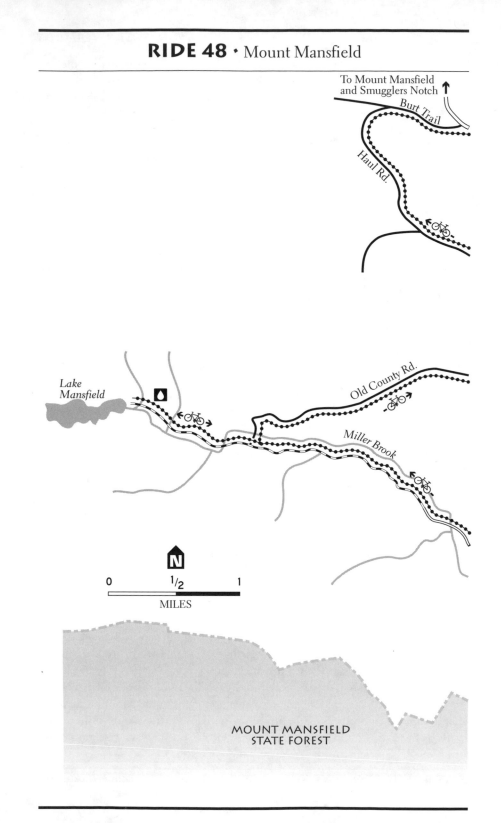

To Mount Mansfield
and Smugglers Notch

Burt Trail

Haul Rd.

Lake
Mansfield

Old County Rd.

Miller Brook

N

0   1/2   1

MILES

MOUNT MANSFIELD
STATE FOREST

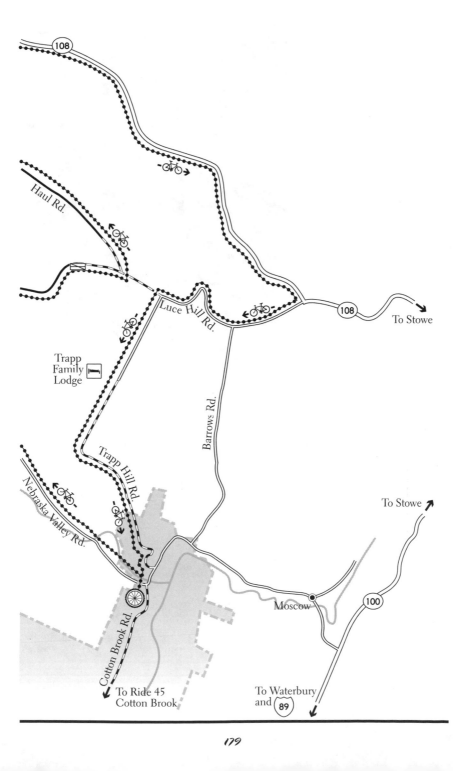

108

Haul Rd.

Luce Hill Rd.

108

To Stowe

Trapp
Family
Lodge

Barrows Rd.

Trapp Hill Rd.

Nebraska Valley Rd.

To Stowe

Moscow

100

Cotton Brook Rd.

To Ride 45
Cotton Brook

To Waterbury
and 89

With views of Mount Mansfield ahead, this steep descent on Ranch Camp connects the Trapp Family Lodge cross-country ski trails to the Mount Mansfield Resort cross-country ski trails.

Elevation change: 1,000´ of climbing with a steep, technical 1-mile section of single-track on Old County Road. Then a rocky 400´ descent drops you quickly to Luce Hill Road. You gain that 400´ right back on the Haul Road, a cross-country ski trail. A 1,000´ descent on Ranch Camp and Burt ski trails brings you to VT 108 and 4 miles of gentle downhill on pavement. You then climb 400´ up Luce Hill Road to the Trapp Family Lodge where the road turns to dirt and descends steadily for 1.5 miles to the finish.

Season: The best riding is from late June through October, but if it's a dry season, the conditions could be favorable in May. Snow is possible at the higher elevations in May and early October.

Services: All services are available in Stowe. Two bike shops, The Mountain Bike Shop (802-253-7919) and Stowe Action Outfitters (802-253-7975), are both on the Mountain Road (VT 108) in Stowe. There is camping at Smugglers Notch State Park, 8 miles north of Stowe on VT 108 near Mount Mansfield Ski Resort (802-253-4014).

Hazards: The terrain is very rocky at times, making descents very tricky. There is the possibility of logging operations on Old County Road, Haul Road, and the very bottom of the Burt Trail. Often signs are posted warning bikers of logging operations. Watch out for bottomless holes caused by spring runoff, and keep your eyes open for moose.

Rescue index: Don't ride these trails alone. There are times when you will be several miles from civilization and help. It's a long way out, and it could be several hours, or even days, before another rider came along and found you. If you decide to ride alone, inform a friend of your plans. A first-aid kit is a good idea.

Land status: Class 4 roads, logging roads, cross-country ski trails, and some paved sections.

Maps: A combination of maps will give you the complete picture. Two USGS 7.5 minute quads, Stowe and Bolton, show Old County Road as a trail, the Haul Road as prematurely ending, and Ranch Camp as nonexistent. Northern Cartographic's atlas is pretty good, but it named Old County Road as Meisler Road (all signs call it Old County Road). Individual maps of the Trapp and Stowe Mountain Cross-Country Ski Centers will fill in the missing gaps. All maps can be found at assorted shops in Stowe. Trapp's gift shop also has a good selection of local maps.

Finding the trail: Take Exit 10 off Interstate 89; go north for 8 miles on VT 100. Turn left, following signs for the town of Moscow. Go through Moscow (don't blink) and continue for 1.5 miles past Barrows Road and Trapp Hill Road, both on your right. Immediately after Trapp Hill Road, the main road bears sharply right while Cotton Brook Road, a dirt road, lies straight ahead. Take Cotton Brook Road for 100 yards and park in the parking area on the right. This is where the rides begin and end.

Source of additional information: The staff at the Mountain Bike Shop on the Mountain Road (VT 108) can answer all your questions (802-253-7919). They lead guided tours in the Stowe area by appointment and they host group mountain bike rides on local trails every Tuesday evening from May through October. They also have a good selection of maps.

Notes on the trail: From the parking area go back to the main road and turn left. This is Nebraska Valley Road which parallels Miller Brook. In 2 miles it turns to dirt. Continue climbing gradually to Mansfield Lake, passing Old County Road on your right. (You will return to this road after a brief visit to the lake and the Mount Mansfield Trout Club.) Just before you reach the lake is a spring where you can fill your water bottle with fresh mountain water that comes out of a pipe and is frequently tested by the Vermont Department of Health.

After checking out the scenery at Mansfield Lake, return to Old County Road, now on your left. Take Old County Road, which eventually turns from a dirt road into a jeep trail and then to single-track. The single-track can be quite tricky, especially when wet, but it's completely rideable from bottom to top. Expert riders will enjoy this challenging section.

After about a mile of single-track, you will come to the Trapp Family Lodge Cross-Country Ski Center trail network. Be sure to stay on Old County Road because all other ski trails are on private land. You will know you are on Trapp property when you see the large trail map and trail signs on your left. Continue going straight, still climbing on Old County Road. The trail levels out as you ride through "The Narrows," as it is known by local skiers. At the far end of The Narrows, the trail drops off steeply and descends through a rocky section. Then the pitch becomes less dramatic and eventually you arrive at a well-marked cable suspended across the trail — bear left onto a dirt road, Luce Hill Road, and continue descending.

Soon you will see a brown house with turquoise trim on your right, and a brown house with blue trim on your left. Just before the house with the blue trim, turn left onto what looks like an old logging road. This is the Haul Road, so named because it was once used by logging operations to haul logs out to the main road. The Haul Road is delightful riding, even as it climbs steeply up "The Chute," another section named by local skiers. Above The Chute, the trail becomes level. You will pass Adams' Camp ski trail on your right and Oslo and Bobcat ski trails on your left. *Reminder:* It is illegal to ride on these trails, and if you are caught you will be fined.

In 2 miles a cable blocks the Haul Road to further travel. Turn right onto Ranch Camp Trail at the signs for the Mansfield Touring Center. After a flat section and a short, steep climb, you will begin a very long descent that is fairly rugged at times, ending at a major trail intersection. Turn right onto Burt Trail, a well-maintained jeep road. Continue descending (to your left is the majority of the Stowe Mountain Cross-Country Center's trail network).

The Burt Trail will bounce you all the way down to VT 108 (a.k.a. the Mountain Road) to the 14-mile mark in the ride. Turn right onto pavement. You now have a choice of riding the next 3.5 miles on VT 108 or on the Stowe Rec Path. The Rec Path is quite entertaining, but there are many moving obstacles — people of all shapes and sizes walking, in-line skating, running, rollerskiing, cycling, and pushing baby strollers. If you want to make time, stick to the highway. After 3.5 miles, turn right onto Luce Hill Road. If you choose the Rec Path, immediately after turning onto VT 108 from the Burt Trail, turn right onto Brook Road. Just before the covered bridge, turn left into a small parking area and hop onto the Rec Path. Wind your way through the obstacles and across several narrow, wooden bridges. Keep your eyes open for a large parking area on your right called Chase Park, which has a brown post-and-rail fence around the perimeter. Exit the Rec Path through the parking area and turn right at the stop sign onto Luce Hill Road.

Follow Luce Hill Road until you come to Trapp Hill Road and turn left. Climb to the Trapp Family Lodge Resort. On your left is the Tea Room, open daily for light fare, and on your right is the lodge, restaurant, and gift shop. Across from the gift shop are greenhouses and gardens. As you begin to descend, the road turns to dirt. Look to the right and you will see a stage where outdoor concerts are held. Shortly after that, on the right, look for the herd of Scottish Highland cattle. Continue descending, steeply at times, until you come to a paved road. Turn right and almost immediately you will be back at Cotton Brook Road and your starting point, for a total of 21 miles. If you are hungry after all this riding, the Moscow general store has great sandwiches!

Note: The second half of this tour can be done as a separate ride by itself. Park at Chase Park on the Stowe Rec Path at the junction of Luce Hill and the Mountain Roads. Ride up Luce Hill Road and turn right onto the Haul Road at the brown house with blue trim. Proceed as above for a total of 12 miles.

RIDE 49 · Chester A. Arthur Memorial Ride

AT A GLANCE

Length/configuration: 18.5-mile loop

Aerobic difficulty: Moderate

Technical difficulty: Easy

VT

Overall rating: Advanced intermediate

Scenery: Farmland of rural Vermont

Special comments: A challenging all–dirt road ride with a stop at a historic landmark

President Chester A. Arthur was born on October 5, 1829, in Fairfield, Vermont, the eldest of seven children and the son of a Baptist minister. He first served as vice president to James Garfield, the twentieth president of the United States. On September 20, 1881, subsequent to the assassination of Garfield, Arthur became the twenty-first president. His greatest achievement during his administration was to pass the Pendleton Civil Service Act, which took thousands of government jobs out of politics. He was not reelected and he died at his home in New York at the young age of 56.

This 18.5-mile dirt road ride takes you by the historic site where Arthur's family lived for much of his early childhood. On this location in 1953, a small, yellow replica of the Arthur house was reconstructed by the state of Vermont. The building currently houses an interpretive exhibit on Arthur's life and career. Nearby is the brick church where his father preached.

It has become an annual tradition for cycling friends of Chuck's Bikes in Morrisville to ride this loop in the spring, after the first mergansers have been spotted on nearby Lake Lamoille. It is a good early-season ride because it takes place primarily on dirt roads with minimal traffic, and in a rural atmosphere

RIDE 49 · Chester A. Arthur Memorial Ride

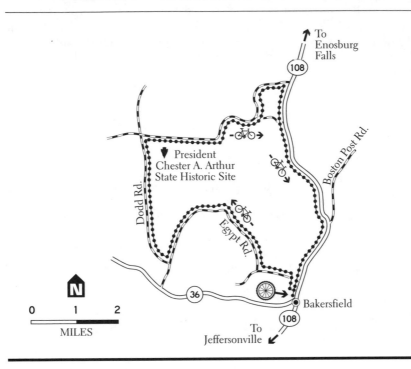

with good views and just a few short hills. Technically the ride is easy, but the distance (18.5 miles) and one steep hill make it an advanced intermediate ride.

General location: Bakersfield.

Elevation change: Nothing significant, just a few rollers.

Season: Anytime the roads are clear of snow.

Services: There is a general store in Bakersfield. Ten miles south on VT 108 is Jeffersonville, a small village that becomes a ski town to Smugglers Notch Ski Area during the winter months. In Jeffersonville you will find all services, including Foot of the Notch Bicycles (802-644-8182). Chuck's Bikes is located 10 miles east of Jeffersonville in downtown Morrisville (802-888-7642).

Hazards: Slow-moving farm equipment.

Rescue index: There are private homes within view throughout the ride.

Land status: Class 3 roads.

Maps: DeLorme's and Northern Cartographic's atlases both show the ride in detail.

Finding the trail: Bakersfield is located at the junction of VT 108 and VT 36, 10 miles north of Jeffersonville and 15 miles east of St. Albans. The ride begins at the village green.

An 18.5-mile, all–dirt road ride takes bikers past this replica of the Chester A. Arthur homestead, built in memory of Chester A. Arthur, twenty-first president of the United States.

Source of additional information: In Morrisville, the staff at Chuck's Bikes, including Chuck himself, are familiar with the details of this ride (802-888-7642).

Notes on the trail: From the village green in Bakersfield, begin riding north on VT 108. Just after the general store, take the second left onto a paved road, heading for a cemetery. The road bears right at the cemetery and turns to dirt. Go left at the **T**-intersection. About a mile farther, take the only right, Egypt Road, just after a brick house.

At 3.5 miles you come to a major dirt road intersection: bear left, keeping the Sheridan farm barn to your right. This next stretch of dirt road affords direct views of Mount Mansfield from an unusual angle to the south.

Just after the 5-mile mark, take the hairpin right turn onto Dodd Road, riding toward a blue garage. This is rural Vermont at its finest, and you will most likely see cows, farmers, and farm equipment on the road. Continue on this dirt road, climb a short steep hill, and come to a 4-way intersection with signs for the Chester A. Arthur State Historic Site. Turn right and soon you will come to the small yellow house built on the site where Arthur and his family lived in the 1830s. This is the halfway point of the ride.

Continue on the dirt road, pass through a beaver dam area, and descend quickly to paved VT 108 (13 miles). Turn right and cruise for 5.5 miles on flat pavement back to the start for a total of 18.5 miles.

RIDE 50 · Highway 61

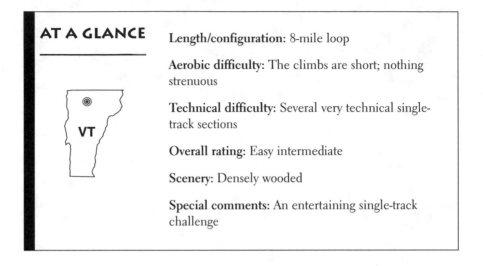

AT A GLANCE

VT

Length/configuration: 8-mile loop

Aerobic difficulty: The climbs are short; nothing strenuous

Technical difficulty: Several very technical single-track sections

Overall rating: Easy intermediate

Scenery: Densely wooded

Special comments: An entertaining single-track challenge

I didn't realize what I was getting into when I made arrangements to tag along on a local's group ride one Sunday morning in Montgomery Center. A bunch of rad dudes with fancy bikes and high testosterone levels showed up, and there I was, the only woman on the ride. I don't normally enjoy riding under such conditions, but I decided to make the best of it for the sake of including the ride in this book, and I'm glad I did. I had a great time.

The most interesting part of Highway 61 is the beginning while you are riding alongside Trout Brook. The trail was once used by logging companies to move logs downstream. It is easy single- and double-track riding with a few bridge crossings and short technical sections. Several optional side trails loop out to the river and back—if you look closely you will see faint single-track trails branching off to the left. According to one of the more gnarly dudes with whom I was riding, no one has successfully negotiated any of these side trails without crashing. So there you have it. The challenge is made. If you dare, take it. I didn't, but that's only because I was carrying a camera . . .

The second half of the loop is on a dirt road, VT 58, a.k.a. Hazen's Notch Road. It will take you downhill all the way back to the start. Because there are no major climbs and the distance is only eight miles, I rate this an easy intermediate ride.

General location: Montgomery Center.

Elevation change: An initial short, steep climb.

Season: Mid-June through October.

Services: All services can be found in Montgomery Center, but the nearest bike shops are at least 20 miles away. Foot of the Notch Bicycles is in Jeffersonville

RIDE 50 · Highway 61

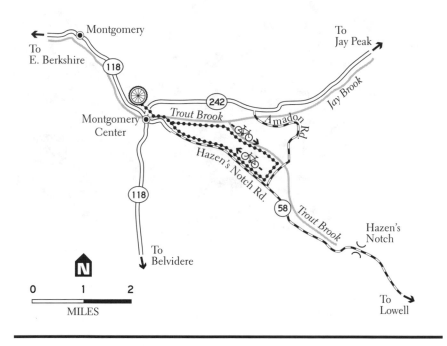

(802-644-8182); Chuck's Bikes is in downtown Morrisville (802-888-7642); and Village Bike Shop is in Derby (802-766-8009).

Hazards: Typical trail riding obstacles.

Rescue index: You are never more than a few miles from a telephone.

Land status: Class 3 roads, trails, and some pavement.

Maps: Stop in at Flick's video store in Montgomery Center and ask for Rob Barnard (802-326-4343). He organizes a lot of rides in the area and will give you the best map for this ride. Flick's opens daily at 11 A.M., including Sundays.

Finding the trail: Highway 61 begins in Montgomery Center at Flick's video store on Main Street (VT 118). You can park in their side lot.

Source of additional information: Rob Barnard, at Flick's video store, is the source for riding information in the Montgomery area.

Notes on the trail: From Flick's, turn left onto VT 118 and ride through the center of town and bear right, staying on VT 118. Immediately turn left onto VT 58 (Hazen's Notch Road). Climb steeply and steadily for .5 mile on pavement. Just past Reagon Road, turn left through an open, grassy area and ride across the field to the far side. Look for VAST snowmobile signs and veer slightly right onto

Dudes on bikes! Highway 61 will challenge most testosterone-driven riders and amuse the rest.

a trail. You are now on Highway 61, a double-track trail that follows Trout River and Wade Brook.

At about the 3.5-mile mark you will arrive at a dirt road, Amadon Road. Go left and climb briefly. At the next **T**-intersection, look to the left for a single-track trail. Cross over the culvert, dip left into an opening in the brush, and look to the right for the trail that winds and curves and takes you back to Highway 61. When you get there, go left and retrace your steps back to Amadon Road.

Turn right on Amadon Road, cross over Wade Brook, and ride to VT 58. Turn right and cruise downhill back to Montgomery Center for a total of 8 miles.

RIDE 51 · Montgomery Covered Bridges

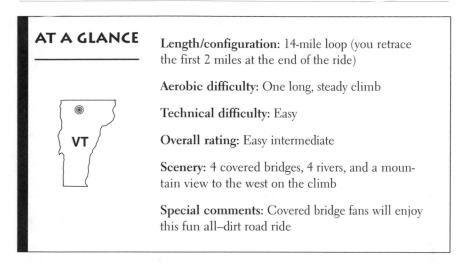

AT A GLANCE

Length/configuration: 14-mile loop (you retrace the first 2 miles at the end of the ride)

Aerobic difficulty: One long, steady climb

Technical difficulty: Easy

Overall rating: Easy intermediate

Scenery: 4 covered bridges, 4 rivers, and a mountain view to the west on the climb

Special comments: Covered bridge fans will enjoy this fun all–dirt road ride

If you enjoy riding through covered bridges, you will love this ride that begins and ends in the sleepy town of Montgomery. It features four covered bridges built in the late 1800s. Two of the bridges span Trout Brook, one crosses Black River, and one crosses West Hill Brook. The loop is 14 miles, mostly on dirt roads in a rural area, with private houses and farms throughout the route. There is one substantial climb with views of the Cold Hollow Mountains to the west, but there is no trail riding, so I rate it an easy intermediate ride.

General location: Montgomery.

Elevation change: One 700´ climb on West Hill Road.

Season: Anytime, but May through October is best.

Services: All services can be found in Montgomery Center, but the nearest bike shops are at least 20 miles away. Foot of the Notch Bicycles is in Jeffersonville (802-644-8182); Chuck's Bikes is in downtown Morrisville (802-888-7642); and Village Bike Shop is in Derby (802-766-8009).

Hazards: Occasional cars travel the dirt roads; farm equipment moves at slow speeds.

Rescue index: You are never more than a few miles from a telephone.

Land status: Class 3 roads and some pavement.

Maps: DeLorme's and Northern Cartographic's atlases both show the area in detail.

Finding the trail: Begin at Flick's video store on Main Street in Montgomery Center (VT 118). You can park in their side lot. Flick's opens daily at 11 A.M., including Sundays.

RIDE 51 · Montgomery Covered Bridges

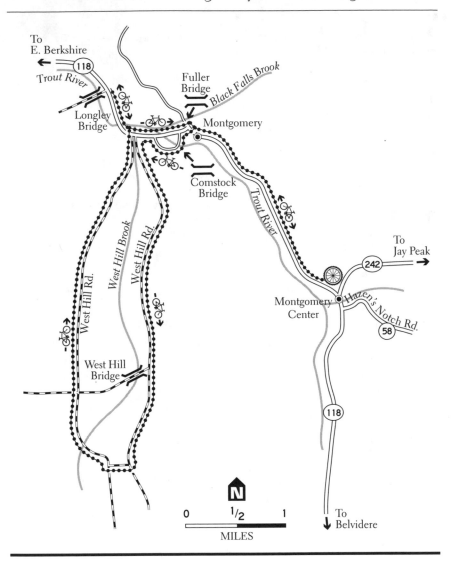

Source of additional information: Stop at Flick's and ask for Rob Barnard (802-326-4343). He organizes a lot of rides in the area and will be happy to give you advice.

Notes on the trail: From Flick's, go right on VT 118. Ride almost 2.5 miles on pavement to Montgomery. Just past the village green where VT 118 bends sharply to the right, go straight onto Comstock Road, keeping the IGS store on your left. Ride through Comstock Covered Bridge, a 63-foot lattice-type bridge,

The Comstock Covered Bridge–one of four covered bridges on the Montgomery Covered Bridges ride.

built in 1883, that spans the Trout River. Continue ahead, return to VT 118, and turn left. Immediately turn left onto West Hill Road, a gravel Class 3 road.

Climb steadily for 1 mile. Look for a freshwater spring on your left. Continue climbing and pass Creamery Bridge Road on your right. From there it is a few hundred yards down to the West Hill Bridge.

Continue on West Hill Road. At the junction where a jeep trail continues straight, turn right on the gravel road. Soon you will come to another intersection. Turn right again and begin descending. You will pass the other end of Creamery Bridge Road on your right. Stay straight and eventually the descent turns to pavement. Turn left onto VT 118 and go about .5 mile to Longley Bridge Road. Turn left to see Longley Bridge, a town lattice structure built in 1863. Longley Bridge is 85 feet long and spans the Trout River.

Retrace your steps back to Montgomery on VT 118. At the village green in Montgomery, turn left to see Fuller Bridge, also a town lattice structure, 50 feet long. Built in 1890, it spans Black Falls Brook.

From Montgomery it is 2.5 miles back to Montgomery Center on VT 118, for a total of 14 miles.

RIDE 52 · Jay Peak's Northway

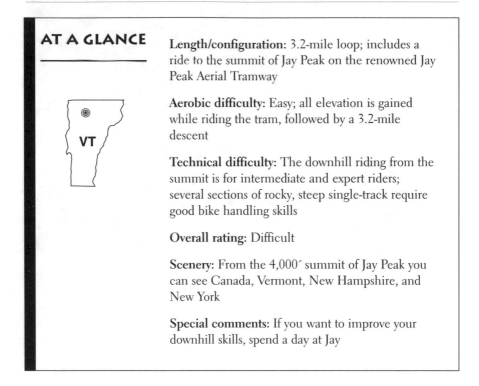

AT A GLANCE

Length/configuration: 3.2-mile loop; includes a ride to the summit of Jay Peak on the renowned Jay Peak Aerial Tramway

Aerobic difficulty: Easy; all elevation is gained while riding the tram, followed by a 3.2-mile descent

Technical difficulty: The downhill riding from the summit is for intermediate and expert riders; several sections of rocky, steep single-track require good bike handling skills

Overall rating: Difficult

Scenery: From the 4,000′ summit of Jay Peak you can see Canada, Vermont, New Hampshire, and New York

Special comments: If you want to improve your downhill skills, spend a day at Jay

Jay Peak Resort is Vermont's northernmost downhill ski area. During the summer, the Jay Peak Aerial Tramway transports experienced mountain bikers to the 4,000-foot summit with its spectacular views of three states and Canada. Various routes descend the 2,150-foot vertical drop, including the 3.2-mile Northway described below. No biking is allowed on Vermont's Long Trail, a hiking trail that extends from Massachusetts to Canada. It passes over the summit of Jay Peak at the site where mountain bikers unload from the tram. Beginners can ride on the gravel roads and cross-country ski trails at the base area, while really rugged riders can skip the tram and ride their bikes to the summit on the maintenance roads. After riding, bikers are welcome to cool off in Jay Peak's Junior Olympic–size pool.

The 3.2-mile Northway begins with a 10-minute ride on the Aerial Tramway to the summit (tram ride not included in mileage). From the summit, the route drops off the back side on Trail 9, Northway, winds around Jay Peak, and traverses the front face of the mountain. On the way down there are several steep, rocky drops that are technically challenging. Soon the route mellows out on Trail 7, Kitzbuehel, which takes you to the base of the Jet Triple Chair. A short climb on a work road brings you to Trail 17, Queens Highway, and your final

RIDE 52 • Jay Peak's Northway

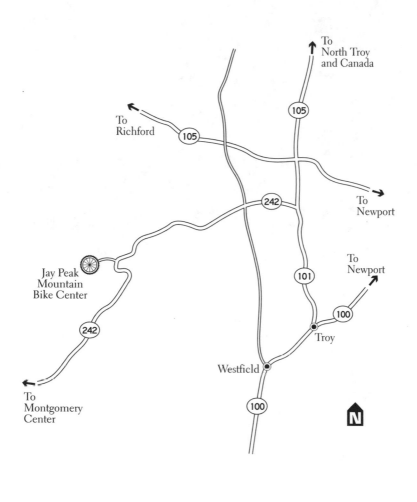

To
North Troy
and Canada

105

To
Richford 105

242

To
Newport

To
Newport

Jay Peak
Mountain
Bike Center

101

242

100

Troy

Westfield

To
Montgomery
Center

100

N

descent to the base area where you started. The tram runs every 30 minutes, the tram ride to the summit takes 10 minutes, the average descent is 20 minutes, and the tram is open from 10 A.M. to 4 P.M., making 14 top-to-bottom runs possible in one day.

A limited selection of mountain bikes are available for rent at the low-key Mountain Bike Center, which offers two- and four-hour guided tours. An all-day trail fee is $5; a single tram ride is $5; and an all-day trail fee with unlimited tram rides plus use of the pool is $19. Accommodations, food, and

From the 4,000-foot summit of Jay Peak, it's all downhill to the bottom.

beverages are conveniently located on site. Jay Peak is open daily from 10 A.M. to 4 P.M. from June through Labor Day weekend, and on weekends after Labor Day (weather permitting).

General location: Jay Peak Resort.

Elevation change: About 2,150´ of elevation are gained riding in the Aerial Tram. From the summit it is all downhill to the start.

Season: Mid-June through mid-October. Jay Peak is notoriously wet, so expect muddy conditions, especially on the cross-country ski trails at the bottom of the mountain.

Services: All services are located at the base area. Hotel Jay has a restaurant and accommodations; Vesuvio Pizza, located directly under the tram loading zone, makes a pretty good pizza and has a satisfactory selection of deli items. There is a modest bike shop (rentals and repairs, no sales) at the base area where you purchase your trail and tram pass. The Village Bike Shop (802-766-8009) is located about 15 miles away in Derby.

Hazards: The work roads have waterbars. You may encounter a maintenance vehicle while descending.

Rescue index: Jay Peak Resort encourages mountain bikers to ride in pairs: if one rider needs assistance, the other can ride to the bottom for help. Several staff members are EMT certified.

Land status: The trails are all on land owned and operated by the Jay Peak Resort.

Maps: The best map is the one produced by the Jay Peak Mountain Bike Center. It is free and can be found at the center and at Hotel Jay. The trails are signed with orange discs and are easy to follow.

Finding the trail: From the town of Jay (junctions VT 100 and VT 242), go west on VT 242 for 4 miles, climbing steadily up Jay Pass. Turn right at the sign for Hotel Jay and Jay Peak Ski Area. At the **T**-intersection turn right, following signs for the Aerial Tram. Follow this road to the end and park in the parking lot for Hotel Jay. The Mountain Bike Center is located in the tiny, round kiosk building behind Hotel Jay. This is where you purchase your trail pass and pick up a trail map. The Aerial Tram is located just to the right of Hotel Jay.

Sources of additional information: Call (802) 988-2611 for any information about mountain bike riding at Jay Peak. Suggested reading: *Mountain Biking the Ski Resorts of the Northeast* by Robert Immler (Woodstock: Countryman Press).

Notes on the trail: After purchasing your trail and tram passes, walk your bike over to the tram. Climb a double flight of steps to the tram loading area. You can take your bike right into the tram with you. The views during the tram ride are quite good and you can see some of the trails on which you will be descending.

At the summit, walk your bike off the tram and down the exit ramp. Ride downhill to the left, and immediately take the hairpin right onto Trail 9, Northway, on the backside of Jay Peak. Northway gradually wraps around to the front of the mountain, where you will pass under the tram. Keep your speed under control, as a single-track path snakes across Northway trail. Several sheets of plywood span waterbars and wet areas. Descend to Trail 11, Angle's Wiggle, a hairpin left turn. Take this steep pitch to Trail 7, Lower Kitzbuehel, which is not as steep as the upper half of the mountain. Follow this to the bottom of the Jet Triple Chair. With the chair to your right, take a hard left onto a gravel work road, climbing steadily for a few hundred yards. At the top of the climb, turn right onto Trail 17, Queen's Highway, a gravelly ski trail that gradually descends to the tram where you started.

You should do this ride at least twice. The first time is a practice run to familiarize you with the route. The second time is much easier, more enjoyable, and as a result, significantly faster.

RIDE 53 · Missisquoi Valley Rail Trail

AT A GLANCE

Length/configuration: 18-mile out-and-back (9 miles each way)

Aerobic difficulty: Flat and easy on an abandoned railroad bed

Technical difficulty: A smooth surface of crushed limestone

Overall rating: Easy

Scenery: Open vistas, rural landscapes, farmland

Special comments: This rail trail was once the Central Vermont railroad bed that has now been upgraded to a smooth surface and is an excellent place for families and beginners; closed to motor vehicles; you can turn around at any point along the way

The Missisquoi Valley Rail Trail was once the Richford Branch of the Central Vermont railroad (CV). It served as the connection between the CV, which ran from Connecticut to Canada along the western border of Vermont, and the Canadian Pacific Railroad (CPR), in Sutton, Quebec. CPR had two major customers in Vermont: Blue Seal Feed and the dairy industry. These products provided steady boxcar freight until the 1960s when 18-wheel trucks brought stiff competition into the transportation industry. Despite the decline in business, the CV continued to run until 1984 when a major derailment occurred in Sheldon Junction, the turnaround point for this ride. It was deemed unprofitable to repair the damage and the railroad bed was abandoned. The rails were pulled out in 1990, and in 1995 the state of Vermont took over the management of the railroad bed as a multiuse recreation trail.

The entire length of the Missisquoi Valley Rail Trail, from St. Albans to Richford, is 24.7 miles one way. However, the good riding surface, crushed limestone, extends for only 9 miles from St. Albans to Sheldon Junction. Beyond that, from Sheldon Junction to Richford, is still the original ballast, which is not much fun to ride on. However, if everything goes according to plan, the rest of the railroad bed will be upgraded to crushed limestone by June, 1998.

This 18-mile out-and-back ride (9 miles each way) makes use of the improved section from St. Albans to Sheldon Junction. Because it was originally designed

RIDE 53 · Missisquoi Valley Rail Trail

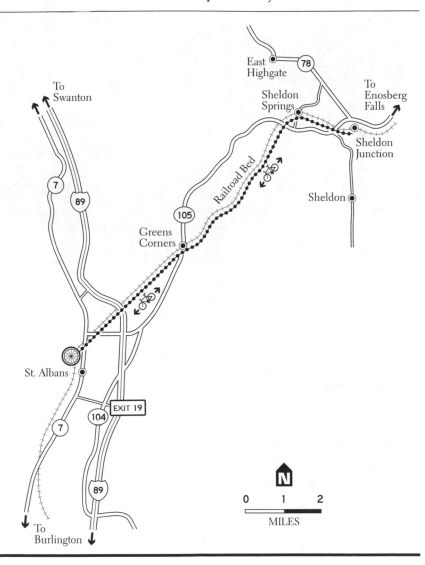

as a railroad bed, the terrain is as flat as anything can possibly be in Vermont. Closed to motor vehicles, the trail is open to walkers, runners, bikers, horseback riders, snowmobilers, and cross-country skiers. It traverses open farmland and provides views of vistas, residential neighborhoods, old buildings, and stream crossings. A few road crossings, including VT 105, can be heavy with traffic during morning and evening commuter times and on Saturdays. Eventually you meet up with the Missisquoi River in Sheldon Junction, the turnaround point of

Railroad ties were pulled up and replaced with crushed limestone to give this abandoned railroad bed in the Missisquoi Valley an ultra-smooth finish.

the ride. The scenery is lovely and will give you a true sense of rural northern Vermont lifestyles.

Families or beginners looking for a shorter ride can turn around at any point along the way.

General location: St. Albans.

Elevation change: None.

Season: Anytime there is no snow—most likely May through November.

Services: All services can be found in St. Albans. North Star Cyclery is on South Main Street (802) 524-9678.

Hazards: The railroad bed has several street crossings. Watch for fast-moving vehicles, especially on VT 105 where the speed limit is 50 mph.

Rescue index: You are never more than .5 mile from a private residence.

Land status: Abandoned railroad bed now managed by the Franklin/Grand Isle Regional Planning and Development Commission.

Maps: The abandoned CV railroad bed is shown on both DeLorme's and Northern Cartographic's atlases.

Finding the trail: This ride begins at the western terminus of the CV railroad bed in St. Albans. Take Interstate 89 to Exit 20. At the end of the ramp go south on VT 7 to the intersection of VT 5. Go one more block and park where appropriate. The trail starts on the east side of VT 7, opposite the railroad tracks that still exist on the other side of VT 7. The recreation trail is clearly marked.

Sources of additional information: The abandoned CV railroad bed is under the jurisdiction of the Franklin/Grand Isle Regional Planning and Development Commission, 140 South Main Street, St. Albans, VT 05478-1850; (802) 524-5958. Suggested reading: *Great Rail-Trails of the Northeast* (Amherst: New England Cartographics).

Notes on the trail: Begin on VT 7 at the western terminus, which is clearly marked. You will be riding northeast. Pass under I-89 and ride to Greens Corners where you cross VT 105. Take care when crossing this busy highway. Continue riding through farmland, skirting along a dirt road to your right. Cross the dirt road at the Sheldon town line. The railroad bed stays parallel to the dirt road, which you will eventually cross one more time.

In Sheldon Springs, you will arrive again at VT 105. This is a good place for families and beginners to turn around. You can get a cold drink by turning right on VT 105 and riding .5 mile to the convenience store on the right.

Or, continue on the trail, passing through the tiny town of Sheldon Springs. At this point you are riding north of, and parallel to, VT 105. At 9 miles you come to the junction of VT 105 on the outskirts of Sheldon Junction where the improved section of the railroad bed ends. You will know you are at the end because the bridge where trains used to cross the Missisquoi River is washed out. If you want to ride into Sheldon Junction, turn left onto VT 105, cross the 105 bridge and ride into town. There is not much in Sheldon Junction, but you can find refreshments at the general store.

Retrace your steps back to St. Albans for a total of 18 easy miles of riding.

NORTHEAST KINGDOM

Located in the northeastern corner of Vermont, the Northeast Kingdom is often touted as quintessential Vermont, with hilltop farms, deep lakes, white church steeples, gentle valleys, and sparsely populated towns. Compared with the rest of Vermont, it is relatively untouched and does not display the manicured appearance found in other regions of the state.

The Northeast Kingdom comprises Caledonia, Orleans, and Essex Counties. The northern extremity is defined by the Canadian border from west of North Troy to the Vermont/New Hampshire state line. The western edge is defined by the Lowell Mountain Range to the north, and Groton State Forest to the south. The Vermont/New Hampshire border defines the eastern edge, while the southern tip is bordered by VT 302.

Geographically the Northeast Kingdom covers approximately 20% of the state, yet its population of about 58,300 is only 10% of the state's population (562,758). Job opportunities are slim in this area of Vermont, which partly explains the low population, but its remote location, far from any metropolitan city, is the real reason for its lack of inhabitants.

Essex County is the most densely timbered county in Vermont, and at one time it was heavily logged. Occasional logging operations are still in business today, but not to the extent of past years. Several trail networks comprise logging roads used by snowmobilers, cross-country skiers, and mountain bikers. The heart of mountain biking in the Northeast Kingdom is the Burke Mountain area, about 30 miles north of St. Johnsbury. In this book, I have featured three rides that begin on Burke Mountain and make use of some of the old logging roads in that area.

Another hotbed for mountain bike riding is the Craftsbury area. Not as mountainous as the Burke Mountain area, Craftsbury is the home of the Craftsbury Outdoor Center which features single- and double-track trail riding on its cross-country ski trails. I have also featured three rides from the Craftsbury area.

Ride 57, Willoughby, and Ride 61, Groton State Forest, round out the sampling of mountain bike rides in the Northeast Kingdom.

CRAFTSBURY AREA

Three small and distinctly different towns make up the Craftsbury area: Craftsbury, East Craftsbury, and Craftsbury Common. All are named for Colonel Crafts of Massachusetts, who settled here with his family in the late 1700s. He constructed a saw and grist mill in what is now called the Mill Village, just north of Craftsbury Common. Craftsbury and East Craftsbury are nestled low in the valley, while Craftsbury Common, a picturesque village known for its abundance of white buildings trimmed with green shutters, sits proudly on a high meadow. Craftsbury Common is home to Craftsbury Academy and Sterling College, where students specialize in ecology and environmental studies.

A stone's throw to the north of Craftsbury Common is the Craftsbury Outdoor Center on Great Hosmer Pond. The center is a mecca for year-round outdoor activities, from cross-country skiing and winter orienteering to sculling, hiking, and mountain biking. The center's highlight is its extensive network of cross-country ski trails, some of which are available for mountain bike riding during the summer. For the more experienced riders, the center has developed several miles of single-track trails. For beginners, endless miles of dirt roads offer a myriad of riding possibilities. These roads are also excellent early- and late-season riding.

The Craftsbury Outdoor Center has overnight accommodations for 90, and serves hearty meals in its dining hall. The center offers guided mountain bike tours and has an extensive selection of printed maps and directions for anyone wishing to do self-guided tours. Gary Fisher mountain bikes are available for rent (with and without front suspension) and there is a modest trail fee if you want to ride on their single- and double-track trails.

I have put together a sampling of the types of riding you will find in the Craftsbury area: Race Course, Lords Creek, and Wild Branch. All three rides begin and end at the Craftsbury Outdoor Center, P.O. Box 31, Craftsbury Common, VT 05827 (800) 729-7751 or (802) 586-2514.

RIDE 54 · Race Course

AT A GLANCE

VT

Length/configuration: 4-mile loop

Aerobic difficulty: You need a good aerobic base to enjoy this loop

Technical difficulty: The single-track trails have natural obstacles such as logs, rocks, and steep pitches; the double-track trails are smoother because they are maintained for cross-country skiing, but they also have short, steep climbs

Overall rating: Advanced intermediate

Scenery: Densely wooded with occasional open fields

Special comments: Single-track at its finest

This 4-mile loop-de-loop of cross-country ski trails and single-track trails weaves around the Craftsbury Outdoor Center property. The route is well marked with mountain bike signs, and a map is available at the Outdoor Center office. The Race Course loop has challenging, short climbs and plenty of technical riding, but it isn't long, so I rate it advanced intermediate. During the Craftsbury Mountain Bike Race held every October, the expert-class racers ride four times around a slightly longer version of this loop, and the beginners travel it once.

Riding cross-country ski trails is a great way for a novice mountain biker to try trail riding. The trails are cleared for winter grooming so you won't encounter as many obstacles as you would on unmaintained backcountry trails. This loop also offers some challenging technical single-track away from the ski trails.

General location: The Craftsbury Outdoor Center, 1 mile north of Craftsbury Common.

Elevation change: There are a few short, strenuous climbs throughout the ride, but nothing sustained.

Season: Summer, when the trails are dry.

Services: All services are available at the Outdoor Center (800-729-7751 or 802-586-2514). The closest bike shop is Chuck's Bikes in Morrisville (802-888-7642).

Hazards: Typical single-track obstacles such as logs, deep holes, steep drops, and windfall.

RIDE 54 • Race Course

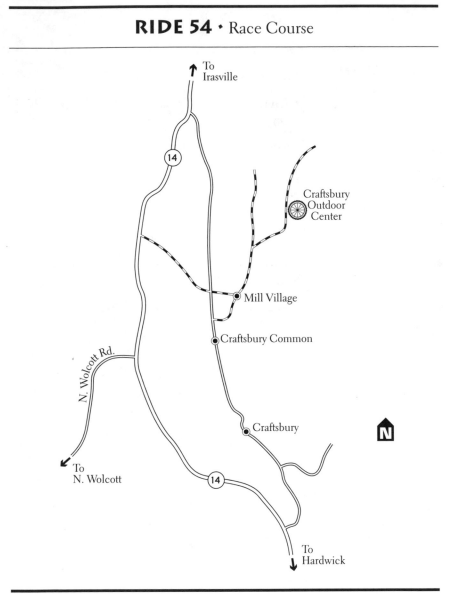

Rescue index: You are never more than 1 mile from the Outdoor Center offices and staff assistance. If you are alone, it would be wise to check in with the office preride and postride. The nearest rescue service is in Hardwick. Copley Hospital is in Morrisville.

Land status: Private property belonging to the Craftsbury Outdoor Center.

Maps: The dirt roads located in the vicinity of the Outdoor Center are indicated on DeLorme's and Northern Cartographic's atlases. A detailed map of the Race Course is available at the center.

Finding the trail: Craftsbury Common is located about 7 miles north of Hardwick, just to the east of VT 14. From the common, follow white signs for the Craftsbury Outdoor Center, located on a dirt road about 2 miles north of the common. You can park in the center's parking lot.

Source of additional information: The Craftsbury Outdoor Center is the best place for information on this ride, as well as information on other activities nearby (800-729-7751 or 802-586-2514).

Notes on the trail: The ride begins and ends in the meadow behind the bike-rental/trail-pass cabin and is well marked with white mountain bike rider signs. Follow the signs and you can't go wrong. Some turns come up quickly, so keep your eyes open and expect surprises along the way.

RIDE 55 · Lords Creek

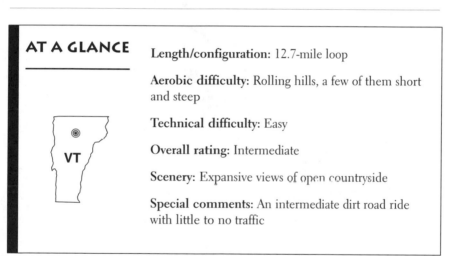

AT A GLANCE

Length/configuration: 12.7-mile loop

Aerobic difficulty: Rolling hills, a few of them short and steep

Technical difficulty: Easy

Overall rating: Intermediate

Scenery: Expansive views of open countryside

Special comments: An intermediate dirt road ride with little to no traffic

The first two miles of this 12.7-mile loop ride are on double-track cross-country ski trails at the Craftsbury Outdoor Center. The trails are maintained and smooth, but there are occasional steep pitches to climb and descend. The rest of the ride is on Class 3 and 4 roads and consists of all left turns. You can, of course, do the ride in reverse if you prefer right turns.

You will cross Lords Creek twice during the first half of the ride. You also will pass an old cemetery, several working farms, and three towns that consist of no more than intersecting roads, a house or two, and maybe a church. At some points you will be in dense forests and at other times you will have wide-open views. The terrain is endlessly rolling, but there are no major climbs, so I rate this as an intermediate ride.

RIDE 55 · Lords Creek

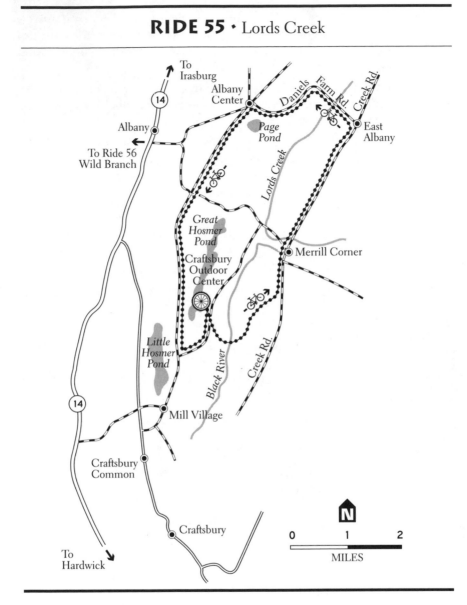

General location: The ride begins and ends at the Craftsbury Outdoor Center, 1 mile north of Craftsbury Common.

Elevation change: A few short, strenuous climbs throughout the ride.

Season: Summer, when the trails are dry, if you want to include the first 2 miles of trail riding; at all other times of the year you can skip the trail section by taking a dirt road to the 3-mile mark (a **Y**-intersection called Merrill Corner), and continue the ride from there.

A view of Craftsbury Common as you approach it from the south.

Services: All services are available at the Outdoor Center (800-729-7751 or 802-586-2514). The nearest bike shop is Chuck's Bikes in Morrisville (802-888-7642).

Hazards: Typical single-track obstacles, slow-moving farm equipment, and an occasional dog.

Rescue index: You are never too far from the Outdoor Center offices and staff assistance (800-729-7751 or 802-586-2514). If you are alone, it would be wise to check in with the office preride and postride. The nearest rescue service is in Hardwick. Copley Hospital is in Morrisville.

Land status: Private property belonging to the Craftsbury Outdoor Center, and Class 3 and 4 roads.

Maps: A detailed map with description is available at the center. Most of the ride is also shown on DeLorme's and Northern Cartographic's atlases.

Finding the trail: Craftsbury Common is located about 7 miles north of Hardwick, just to the east of VT 14. From the common, follow white signs for the Craftsbury Outdoor Center, located on a dirt road about 2 miles north of the common. You can park in the center's parking lot.

Source of additional information: The staff at the Craftsbury Outdoor Center can tell you anything you need to know about this area of Vermont (800-729-7751 or 802-586-2514).

Notes on the trail: The ride begins and ends at the Outdoor Center parking lot. Follow cross-country ski trail 13 down to a swamp and across a bog bridge over the Black River. Climb to an electric fence (don't worry, it's not turned on) and ride through the open section into a pasture. Ride to the far end of the pasture and turn left onto unpaved Creek Road, a Class 4 dirt road. Pass a cemetery on your left and continue straight past the right turn to South Albany. At 3 miles you will come to a **Y**-intersection. This is Merrill Corner. Bear right, pass over Lords Creek, and enjoy 2 miles of gentle, open terrain.

At the 4-way intersection in East Albany, turn left at the church onto Daniels Road. This road can be very rough, especially in the spring, if it hasn't been graded. Descend to Lords Creek and then climb a hill on a washed-out town road. At 6.2 miles the road bears left and remains rough.

After about 1.5 miles, you will come to Albany Center, where many roads converge. At the first 4-way intersection go left, then continue straight through the next two intersections. This is the area where you may encounter dogs. The next long, straight stretch of dirt road brings you to a 4-way intersection at Page Pond. Continue straight, keeping Page Pond on your left, and soon you will begin a half-mile descent. At 12.2 miles from the start, turn left onto Town Highway 12 (TH 12). Climb a half-mile hill and arrive back at your starting point for a total of 12.7 miles.

RIDE 56 · Wild Branch

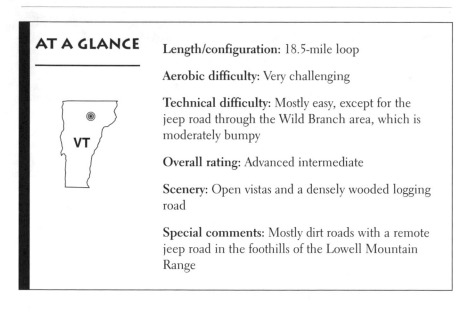

AT A GLANCE

Length/configuration: 18.5-mile loop

Aerobic difficulty: Very challenging

Technical difficulty: Mostly easy, except for the jeep road through the Wild Branch area, which is moderately bumpy

Overall rating: Advanced intermediate

Scenery: Open vistas and a densely wooded logging road

Special comments: Mostly dirt roads with a remote jeep road in the foothills of the Lowell Mountain Range

Rarely traveled dirt roads abound in the Northeast Kingdom, and this 18.5-mile loop ride makes the most of the ones in the vicinity of Craftsbury and Albany. At the halfway point you will climb into the foothills of the Lowell Mountain Range on a single-lane, unmaintained Class 4 road which passes through the remote Wild Branch Wildlife Management Area. Expect to see a variety of wildlife and a wide range of lifestyles on this ride.

RIDE 56 • Wild Branch

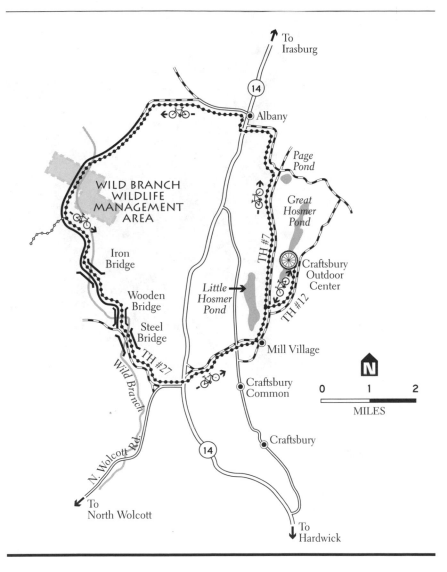

There is one long climb and many rollers, but technically the ride is easy. Because of the distance, I rate this as an intermediate dirt road ride.

General location: The ride begins and ends at the Craftsbury Outdoor Center, 1 mile north of Craftsbury Common.

Elevation change: There is a 200´ climb at the start and a 650´ climb at mile 5, plus lots of rollers.

Rural Vermont
plumbing.

Season: May through mid-November if there is no snow. Much of the section in the foothills of the Lowell Mountains is not plowed in the winter. I rode this loop in mid-May and had a great time.

Services: All services are available at the Outdoor Center. The nearest bike shop is Chuck's Bikes in Morrisville (802-888-7642).

Hazards: Possible logging operations to the west of Albany.

Rescue index: You are never far from a private telephone. The nearest rescue service is in Hardwick. Copley Hospital is in Morrisville.

Land status: Mostly maintained and unmaintained Class 3 and 4 roads, as well as a bit of paved highway.

Maps: A detailed map is available at the Craftsbury Outdoor Center. The dirt roads are shown in DeLorme's and Northern Cartographic's atlases, both of which are easily found throughout Vermont. The USGS 7.5 minute quad, Albany, shows most of the ride in detail.

Finding the trail: Craftsbury Common is located about 7 miles north of Hardwick and about 15 miles northeast of Morrisville, to the east of VT 14. From the common, follow white signs for the Craftsbury Outdoor Center, located on a dirt road about 2 miles to the north. You can park in the center's parking lot, where the ride begins.

Source of additional information: The Outdoor Center has information on the area (800-729-7751 or 802-586-2514).

Notes on the trail: The ride begins and ends at the Craftsbury Outdoor Center. From the center, ride downhill toward Little Hosmer Pond. At the **T**-intersection turn right. Begin a half-mile climb that takes you to a high plateau with good views. Ride to a 4-way intersection with Page Pond on your right. Go left, following signs for Albany. Descend steeply through a set of **S**-turns. When you reach a junction, bear left, crossing over an iron bridge.

Come to a paved highway (VT 14). You will see a sign for the Albany Town Clerk directly across the road. Turn right and pass by the Albany Mini Mart (open 7 days) and the Albany Library. Take the next left just after the town hall at Noble Associates. Begin climbing gradually and then more steeply. At 7 miles bear left at the fork, following the VAST trail signs. The road becomes very narrow and eventually turns into a single lane, which is where you will most likely encounter logging machinery. It is also where you are most likely to encounter a moose, or at least moose tracks.

Ride through an open meadow that, depending on the weather, may be very wet. Pass through the Wild Branch Wildlife Management Area, gradually descending until you come to an intersection. Bear left, still descending gradually on a maintained dirt road. Cross a wooden snowmobile bridge and a steel bridge. At the next **T**-intersection, turn left onto Town Highway 27. Here you will begin to see houses and motor vehicles.

At the Petrol King (open 7 days), bear left. Come to a paved road and turn left. Directly ahead of you, up on the hillside, is Craftsbury Common. Descend to paved VT 14 and turn left. Take the next dirt road to the right, following signs for Craftsbury Common. Cross the Black River and climb a steep hill. At the top is a 4-way intersection. Cross over the paved road and bear left onto the dirt road marked with white signs for the Craftsbury Outdoor Center.

Take the next right, still following the signs. Jog left, following the natural bend of the road as you descend into Mill Village. Take the next right onto TH 12 and begin climbing. Retrace the last half-mile back to the Craftsbury Outdoor Center for a total of 18.5 miles.

RIDE 57 · Willoughby

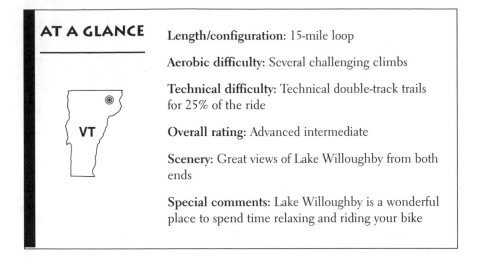

AT A GLANCE

Length/configuration: 15-mile loop

Aerobic difficulty: Several challenging climbs

Technical difficulty: Technical double-track trails for 25% of the ride

Overall rating: Advanced intermediate

Scenery: Great views of Lake Willoughby from both ends

Special comments: Lake Willoughby is a wonderful place to spend time relaxing and riding your bike

In the Northeast Kingdom, Lake Willoughby is the crowning jewel among a treaure chest of gems. It slices like a knife between Mount Hor (2,648 feet) and Mount Pisgah (2,741 feet), creating a dramatic backdrop from every point of view on this ride. Lake Willoughby is 5 miles long by barely a mile wide, and the deepest point is 308 feet. The water is very cold, which makes for good trout fishing and invigorating swimming. This 15-mile loop, which begins and ends at the south shore, takes you clockwise around the circumference of the lake on dirt roads, rugged jeep trails, and pavement.

It is unlikely you will see anyone else on the first part of the ride, which traverses old Civilian Conservation Corps (CCC) roads and jeep trails in the Willoughby State Forest. You will ride by Duck and Blake Ponds and several hiking trails, but the area gets minimal use by human beings. There are public beaches at the north and south ends of the lake, and great hiking and camping nearby.

This is a challenging ride, and you might find yourself walking in a few sections near Duck and Blake Ponds. Because it is only 15 miles long, I rate it as an advanced intermediate ride.

General location: 4 miles north of West Burke on VT 5A.

Elevation change: One initial 500´ climb.

Season: June through October, with July and August being the best swimming months. Expect a lot of mud on the state forest trails.

Services: All services can be found in West Burke and Westmore.

Hazards: Occasional windfall.

Rescue index: The farthest you will be from a telephone is 3 miles while you're in Willoughby State Forest.

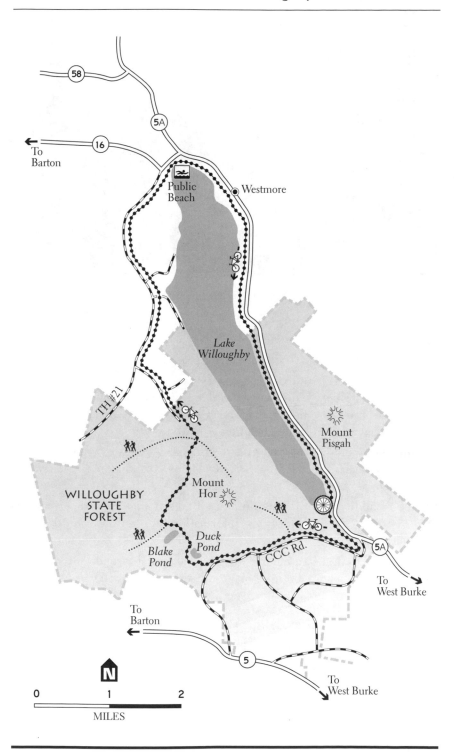

58

5A

16

To
Barton

Public
Beach

Westmore

Lake
Willoughby

TH #21

Mount
Pisgah

Mount
Hor

WILLOUGHBY
STATE
FOREST

Duck
Pond

Blake
Pond

CCC Rd.

5A

To
West Burke

To
Barton

5

To
West Burke

N

0   1   2

MILES

A view from the trail of Lake Willoughby and Mount Pisgah.

Land status: Willoughby State Forest roads, jeep trails, and some pavement.

Maps: Two USGS 7.5 minute quads, Westmore and Sutton, are useful. The Westmore Association Trails puts out a detailed map of trails in Willoughby State Forest. You can get a copy of the map at East Burke Sports Shop in East Burke, or at Northern Lights general store in Westmore.

Finding the trail: The ride begins at the public parking area at the south end of Lake Willoughby on VT 5A. There is additional parking in a lot on VT 5A just south of the beach.

Source of additional information: East Burke Sports Shop in East Burke (802-626-3215) is the place for information on trail use in the Lake Willoughby area.

Notes on the trail: Leave the parking area and go right (south) on VT 5A. In .5 mile, turn right onto a dirt road. Stay to the right of the small parking area and begin climbing on the CCC Road. At the fork, stay to the right and ride to a scenic overview of Lake Willoughby and Mount Pisgah.

At the summit of the climb, pass by a trailhead to Mount Hor. Descend for .5 mile and turn right onto a four-wheel-drive road. Rise and dip along this road for about 2 miles, then turn right onto an unmarked four-wheel-drive road (look for the remains of a gate and an orange surveyor's ribbon). Stay right and descend to Duck Pond.

Keeping the pond on your right, continue on the four-wheel-drive road through wet, rugged terrain for about .5 mile. Depending on how wet the season has been, you might have to walk several parts of this section. The road levels out and Blake Pond appears on your left. Just past the pond access, take the jeep trail on the right and begin climbing. This section is very rocky and wet, and you might find yourself walking most of it.

You will come to a wide-open area. Continue straight up an overgrown gravel road. The condition of the road improves the farther you ride. Descend steadily and come to a 4-way intersection; proceed straight through and continue until you reach an obviously well-traveled road. Turn right on this road, which is Town Highway 21. Stay on TH 21 until you come to a **T**-intersection. Turn right. Look for a llama farm on the left. Follow this road past the north end of Lake Willoughby and turn right onto paved VT 5A. Stay on VT 5A and cruise along the west side of Lake Willoughby for 5 miles, all the way back to the start. Finish your ride with a brisk dip in the lake.

BURKE MOUNTAIN AREA

For years, winter sports fans have been coming to East Burke to downhill ski at Burke Mountain or to cross-country ski at the Burke Mountain Cross-Country Center. More recently, mountain bikers have taken notice of this expansive, unspoiled region in the Northeast Kingdom. Several excellent rides have surfaced, making use of Civilian Conservation Corps (CCC) roads, jeep trails, logging roads, natural gas lines, and remote dirt roads.

Three excellent rides that begin on Burke Mountain are as diverse in their scenery as they are in their level of difficulty, although none is easy. The 18-mile Kirby Mountain, an advanced intermediate ride, is the easiest of the three. The 22-mile Victory Bog and the 40-mile Fred Mold Memorial Ride are both very difficult, with Fred Mold being the toughest—very difficult and very long. Although they start out the same, they are distinctly different. For clarity, I will describe them individually in this book.

All three rides begin by climbing the Burke Mountain access road to the CCC Road, a single-track trail that traverses Burke Mountain and then drops down its backside. The Kirby Mountain loop branches off for a climb over Kirby Mountain then heads back to the start. The Victory Bog and Fred Mold Memorial rides continue into Victory State Forest where they pick up the natural gas line. At Victory Road, the rides split again. The Victory Bog loop returns to the start, while the Fred Mold Memorial Ride takes you on dirt roads through the remote Victory Bog Wilderness Area to the towns of Gallup Mills and Victory. Eventually, this 40-miler joins up with the Kirby Mountain ride for the final climb over Kirby Mountain.

Much of the credit for the development of these three rides goes to the Kingdom Riders, a trails association affiliated with the East Burke Sports Shop. Kingdom Riders is making use of abandoned legal roads and trails for hundreds of miles of riding in the Northeast Kingdom. Maps of several rides are available at the East Burke Sports Shop (802-626-3215). All three rides described below begin and end at the shop, so be sure to stop in and say hello to co-owner John Worth, who rides these trails regularly.

RIDE 58 · Kirby Mountain

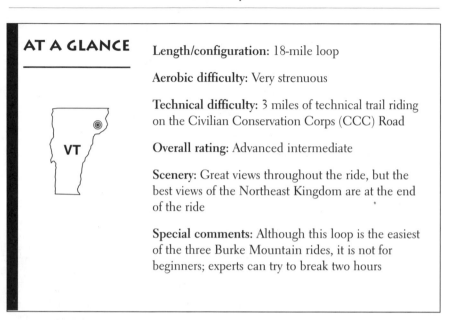

AT A GLANCE

Length/configuration: 18-mile loop

Aerobic difficulty: Very strenuous

Technical difficulty: 3 miles of technical trail riding on the Civilian Conservation Corps (CCC) Road

Overall rating: Advanced intermediate

Scenery: Great views throughout the ride, but the best views of the Northeast Kingdom are at the end of the ride

Special comments: Although this loop is the easiest of the three Burke Mountain rides, it is not for beginners; experts can try to break two hours

VT

This 18-mile loop is the easiest of the three Burke Mountain rides; nevertheless, it includes some challenging single-track and two big climbs with a total elevation gain of 3,240 feet. A great deal of the riding is in the woods where you have occasional glimpses of views through the trees. The most scenic views are of open farmland near the end of the ride on Town Highway 7, following the descent from Kirby Mountain.

Overall, this is an excellent ride for introducing intermediate riders to technical off-road terrain, and to the fine art of climbing. Take your time, and bring plenty of water and extra food. You will be glad you did!

General location: Burke Mountain in East Burke, roughly 10 miles north of St. Johnsbury on VT 114.

Elevation change: An initial 2,240′ climb up the Burke Mountain access road is followed by flat and downhill sections on the CCC Road. There is a second 1,000′ climb over Kirby Mountain on a narrow dirt road.

Season: June through mid-November is best since spring runoff can keep the CCC Road very wet. Expect snow at higher elevations in October and November.

RIDE 58 · Kirby Mountain

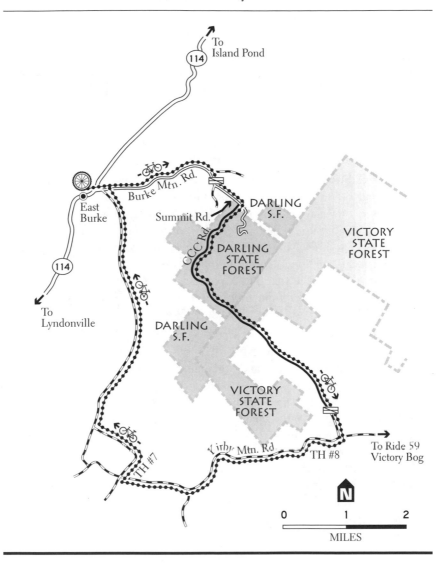

Services: All services are available in East Burke, where the ride begins and ends. Bailey's Country Store on VT 114 has a deli counter, home-baked goods, fresh produce, a wine cellar, and a candy counter. Upstairs is an interesting gift and clothing shop. All are contained within an old, post-and-beam structure, open in the center from floor to ceiling. No other services are available on the ride.

Hazards: Watch for fallen trees, deep potholes, and uneven bridges that drop off suddenly at both ends.

Rescue index: Don't ride this loop alone. The Northeast Kingdom is sparsely populated with private houses far and few between. There are several rugged sections on the CCC Road where you will be at least 3 miles from a phone.

Land status: Dirt roads, CCC roads, trails, and single-track.

Maps: Two USGS 7.5 minute quads, Gallup Mills and Burke Mountain, will give you a good sense of the remoteness of the ride. The dirt roads and the CCC Road are shown on Northern Cartographic's and DeLorme's atlases. East Burke Sports Shop has a good collection of its own handmade maps available free of charge (802-626-3215).

Finding the trail: Begin and end at East Burke Sports Shop, located on VT 114, directly across from Bailey's Country Store.

Sources of additional information: The East Burke Sports Shop staff are *the* source for all riding in the Burke Mountain area. They sell, repair, and rent bicycles, and they have a complete selection of maps (802-626-3215). The Mountain View Creamery Bed & Breakfast, once a dairy farm, sits high on a ridge overlooking Burke Mountain. It is still a working farm, and the owners are active with local trail committees. Mountain bike trails on their property connect to other riding in the area. The Mountain View Creamery Bed & Breakfast is a lovely place to stay for a romantic mountain bike weekend. It is located on Darling Hill Road in East Burke (802-626-9924).

Notes on the trail: Leave the East Burke Sports parking lot and turn left (due north) on VT 114. Immediately turn right onto Burke Mountain Road at the sign for the Burke Mountain ski area and begin climbing. At the fork, stay right on the paved road then go left through the gate and up the Summit Road. Turn right onto the CCC Road, just after a green house on the right and a red building on the left. Look for a small, hidden sign nailed to a tree marking the road. Traverse the alpine ski trails and continue climbing to the highest point of this ride (4.2 miles and 2,240´ of elevation gain).

Pass a lean-to on your right and begin to descend. The CCC Road is rocky and washed out in places, so use caution on the downhills. Go straight at all trail junctions and soon you will come to an open area that serves as a logging landing and may be strewn with piles of logs on either side. Shortly after this you will pass through a gate and ride by one of Vermont's hidden junkyards. Stay to the left and ride around the cable stretched across the road. (Don't worry; you are on public land.) At a T-intersection with a sign indicating North Concord, turn right on TH 8, following arrows on the worn-out shed for Kirby Mountain and Lyndonville.

Climb steadily for about 2 miles until you come to a set of VAST trail signs at the summit of the climb. Stay to the right and begin a steep, long descent. Turn right onto TH 7 just before the big red barn and farmhouse. This road affords the most beautiful views on the ride. Take the time to look behind you.

Soon you will find yourself facing a steep climb directly ahead. Relax and turn left just before it. Ride to a T-intersection with a large, orange directional arrow. Turn right. Follow this road until you come to another T-intersection that is paved. This is Burke Mountain Road where you first started. Turn left and immediately turn left again onto VT 114. East Burke Sports Shop and your car are just ahead on the right.

RIDE 59 · Victory Bog

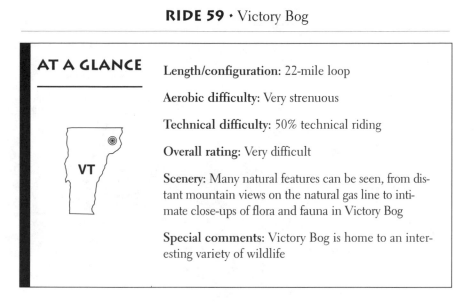

AT A GLANCE

Length/configuration: 22-mile loop

Aerobic difficulty: Very strenuous

Technical difficulty: 50% technical riding

Overall rating: Very difficult

Scenery: Many natural features can be seen, from distant mountain views on the natural gas line to intimate close-ups of flora and fauna in Victory Bog

Special comments: Victory Bog is home to an interesting variety of wildlife

This 22-mile loop takes you up Burke Mountain, down the Civilian Conservation Corps (CCC) Road, across an old jeep road, and down the natural gas line through one end of Victory Bog State Forest. The natural gas line is as wide as an interstate with expansive views to the north of the East Haven Range. Although there is only one major ascent—the 2,240-foot initial climb up Burke Mountain—it is more difficult than the CCC Road loop because of the single-track section on the natural gas line through Victory Bog wildlife preserve.

General location: Burke Mountain in East Burke, roughly 10 miles north of St. Johnsbury on VT 114.

Elevation change: You will gain 2,420′ right off the bat as you climb up the Burke Mountain Road. Other than that, there are only a few short climbs hardly worth noting.

Season: June through mid-November is best since spring runoff can keep the CCC Road and the Victory Bog very wet in April and May. Expect snow at higher elevations in October and November.

Services: All services are available in East Burke, where the ride begins and ends. Bailey's Country Store on VT 114 has a deli counter, home-baked goods, fresh produce, a wine cellar, and a candy counter. Upstairs is an interesting gift

RIDE 59 · Victory Bog

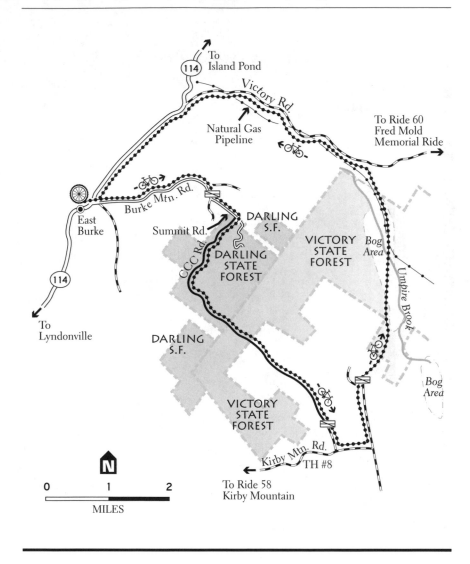

and clothing shop. All are contained within an old, post-and-beam structure, open in the center from floor to ceiling. No other services are on the ride.

Hazards: Watch out for fallen trees, deep potholes, and uneven bridges that drop off suddenly at both ends. The natural gas line has a single-track trail down the middle. It also has tall grass that makes it difficult to discern what you are actually riding on.

Rescue index: Don't ride this loop alone. The Northeast Kingdom is sparsely populated with private houses far and few between. There are several rugged sections on the CCC Road and in Victory Bog where you will be at least 5 miles from a phone.

Land status: Dirt roads, CCC roads, trails, and single-track, some through the Victory State Forest.

Maps: Two USGS 7.5 minute quads, Gallup Mills and Burke Mountain, will give you a good sense of the remoteness of the ride. The dirt roads and the CCC Road are shown on Northern Cartographic's and DeLorme's atlases. East Burke Sports Shop has a good collection of its own handmade maps available free of charge (802-626-3215).

Finding the trail: Begin and end at East Burke Sports Shop, located on VT 114, directly across from the Bailey's Country Store.

Sources of additional information: The East Burke Sports Shop staff are *the* source for all riding in the Burke Mountain area. They sell, repair, and rent bicycles, and they have a complete selection of maps (802-626-3215). The Mountain View Creamery Bed & Breakfast, once a dairy farm, sits high on a ridge overlooking Burke Mountain. It is still a working farm, and the owners are active with local trail committees. Mountain bike trails on their property connect to other riding in the area. The Mountain View Creamery Bed & Breakfast is a lovely place to stay for a romantic mountain bike weekend. It is located on Darling Hill Road in East Burke (802-626-9924).

Notes on the trail: Leave the East Burke Sports parking lot and turn left (due north) on VT 114. Immediately turn right onto Burke Mountain Road at the sign for the Burke Mountain ski area and begin climbing. At the fork, stay right on the paved road then go left through the gate and up the Summit Road. Turn right onto the CCC Road, just after a green house on the right and a red building on the left. There is a small, hidden sign nailed to a tree marking the road. Traverse the alpine ski trails and continue climbing to the highest point of this ride (4.2 miles and 2,240′ of elevation gain).

Pass a lean-to on your right and begin to descend. The CCC Road is rocky and washed out in places, so use caution when descending. Go straight at all trail junctions and soon you will come to an open area with very large logs stacked on the side. Shortly after this you will pass through a gate and ride by one of Vermont's hidden junkyards. Stay to the left and ride around the cable stretched across the road. (Don't worry; you are on public land.) At a **T**-intersection with a sign indicating North Concord, turn left. After a good downhill, come to another **T**-intersection and turn left onto a road with a Dead End sign.

Roll along on a dirt road keeping your eyes peeled for a big white house with gray trim. Between the white house and a large brown house, turn right onto a jeep road and pass through a gray gate.

You are now in Victory State Forest. Follow the main vein of this jeep road for about 3 miles until you come to a set of VAST trail signs. Stay left and soon you will come to the natural gas line, a clearing as wide as the interstate with a single-track path through it. Follow the gas-line path down into Victory Bog, where you will most likely spot a moose, birds, or other wildlife. Take your time here, as the grassy terrain makes it difficult to tell what is about to be under your front wheel. Stay alert and pay attention!

Just past gas-line marker 122, turn right into a wooded area on an obvious four-wheel-drive trail. This canopied trail will take you to a dirt road known locally as Victory Road. Turn left on Victory Road and descend for about 2.5 miles to VT 114. Turn left and take VT 114 back to East Burke Sports Shop.

RIDE 60 · Fred Mold Memorial Ride

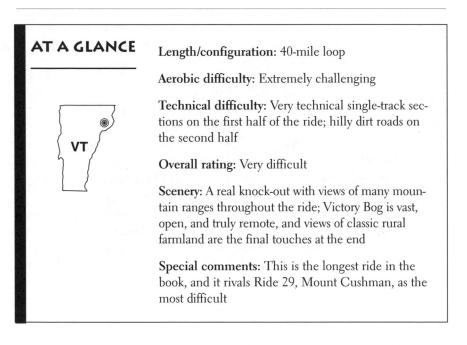

AT A GLANCE

Length/configuration: 40-mile loop

Aerobic difficulty: Extremely challenging

Technical difficulty: Very technical single-track sections on the first half of the ride; hilly dirt roads on the second half

Overall rating: Very difficult

Scenery: A real knock-out with views of many mountain ranges throughout the ride; Victory Bog is vast, open, and truly remote, and views of classic rural farmland are the final touches at the end

Special comments: This is the longest ride in the book, and it rivals Ride 29, Mount Cushman, as the most difficult

Fred Mold was the director of the Fairbanks Museum in St. Johnsbury, Vermont, from 1948 until he died in 1975. He was a pioneer in the Victory Bog region and was revered as a champion of the Northeast Kingdom environment. He led a spirited and publicly vocal opposition against the U.S. Army Corp of Engineers, who at one time planned to create a recreational reservoir by damming the Moose River. Mold was a gifted science teacher who dazzled peers with his charismatic style and persuaded them to join his environmental mission.

The Fred Mold Memorial Ride, an astonishingly beautiful, rugged, and remote ride, is dedicated to the memory of Fred Mold and his efforts on behalf of the environment. It is a 40-mile loop that takes you to the back side of Burke

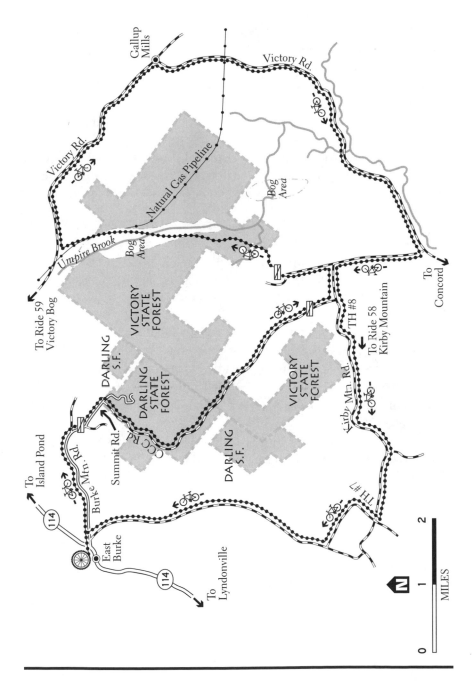

Mountain via the CCC Road, an old jeep road, and the natural gas line. The second half of the ride is on wide, flat, scarcely traveled dirt roads. Much of the riding is done in Victory State Forest and the Victory Bog Wildlife Management Area, on single-track trails as well as dirt roads.

General location: Burke Mountain in East Burke, roughly 10 miles north of St. Johnsbury on VT 114.

Elevation change: A total of 3,420′ in elevation is gained. The first climb happens immediately when you ascend 2,420′ up the Burke Mountain Road. After about 28 miles you will climb 1,000′ feet over Kirby Mountain.

Season: June through mid-November is best since spring runoff can keep the CCC Road and the Victory Bog very wet in April and May. Expect snow at higher elevations in October and November. The dirt road sections can be ridden as soon as the snow melts.

Services: All services are available in East Burke, where the ride begins and ends. Bailey's Country Store on VT 114 has a deli counter, home-baked goods, fresh produce, a wine cellar, and a candy counter. Upstairs is an interesting gift and clothing shop. All are contained within an old, post-and-beam structure, open in the center from floor to ceiling. No services are available on this ride. Take plenty of food and water.

Hazards: Watch for fallen trees, deep potholes, and uneven bridges that drop off suddenly at both ends. The natural gas line has a single-track trail down the middle. It also has tall grass that makes it difficult to discern what you are actually riding on.

Rescue index: Don't ride this loop alone. The Northeast Kingdom is sparsely populated with private houses far and few between. There are several rugged sections on the CCC Road and in Victory Bog where you will be at least 5 miles from a phone.

Land status: Dirt roads, CCC roads, trails, and single-track, some through the Victory State Forest.

Maps: Two USGS 7.5 minute quads, Gallup Mills and Burke Mountain, will give you a good sense of the remoteness of the ride. The dirt roads and the CCC Road are shown on Northern Cartographic's and DeLorme's atlases. East Burke Sports Shop has a good collection of its own handmade maps available free of charge (802-626-3215).

Finding the trail: Begin and end at East Burke Sports Shop, located on VT 114, directly across from the Bailey's Country Store.

Sources of additional information: The East Burke Sports Shop staff are *the* source for all riding in the Burke Mountain area. They sell, repair, and rent bicycles, and they have a complete selection of maps. (802-626-3215). The Mountain View Creamery Bed & Breakfast, once a dairy farm, sits high on a ridge overlooking Burke Mountain. It is still a working farm, and the owners are active with local trail committees. Mountain bike trails on their property connect to other riding in the area. The Mountain View Creamery Bed & Breakfast is a lovely place to stay for a romantic mountain bike weekend. It is located on Darling Hill Road in East Burke (802-626-9924).

Notes on the trail: Leave the East Burke Sports parking lot and turn left (due north) on VT 114. Immediately turn right onto Burke Mountain Road at the sign for the Burke Mountain ski area and begin climbing. At the fork, stay right on the paved road, then go left through the gate and up Summit Road. After about 3 miles, turn right onto the CCC Road, just after a green house on the right and a red building on the left. There is a small, hidden sign nailed to a tree marking the road. Traverse the alpine ski trails and continue climbing to the highest point of this ride (4.2 miles and 2,240´ of climbing).

Pass a lean-to on your right and begin to descend. The CCC Road is rocky and washed out in places, so use caution when descending. Go straight at all trail junctions and soon you will come to an open area with very large logs stacked on the side. Shortly after this you will pass through a gate and ride by one of Vermont's hidden junkyards. Stay to the left and ride around the cable stretched across the road. (Don't worry; you are on public land.) At a **T**-intersection with a sign indicating North Concord, turn left. After a good downhill, come to another **T**-intersection and turn left onto a road with a Dead End sign.

Roll along on a dirt road keeping your eyes peeled for a big white house with gray trim. Between the white house and a large brown house, turn right onto a jeep road and pass through a gray gate into Victory State Forest.

Follow the main vein of this jeep road for about 3 miles until you come to a set of VAST trail signs. Stay left and soon you will come to the natural gas line, a clearing as wide as the interstate with a single-track path through it. Follow the gas-line path down into Victory Bog, where you will most likely spot a moose, birds, or other wildlife. Take your time here, as the grassy terrain makes it difficult to tell what is about to be under your front wheel. Stay alert and pay attention!

Just past gas-line marker 122, turn right into a wooded area on an obvious four-wheel-drive trail. This canopied trail will take you to a dirt road known locally as Victory Road. Turn right and stay on this wide gravel road for over 4 miles; enjoy the long, gradual descent.

You will ride over two short patches of pavement; at the bottom of the second is the hamlet of Gallup Mills. Turn right at the long row of mailboxes. After a mile of totally flat riding you will reenter the Victory Bog Wildlife Management Area. The road continues to be remarkably flat as it parallels the Moose River. Look for the "Chickadee Retweet" on the left and the Fred Mold Memorial Rock on the right.

A half-mile after leaving the Victory Bog Wildlife Management Area, turn right onto Town Highway 3 (there's a small sign readable from the opposite direction). Begin climbing. Turn left just before a Dead End sign and continue climbing until you reach a junction. Go straight on TH 8, following arrows on the worn-out shed for Kirby Mountain and Lyndonville. Keep on climbing!

Climb steadily for about 2 miles until you come to a set of VAST trail signs at the summit of the climb. Stay to the right and begin a steep, long descent.

Turn right onto TH 7 just before the big red barn and farmhouse. This road affords the most beautiful views on the ride. Take the time to look behind you.

Soon you will find yourself facing a steep climb directly ahead. Relax and turn left just before it. Ride to a **T**-intersection with a large, orange directional arrow. Turn right. Follow this road until you come to another **T**-intersection that is paved. This is Burke Mountain Road where you first started. Turn left and immediately turn left again onto VT 114. Just ahead on your right is the East Burke Sports Shop.

RIDE 61 · Groton State Forest

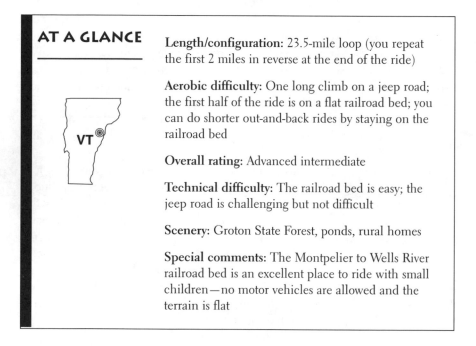

AT A GLANCE
_____

Length/configuration: 23.5-mile loop (you repeat the first 2 miles in reverse at the end of the ride)

Aerobic difficulty: One long climb on a jeep road; the first half of the ride is on a flat railroad bed; you can do shorter out-and-back rides by staying on the railroad bed

Overall rating: Advanced intermediate

Technical difficulty: The railroad bed is easy; the jeep road is challenging but not difficult

Scenery: Groton State Forest, ponds, rural homes

Special comments: The Montpelier to Wells River railroad bed is an excellent place to ride with small children—no motor vehicles are allowed and the terrain is flat

Groton State Forest comprises more than 26,000 acres and lies halfway between Barre and St. Johnsbury. Within the forest are several natural features that make it an interesting place to spend time exploring by mountain bike: Peacham Bog is a "raised" bog with unusual plants and wildlife; Lords Hill Natural Area has many large tree species; ten ponds of assorted width and depth add to the visual diversity of the landscape.

For nearly 200 years the area was heavily logged, and at one point, lumber was transported via trains which traversed the forest from Montpelier to Wells River. The railroad bed has since been rebuilt to accommodate recreational activity. During the winter it is well used by snowmobilers, cross-country

RIDE 61 · Groton State Forest

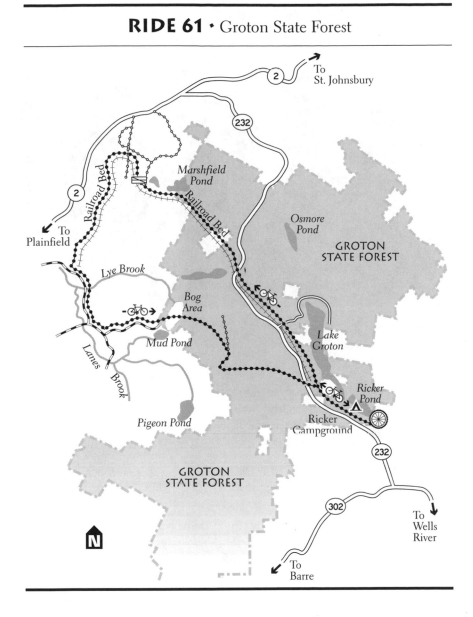

skiers, and snowshoers. During spring, summer, and fall, it is an ideal place for walkers, runners, and mountain bikers.

Now the Montpelier to Wells River railroad bed extends uninterrupted, except for occasional road crossings, from Ricker Pond to Plainfield. Because the grade is nearly flat and the technical aspects of the terrain are minimal, it is an excellent place for novice riders.

The ride described below, Groton State Forest loop, is 23.5 miles, and makes use of the railroad bed for the first half of the loop. Beginners can make the ride

Mountain bikes enjoy a trailside view in Groton State Forest.

as long as they want by turning around at any point along the way. However, everyone should plan to check out the view from the west shore of Marshfield Pond. Those who complete the ride will be faced with a steady climb (not technical) to Hardwood Ridge on a jeep road.

General location: Groton State Forest.

Elevation change: The railroad bed is flat; the second half of the loop climbs steadily for 800´.

Season: This is a great place for early-season riding because the drainage on the railroad bed and dirt roads is so good. The best time, of course, is during fall foliage, late September to early October.

Services: All services can be found in Marshfield and Plainfield. Several private campgrounds are near (consult DeLorme's and Northern Cartographic's atlases). The nearest bicycle shops are Onion River Sports in Barre (802-476-9750) and Park Pedals in Cabot (802-563-2252). In Marshfield, Rainbow Bakery is worth checking out for its interesting deli features.

Hazards: Occasional road crossings on the railroad bed.

Rescue index: The southern half of the railroad bed runs parallel to VT 232, so you could flag down a passing car if necessary. On the northern half, though, you may be as far as 3 miles from a telephone. On the second half of the loop, when you reach Hardwood Ridge, you will be about 4 miles from the nearest phone.

Land status: Montpelier to Wells River railroad bed in Groton State Forest, well-traveled dirt roads, and one jeep road.

Maps: The best map of this area, the Groton State Forest Trail Map, is published by the state of Vermont, Department of Forests, Parks and Recreation, and can be obtained by calling (802) 241-3655. The two atlases printed by DeLorme and Northern Cartographic do not show the railroad bed or the jeep trail.

Finding the trail: This ride begins at the south end of Ricker Pond on VT 232. From Exit 17 off Interstate 91, take VT 302 west through Groton. Two miles past Groton, turn right on VT 232. In 2 miles you will see a parking area on the right (look for the "attractive" camper and old blue school bus). The ride begins from the parking area.

Source of additional information: Contact the Vermont Department of Forests, Parks and Recreation for information on Groton State Forest by calling (802) 241-3655.

Notes on the trail: Begin by riding north on the railroad bed (it looks like a pleasant country lane), keeping Ricker Pond on your right. Soon you will enter Ricker Campground; keep in mind that the facilities here are for paying guests. Continue on the railroad bed, periodically crossing dirt roads, which to the left lead to VT 232 and to the right lead to Groton Pond. To add variety, you can ride down to Groton Pond or check out the nature center near Boulder Beech.

At the 3-mile mark there is a trail on the left that goes to a scenic viewpoint. Turn onto this steep, rocky, quarter-mile climb that goes to VT 232. When the leaves have fallen from the trees the view is quite good, otherwise you can't see much.

Cross VT 232 and continue on the railroad bed. At the 8-mile mark you will see beautiful views at Marshfield Pond. This is a good turnaround for novice riders, who will be surprised at how easy it is to ride 16 miles. For those who wish to continue, take the left fork just past Marshfield Pond, (the right goes to Marshfield). At 9.5 miles there is a major trail intersection. Fork left and continue straight, then ride around an iron gate.

At 13 miles from the start, descend steeply and cross a stream on a wooden snowmobile bridge. Ride straight through a meadow and then through a sandpit. When you come to a wide gravel road, proceed left, going uphill. Stay right on the main road and cross Lye Brook. At the **T**-intersection turn left and continue climbing. Take the second left at the green house and Dunkling's mailbox. Once you make this turn, Maple Hill Lumber will be on your right. This road becomes narrow and rough and eventually turns into a jeep road. Pass through a small logging operation and continue climbing gradually. Pass a rust-colored house on the left, enter a wooded area and arrive at a trail junction. Take a hard left and continue climbing on the rocky jeep road. At the height of the land, you will pass through a set of beaver ponds.

Begin descending until you reach a **T**-intersection and turn right. Stay on the main road, which improves as you descend. Cross over VT 232 and drop down to the railroad bed on a trail marked with a sign indicating a railroad bed. At the railroad bed, turn right. It's about 2 miles back to the starting point.

AFTERWORD

A few years ago I wrote a long piece on this issue for *Sierra* magazine that entailed calling literally dozens of government land managers, game wardens, mountain bikers, and local officials to get a feeling for how riders were being welcomed on the trails. All that I've seen personally since, and heard from my authors, indicates there hasn't been much change. We're still considered the new kid on the block. We have less of a right to the trails than horses and hikers, and we're excluded from many areas, including:

a) wilderness areas
b) national parks (except on roads, and those paths specifically marked "bike path")
c) national monuments (except on roads open to the public)
d) most state parks and monuments (except on roads, and those paths specifically marked "bike path")
e) an increasing number of urban and county parks, especially in California (except on roads, and those paths specifically marked "bike path")

Frankly, I have little difficulty with these exclusions and would, in fact, restrict our presence from some trails I've ridden (one time) due to the environmental damage and chance of blindsiding the many walkers and hikers I met up with along the way. But these are my personal views. The author of this volume and mountain bikers as a group may hold different opinions.

You can do your part in keeping us from being excluded from even more trails by riding responsibly. Many local and national off-road bicycle organizations have been formed with exactly this in mind, and one of the largest—the National Off-Road Bicycle Association (NORBA)—offers the following code of behavior for mountain bikers:

1. I will yield the right of way to other non-motorized recreationists. I realize that people judge all cyclists by my actions.
2. I will slow down and use caution when approaching or overtaking another cyclist and will make my presence known well in advance.
3. I will maintain control of my speed at all times and will approach turns in anticipation of someone around the bend.
4. I will stay on designated trails to avoid trampling native vegetation and minimize potential erosion to trails by not using muddy trails or short-cutting switchbacks.
5. I will not disturb wildlife or livestock.
6. I will not litter. I will pack out what I pack in, and pack out more than my share whenever possible.
7. I will respect public and private property, including trail use signs and no trespassing signs, and I will leave gates as I have found them.
8. I will always be self-sufficient and my destination and travel speed will be determined by my ability, my equipment, the terrain, the present and potential weather conditions.
9. I will not travel solo when bikepacking in remote areas. I will leave word of my destination and when I plan to return.
10. I will observe the practice of minimum impact bicycling by "taking only pictures and memories and leaving only waffle prints."
11. I will always wear a helmet whenever I ride.

Now, I have a problem with some of these—number nine, for instance. The most enjoyable mountain biking I've ever done has been solo. And as for leaving word of destination and time of return, I've enjoyed living in such a way as to say, "I'm off to pedal Colorado. See you in the fall." Of course it's senseless to take needless risks, and I plan a ride and pack my gear with this in mind. But for me number nine smacks too much of the "never-out-of-touch" mentality. And getting away from civilization, deep into the wilds, is, for many people, what mountain biking's all about.

All in all, however, NORBA's is a good list, and surely we mountain bikers would be liked more, and excluded less, if we followed the suggestions. But let me offer a "code of ethics" I much prefer, one given to cyclists by Utah's Wasatch-Cache National Forest office.

Study a Forest Map Before You Ride
Currently, bicycles are permitted on roads and developed trails within the Wasatch-Cache National Forest except in designated Wilderness. If your route crosses private land, it is your responsibility to obtain right of way permission from the landowner.

Keep Groups Small
Riding in large groups degrades the outdoor experience for others, can disturb wildlife, and usually leads to greater resource damage.

Avoid Riding on Wet Trails
Bicycle tires leave ruts in wet trails. These ruts concentrate runoff and acceler-
ate erosion. Postponing a ride when the trails are wet will preserve the trails
for future use.

Stay on Roads and Trails
Riding cross-country destroys vegetation and damages the soil.

Always Yield to Others
Trails are shared by hikers, horses, and bicycles. Move off the trail to allow
horses to pass and stop to allow hikers adequate room to share the trail.
Simply yelling "Bicycle!" is not acceptable.

Control Your Speed
Excessive speed endangers yourself and other forest users.

Avoid Wheel Lock-up and Spin-out
Steep terrain is especially vulnerable to trail wear. Locking brakes on steep
descents or when stopping needlessly damages trails. If a slope is steep
enough to require locking wheels and skidding, dismount and walk your
bicycle. Likewise, if an ascent is so steep your rear wheel slips and spins, dismount and walk your bicycle.

Protect Waterbars and Switchbacks
Waterbars, the rock and log drains built to direct water off trails, protect trails
from erosion. When you encounter a waterbar, ride directly over the top or
dismount and walk your bicycle. Riding around the ends of waterbars
destroys them and speeds erosion. Skidding around switchback corners short-
ens trail life. Slow down for switchback corners and keep your wheels rolling.

If You Abuse It, You Lose It
Mountain bikers are relative newcomers to the forest and must prove themselves responsible trail users. By following the guidelines above, and by par-
ticipating in trail maintenance service projects, bicyclists can help avoid
closures which would prevent them from using trails.

I've never seen a better trail-etiquette list for mountain bikers. So have fun.
Be careful. And don't screw up things for the next rider.

Dennis Coello
Series Editor

GLOSSARY

This short list of terms does not contain all the words used by mountain bike enthusiasts when discussing their sport. But it should serve as an introduction to the lingo you'll hear on the trails.

ATB	all-terrain bike; this, like "fat-tire bike," is another name for a mountain bike
ATV	all-terrain vehicle; this usually refers to the loud, fume-spewing three- or four-wheeled motorized vehicles you will not enjoy meeting on the trail—except, of course, if you crash and have to hitch a ride out on one
blaze	a mark on a tree made by chipping away a piece of the bark, usually done to designate a trail; such trails are sometimes described as "blazed"
blind corner	a curve in the road or trail that conceals bikers, hikers, equestrians, and other traffic
buffed	used to describe a very smooth trail
catching air	taking a jump in such a way that both wheels of the bike are off the ground at the same time
clean	while this may describe what you and your bike won't be after following many trails, the term is most often used as a verb to denote the action of pedaling a tough section of trail successfully
combination	this type of route may combine two or more configurations; for example, a point-to-point route may integrate a scenic loop or an out-and-back spur midway through the ride; likewise, an out-and-back may have a loop at its farthest point (this configuration looks like a cherry with a stem attached; the stem is the out-and back, the fruit is the terminus loop);

or a loop route may have multiple out-and-back spurs and/or loops to the side; mileage for a combination route is for the total distance to complete the ride

CTA	Catamount Trail Association—a group that maintains the Catamount Trail, a 240-mile cross-country ski trail stretching from Massachusetts to Canada
dab	touching the ground with a foot or hand
deadfall	a tangled mass of fallen trees or branches
diversion	ditch a usually narrow, shallow ditch dug across or around a trail; funneling the water in this manner keeps it from destroying the trail
double-track	the dual tracks made by a jeep or other vehicle, with grass or weeds or rocks between; mountain bikers can ride in either of the tracks, but you will of course find that whichever one you choose, and no matter how many times you change back and forth, the other track will appear to offer smoother travel
dugway	a steep, unpaved, switchbacked descent
endo	flipping end over end
feathering	using a light touch on the brake lever, hitting it lightly many times rather than very hard or locking the brake
four-wheel-drive	this refers to any vehicle with drive-wheel capability on all four wheels (a jeep, for instance, has four-wheel drive as compared with a two-wheel-drive passenger car), or to a rough road or trail that requires four-wheel-drive capability (or a one-wheel-drive mountain bike!) to negotiate it
game trail	the usually narrow trail made by deer, elk, or other game
gated	everyone knows what a gate is, and how many variations exist upon this theme; well, if a trail is described as "gated" it simply has a gate across it; don't forget that the rule is if you find a gate closed, close it behind you; if you find one open, leave it that way
Giardia	shorthand for Giardia lamblia, and known as the "backpacker's bane" until we mountain bikers expropriated it; this is a water-borne parasite that begins its life cycle when swallowed, and one to four weeks later has its host (you) bloated, vomiting, shivering with chills, and living in the bathroom; the disease can be avoided by "treating" (purifying) the water you acquire along the trail (see "Hitting the Trail" in the Introduction)

gnarly	a term thankfully used less and less these days, it refers to tough trails
grated	refers to a dirt road which has been smoothed out by the use of a wide blade on earth-moving equipment; "blading" gets rid of the teeth-chattering, much-cursed washboards found on so many dirt roads after heavy vehicle use
hammer	to ride very hard
hardpack	a trail in which the dirt surface is packed down hard; such trails make for good and fast riding, and very painful landings; bikers most often use "hardpack" as both a noun and adjective, and "hard-packed" as an adjective only (the grammar lesson will help you when diagramming sentences in camp)
hike-a-bike	what you do when the road or trail becomes too steep or rough to remain in the saddle
jeep road, jeep trail	a rough road or trail passable only with four-wheel-drive capability (or a horse or mountain bike)
kamikaze	while this once referred primarily to those Japanese fliers who quaffed a glass of sake, then flew off as human bombs in suicide missions against U.S. naval vessels, it has more recently been applied to the idiot mountain bikers who, far less honorably, scream down hiking trails, endangering the physical and mental safety of the walking, biking, and equestrian traffic they meet; deck guns were necessary to stop the Japanese kamikaze pilots, but a bike pump or walking staff in the spokes is sufficient for the current-day kamikazes who threaten to get us all kicked off the trails
loop	this route configuration is characterized by riding from the designated trailhead to a distant point, then returning to the trailhead via a different route (or simply continuing on the same in a circle route) without doubling back; you always move forward across new terrain, but return to the starting point when finished; mileage is for the entire loop from the trailhead back to trailhead
ORV	a motorized off-road vehicle
out-and-back	a ride where you will return on the same trail you pedaled out; while this might sound far more boring than a loop route, many trails look very different when pedaled in the opposite direction

point-to-point	a vehicle shuttle (or similar assistance) is required for this type of route, which is ridden from the designated trailhead to a distant location, or endpoint, where the route ends; total mileage is for the one-way trip from the trailhead to endpoint
portage	to carry your bike on your person
quads	bikers use this term to refer both to the extensor muscle in the front of the thigh (which is separated into four parts) and to USGS maps; the expression "Nice quads!" refers always to the former, however, except in those instances when the speaker is an engineer
runoff	rainwater or snowmelt
scree	an accumulation of loose stones or rocky debris lying on a slope or at the base of a hill or cliff
signed	a "signed" trail has signs in place of blazes
single-track	a single, narrow path through grass or brush or over rocky terrain, often created by deer, elk, or backpackers; single-track riding is some of the best fun around
slickrock	the rock-hard, compacted sandstone that is great to ride and even prettier to look at; you'll appreciate it even more if you think of it as a petrified sand dune or seabed (which it is), and if the rider before you hasn't left tire marks (from unnecessary skidding) or granola bar wrappers behind
snowmelt	runoff produced by the melting of snow
snowpack	unmelted snow accumulated over weeks or months of winter—or over years in high-mountain terrain
spur	a road or trail that intersects the main trail you're following
switchback	a zigzagging road or trail designed to assist in traversing steep terrain: mountain bikers should not skid through switchbacks
technical	terrain that is difficult to ride due not to its grade (steepness) but to its obstacles—rocks, roots, logs, ledges, loose soil . . .
topo	short for topographical map, the kind that shows both linear distance and elevation gain and loss; "topo" is pronounced with both vowels long

trashed	a trail that has been destroyed (same term used no matter what has destroyed it . . . cattle, horses, or even mountain bikers riding when the ground was too wet)
two-wheel-drive	this refers to any vehicle with drive-wheel capability on only two wheels (a passenger car, for instance, has two-wheel-drive); a two-wheel-drive road is a road or trail easily traveled by an ordinary car
VAST	Vermont Association of Snow Travelers—a group of snow-mobilers (primarily) who maintain trails year-round for winter use
waterbar	an earth, rock, or wooden structure that funnels water off trails to reduce erosion
washboarded	a road that is surfaced with many ridges spaced closely together, like the ripples on a washboard; these make for very rough riding, and even worse driving in a car or jeep
whoop-de-doo	closely spaced dips or undulations in a trail; these are often encountered in areas traveled heavily by ORVs
wilderness area	land that is officially set aside by the federal government to remain natural—pure, pristine, and untrammeled by any vehicle, including mountain bikes; though mountain bikes had not been born in 1964 (when the United States Congress passed the Wilderness Act, establishing the National Wilderness Preservation system), they are considered a "form of mechanical transport" and are thereby excluded; in short, stay out
windchill	a reference to the wind's cooling effect upon exposed flesh; for example, if the temperature is 10 degrees Fahrenheit and the wind is blowing at 20 miles per hour, the windchill (that is, the actual temperature to which your skin reacts) is minus 32 degrees; if you are riding in wet conditions things are even worse, for the windchill would then be minus 74 degrees!
windfall	anything (trees, limbs, brush, fellow bikers . . .) blown down by the wind

INDEX

ABOUT THE AUTHOR

As editor of the monthly sports publication *Vermont Sports Today*, 42-year-old Kate Carter is closely associated with Vermont's mountain bike community. A devoted "biker for life," both on- and off-road, she welcomed the opportunity to explore Vermont's hidden roads and trails and to write about them for this book.

Kate's cycling experiences include four double-century rides (each completed in a single day), a tour of the Dolomites, and a two-week solo excursion through Tuscany in central Italy. During the winter, she cross-country skis daily at the Trapp and Mount Mansfield nordic centers, and snowshoes Vermont's back-country hiking trails. Her articles have appeared in *Bicycling* magazine, *Ski* magazine, and *Ski Tech*. She writes from her home in Waterbury Center, Vermont.